COLLECTION POLITICAL SCIENCE

DEVELOPMENT AND INTEGRATION OF LATIN AMERICA

An odyssey unfinished

DEVELOPMENT AND INTEGRATION OF LATIN AMERICA

AN ODYSSEY UNFINISHED

Armando Di Filippo

DEVELOPMENT AND INTEGRATION OF LATIN AMERICA

AN ODYSSEY UNFINISHED

ISBN: 978-1-948915-30-4

NORTH
AMERICAN BUSINESS
P R E S S

North American Business Press
Atlanta, Georgia
Miami, Florida
New York, New York
Toronto, Canada

FIRST PRINTING, 2023
This book was originally published in Spanish by Alberto Hurtado University Editions.

Index

Part Three
Latin American Structuralism and Integration

Part Four
Power, democracy and social responsibility

Presentation

The Department of Politics and Government of the Alberto Hurtado University has offered me to edit a compilation and selection of works that I have been writing and publishing in different books or academic journals during the last four decades (1980-2020). I am deeply grateful for this recognition. However, I believe that a selection of works written by the same author covering such a long period acquires greater legitimacy if the topics dealt within this intellectual itinerary are still relevant for a better comprehension of contemporary processes from the point of view of Latin America's interests. Therefore, I will restrict the temporal and thematic scope of this selection only to the works I wrote in this century, (when I concluded my work ties with the UN/ECLAC(Economic Commission for Latin America and the Caribbean)) and broadened my approach to an interdisciplinary or multidimensional perspective. In any case, the long-term historical perspective that is characteristic of the Latin American approach in which I was academically trained still underlies this selection.

I would also like to express my special thanks to the director of the Department of Politics and Government, Ignacio Cienfuegos, for his support to this project, and to the members of the Interdisciplinary Program of International Relations for Latin America (PROIAL) who provided invaluable suggestions regarding the selection of articles that make up this compilation. I am particularly grateful to Shirley Gotz and Isaac Caro who encouraged me to publish this work. I would also like to extend my gratitude to Claudia Fuentes, former director of PROIAL, who was an important collaborator in the final selection of the articles included. My friends, Professors Pablo Salvat,

Héctor Oyarce and Diego Herrera were constant interlocutors in relation to several of the main ideas developed in this selection, making sensible and useful observations that were decisive in giving it its final form. Likewise,

Macarena Aliaga was an invaluable help in ordering the bibliography of the 17 chapters included in the book.

In addition, I would like to highlight with gratitude the profound and pertinent comments made by the author of the blind peer review, whose opinions contributed to enrich this work.

All of my essays compiled in this book emphasize the importance of the different dimensions in the notion of power and its asymmetrical distribution, understood as the central feature or thread that connects the approaches of Latin American historical structuralism. The emphasis on the notion of power predicated on Latin American nation-states is what confers the multidimensional character (not only economic, but also political, cultural and biological-environmental) to the version of Latin American structuralism presented in the essays selected here.

The first part of this compilation consists of a single chapter, which reviews a contrast between the notions of capitalism and development, including the transition between the initial notions referring to economic development and the broader notions of development that place human beings at the center of reflection, penetrating its ethical dimensions. This section includes the central arguments of the postgraduate courses that, during the last twenty years, I have been teaching in various academic environments (the University of Paris, the University of Barcelona, Stanford University, the University of Buenos Aires, the University of Chile, the University Academy of Christian Humanism and, above all, the Alberto Hurtado University).

The second part is a rather extensive essay that was published in an electronic magazine of the University of Chile, where the enormous influence of ECLAC in the foundation of what we are calling the Latin American School of Development (ELADES), which was developed during the period 1950-1980. This approach was set within the international framework of the center-periphery vision of international relations and the industrialist and integrationist message that this institution began to develop in the 1950s. The possible merit of this second part is to present a panoramic view of the contributions of the founding economists of ECLAC's structuralist thinking (Celso Furtado, Aníbal Pinto, Osvaldo Sunkel, and Aldo Ferrer) during the intellectual leadership of Raúl Prebisch. This period of approximately thirty years (1950-1980) corresponds to what we can genuinely consider as the structuralist phase of ECLAC's thinking and its socio-political projections by other social scientists, both from within the organization itself (José Medina Echavarría, Jorge Graciarena, Fernando Henrique Cardoso, Enzo Faletto, etc.) and from the academic world, influenced to different degrees by these ideas (Gino Germani, Rodolfo Stavenhagen, Theotonio Dos Santos, etc.). A notable feature of these socio-political projections was that authors belonging to different theoretical currents such as Gino Germani with his "scientific sociology", or José Medina Echavarría with his Weberian approach, or even the proponents of dependency theory in its different versions (Cardoso and Faletto on the one hand, or Dos Santos and Marini on the other) all assumed and assimilated in their approaches the diagnostic interpretations referred to above, both to the historically inherited primary product exporting economies and to the processes of import substitution industrialization with which ECLAC and the Latin American structuralists tried to promote the economic development of Latin America.

The historical period covered by this second part referring to the evolution of ECLAC's thinking covers the second half of the 20th century, a period during which I was an active member of that UN agency, and my personal work at the time was strongly limited to the economic aspects of development.

The third part includes my personal reflections on the nature of Latin American historical structuralism. In this section I present in a much more frontal and direct way my own interpretation of the contents and fundamental messages of this movement of thinking and its relevance in the 21st century. This approach is presented through four points of view:

i) as a philosophy of history based on the power of technology, ii) as a political economy based on power, inseparable from the existence of a democratically founded State that sets the formal rules of the societal game, iii) as a theory of power-value that explains the process of formation of relative prices in capitalist markets, iv) as a development strategy associated with the expansion of industrial productive power. This section also includes articles that highlight the features that unify Latin American societies because they share common economic, political, and cultural legacies. These features are intended to explain and legitimize a development strategy that promotes the ideal of Latin American integration.

The fourth part, which concludes the book, presents the theme of political power which, starting from the Universal Declaration of Human Rights (Paris/San Francisco, 1948), provides, in opposition to the liberal vision, a republican and multidimensional conception of democracy which, obviously, also includes the notions of power and domination. In this approach to democracy, the notion of liberty is understood as a liberation from the ties and dependencies inherited by our region from the very moment of its conquest and colonization. Furthermore, the idea of democracy, being multi-dimensional, is not limited to its political dimension and includes the biological-environmental, economic and cultural spheres. Within this broader context, this section discusses the ethics and social responsibility of economic and political power holders in Latin American societies in the global era of the twenty-first century. The vision of this part of the paper is strongly supported by the ideology of peace and human rights (political, economic, social and cultural) in the post-war version propagated by the United Nations.

In brief, the works selected here summarize some of the ideas that I have been developing over the last two decades of intellectual work. Except for the introduction, the anticipated conclusions and the first chapter, all the chapters included here have already been published with author's mention in different books or academic journals in Latin America. These chapters express part of my intellectual trajectory over the last twenty years. They are my own opinions which do not compromise either the persons or the institutions with which I have collaborated.

Armando Di Filippo

Introduction[1]

This book considers Latin American structuralism as a school of thought that, starting from the basic notions of economic science, set out to explain the foundations of Latin American development.

It is worth beginning by distinguishing four possible interpretations (or alternative "readings") of this school of thought, some of which go beyond the field of economics to encompass all the dimensions of the notion of development. Thus, Latin American structuralism can be studied: a) as a philosophy concerning history; b) as an economic theory; c) as a political economy; d) as a development strategy.

1. Latin American structuralism understood as a philosophy of history

From this perspective, Latin American structuralism is influenced by historicism, nationalism, Marxism, institutionalism, and "classical" liberalism.

It is not that structuralist authors have explicitly adhered to these currents, but the world and historical visions of L.A.S contain common elements that are also present in those schools of thought. Note that L.A.S is not an eclectic combination of these different visions either, but that the study of Latin American historical reality is the one that leads to interpretations in certain aspects analogous to others pre-existing in the Western social sciences.

Historicism: The relationship with the authors of the German historical school is obvious and immediate because of the decisive

---

[1] Conference presented at the Faculty of Social Sciences of the University of Buenos Aires and at the Faculty of Economic Sciences of the University of Rosario, in November 2016.

importance that the study of history has for Latin American structuralists. Apart from the ideas of Friedrich List, considered one of the founders of the German historical school, another of its most outstanding members was undoubtedly Max Weber, who studied in depth the historical and structural notion of "capitalism" and its "spirit" (its ethical-cultural foundations). Another important author of this school, Werner Sombart, consolidated the notion of capitalism as an essential historical category for the understanding of contemporary economic processes.

The main authors of L.A.S (Prebisch, Furtado, Sunkel, Ferrer, Pinto, etc.) have used the notion of capitalism as an indispensable historical category for understanding contemporary Western societies. In contrast, neo-positivist academic economic theory, characterized by an ahistorical approach, has permanently rejected the use of this notion as a central tool of knowledge.

Nationalism: There is in Latin American structuralism an enormous affinity with the ideas of Friedrich List, who not only appears as one of the founding fathers of historicism but also as an important proponent of what he called the "national system of political economy" (1856), emphasizing an economic nationalism in opposition to the liberal visions of the time.

L.A.S has cultivated what we could call a "Latin American nationalism" or "Latin Americanism". Behind this notion, there is a defense of the idea of liberation against the structures of domination that since the colonial phase fragmented Latin America to submit it to the interests of the hegemonic centers. The idea of integration of this subcontinent has been a strong idea that dates back to the dawn of independent life and is linked to the ideas of Simón Bolívar. Integrationism is an essential component of the authors who gave life to the L.A.S not only in the sphere of "developmentalist" political economy (promotion of economic development through the integration of markets and productive structures) but also in the search for the integration of nations, including the political and cultural dimensions.

Marxism: From Marxism, L.A.S partially rescued the philosophy of history that privileges the development of the productive forces (technical progress in the language of L.A.S) as its great transforming mechanism.

Unlike original Marxism, L.A.S. does not advocate an irreversible rupture of the bourgeois capitalist order but examines a reformist transformative process, where the class struggle does not inexorably culminate in the annihilation of capitalism. The L.A.S. has unveiled and studied a structurally more complex and heterogeneous distributive struggle, placing its hopes and expectations in a process that favors social democratization in the long term. The real transforming engine of the capitalist order has been and continues to be the technical change driven by the hegemonic centers.

Institutionalism: From the American institutionalists (particularly Thorstein Veblen and John Commons) the Latin American structuralists rescue the notion of institutions and integrate it with that of structures. Although, indeed, the use of the term institutions is not as frequent in Latin American structuralist discourse as it was in American institutionalism, it is implicitly present in the core of the notion of social structure that structuralists use, which is multidimensional in nature (not only economic but also political and cultural). Thus, the notion of social structure examined by L.A.S is historically dynamic, is associated with the notions of power and domination, and, starting from the study of political economy, includes a multidimensional reading of the idea of the institution (Prebisch 1981, Furtado 1978, Sunkel 1989).

Liberalism: Regarding economic liberalism, L.A.S was influenced theoretically by the importance it gave to the study of the Industrial Revolution and the introduction of the notions of surplus and profit (above all in Adam Smith), but it always categorically rejected the liberal dogmas of the "invisible hand" and the self-regulation of the markets.

Concerning political liberalism, Latin American structuralism has marked the profound contrast between ideals and realities. Indeed, Latin American nations were born to independent life as republics, quickly rejecting some imperial and monarchical pretensions of internal organization. However, the precepts of "liberty, equality and fraternity" characteristic of the French Revolution, or those of government "of the people, by the people and for the people" (Abraham Lincoln) characteristic of the American popular-democratic ideology, clashed with the beginning of independent political life with the harsh Latin American oligarchic reality inherited from the colonial phase and consolidated during the 19th century. Latin American structuralism highlighted these sharp social contrasts which, in practice, negated those democratic precepts.

Since the mid-twentieth century, a new generation of scholars has coalesced around the Economic Commission for Latin America, a member organization of the United Nations (ECLAC-UN). Within this institutional framework, these thinkers absorbed its principles and precepts in favor of peace, cooperation, and international negotiation, leading the fight against underdevelopment and in favor of human rights.

The UN Economic and Social Council was one of the institutional bodies through which support was promoted for countries that had been subjected to colonialist or neocolonialist institutions. ECLAC was part of this support mechanism, constituting a forum of thought where the first ideas and initiatives that would lead to the L.A.S were conceived.

In the post-war period, the founding fathers of the L.A.S elaborated multiple studies in which they recorded the impact of human populations, technologies, and institutions coming from the centers (both colonial and capitalist) in the conformation of the peripheral structures of Latin America[2].

These studies gave substance and concrete content to Latin American historical structuralism. They examined rural social structures with their estates and plantations based on servile and slave labor regimes. These investigations clarified the economic, ethnic, and cultural conditions of the settlement of the region throughout the colonial period, together with the structures of domination derived from the clash between the new demographic currents and the native peoples.

---

[2] Among the pioneering works of historical classification on a national scale are those of Celso Furtado (1959), Aldo Ferrer (1963) and Anibal Pinto (1965). All of them were placed within the great historical perspective of the Center-Periphery System proposed by Raúl Prebisch from ECLAC (1949). On a Latin American scale, Osvaldo Sunkel and Pedro Paz (1970) elaborated an attempt at a historical interpretation of underdevelopment which was continued by other Latin American authors such as María Concepción Tavares, Antonio Barros de Castro, Carlos Lessa, Octavio Rodríguez, and Armando Di Filippo. On the other side, the so-called Dependency Theory was a more critical and radical projection of the ideas of the L.A.S formulated in the socio-political sphere to which, among other authors, Fernando Henrique Cardoso and Enzo Faletto (1969) or, from a more Philo-Marxist perspective, Theotonio Dos Santos (1978) and Ruy Mauro Marini (1999) contributed.

Historical structuralism studied this legacy of colonialist domination, which continued under neocolonial forms from the 19th century onwards. Finally, with political independence, peripheral capitalism was installed and consolidated in Latin America, where it was possible to frame within a common interpretative framework the typologies of primary product exporting economies that, to this day, continue to characterize the Latin American economic order. The introduction in Latin America of technical change (coming first from the colonialist powers and later from the capitalist centers) was carried out insofar as it was functional to the interests of the centers, generating in this subcontinent the coexistence of productive forms, social relations and mechanisms of domination which, jointly, were studied through the notion of structural heterogeneity.

Thus, the Latin American structuralist conception of history became the original conceptual matrix, of an economic nature, in which a Latin American School of Development (LAD) has been multidimensionally gestated, which also embraced the cultural and political specificities of our societies.

Latin American Structuralism (L.A.S) and its Philosophy of History

The influence of the philosophy of history originating in Marxism is evident in Latin American structuralism. However, regarding the notion of development, there are important conceptual differences between the two approaches (associated with the labor theory of value), which should be summarized as follows.

Concrete human labor produces concrete goods, and the relation between the quantity of product generated (Q) and the quantity of labor required to generate it (T), is called productivity (or productive power) of labor (Q/T), a basic indicator of that phenomenon which, in the economic sphere, we have called development. When the average productivity of labor is considered at the macroeconomic level, weighted by relative market prices, the counterpart of this increase in productive power is the increase in the average purchasing power of the population. If we call (N) the total population, we can arrive at another indicator (Q/N) which would be the number of available goods and services that can be acquired on average per person. If Q is expressed in physical units, we are in the presence of technical and not economic measures of development, since the economic measurements of the social product pass through market valuations weighted by relative prices. A deeper understanding of these economic measures brings us back to the theory that studies the features of capitalism.

Now, what does this elementary numerical review have to do with the historical projections derived from the Latin American structuralist approach?

The above simple mathematical symbology, which is part of the most elementary alphabet of the notion of economic development, indicates that "ceteris paribus" and macroeconomically speaking, the increase in the average productive power of social labor has as its counterpart the reduction in the amount of labor required per unit of product produced. This obvious verification marks the historical limits of capitalist development as we have studied it since the British Industrial Revolution, and indicates the moment (already begun at present in the hegemonic capitalist centers) from which we begin to penetrate a new economic and social system of a post-capitalist character. This new system will transform the instrumental rationality of capitalism from its very roots by softening the antagonistic character of the capital-labor dialectic through the irruption of robotics and artificial intelligence. The risks for future human societies that, in the long term, derive from this process have been examined in the introduction to the Spanish version, also included in this book, to which reference should be made for further discussion of this argument.

Beyond the implications of this process for the labor theory of value, it is worth noting that, in the historical interpretation of the L.A.S. regarding the notion of development applied to the economic formation of Latin America, an important difference is marked with Marx's ideas. This interpretation is framed for Latin American structuralists in the notion of the center-periphery system of international relations. In this sense, Marx, referring to India, subordinated in the 19th century to the British Empire, had once stated that the countries subject to colonial domination, as they became independent, could find in the more developed countries the mirror of their future. The L.A.S. considers that this alignment of countries, following a line of transition from less to more developed, is not a correct interpretation of the history of international economic relations. In contrast, for historical structuralism, what has contemporarily been called "development" and "underdevelopment" are two sides of the same coin evolving simultaneously in the dynamics of global capitalism. L.A.S. looks at capitalist development from the point of view of its impact on our peripheral societies and, from that point of view, constructs a great historical interpretation of the Latin American socioeconomic formation. Unlike historical materialism, Latin American historical structuralism emphasizes and greatly privileges the role of cultural factors as structuring elements of Latin American societies[3].

Moreover, in Latin America, there is an obvious link between the cultural issue and the different ethnic groups that have populated Latin America throughout its history (pre-Hispanic societies, European colonization, and internment of African and Asian slaves). This historical-cultural fact alone is enough to understand why the social formations that originated in the European historical development are not mechanically transplantable to the Latin American reality.

2. *Latin American structuralism considered as an economic theory*

In this section, we will consider two issues: First, the epistemological conditions of the theoretical formalizations-including their mathematical expression developed by L.A.S, and, second, the theories of value and distribution aimed at explaining market prices.

---

[3] In this context, it is enough to recall the notion of cultural creativity as elaborated by Celso Furtado (1978), one of the founding fathers of Latin American structuralism. It is no coincidence that Furtado was Minister of Culture in the Brazilian government. Furtado's contributions in this field established significant and profound connections between the notions of technical progress and cultural creativity (Furtado 1979). Thus, for Latin American structuralists, the notion of development they cultivate is not exhausted, far from it, in the productive forces referring to the economic sphere, but also encompasses the cultural dimensions.

Epistemology: structuralism vs. Neopositivism

If the search for scientific truth consists in confronting theoretical interpretations with the external reality that is to be known, a decisive feature of L.A.S has been the aforementioned search for interpretations that always take history as a starting point. L.A.S. does not attempt to adjust real economic processes to predetermined abstract models.

In contrast, the only features of science recognized by neoclassical positivism (Paul Samuelson, Milton Friedman, etc.) are logical-mathematical coherence, disciplinary compartmentalization in the sphere of instrumental rationality, and empirically limited verification of the proposed hypotheses through the use of econometrics and statistical inference. This "verification", according to Friedman (1953) consists of the capacity of theories to anticipate the future from abstract models based on ahistorical premises such as all those related to trends towards stable general equilibrium under conditions of perfect competition.

L.A.S formulations do not exclude (on the contrary, they assimilate and take advantage of) several methods of a formal-procedural and econometric nature, but they remain permanently framed in the conceptual categories derived from the historical study without accepting the unrealistic premises of neoclassical positive economics.

L.A.S. in the economic sphere is not limited to the positivist instrumental rationality proper to the microeconomic approach. It is also projected into the sphere of moral rationality (distributive justice, democracy, human rights, and duties, etc.) inherent in macroeconomic behavior, or, more broadly, in the macro-societal behavior of democratic states.

As far as the formalizations of macroeconomics are concerned, the L.A.S approach is systemic (Sunkel and Paz 1970, Castro and Lessa 1970, Sunkel and Infante 2009), and the most widely used models that have been the intersectoral flow matrices, especially the Leontief-type input-output matrices, whose precedents go back to Marx's models of simple and expanded reproduction (see Sunkel and Paz, 1970).

In the case of the Leontief model applied to capitalist economies, aggregate demand (as in the Keynesian approach) drives and determines intersectoral productive flows. The composition of this demand admits including the Keynesian categories of consumption, investment, net government expenditure, and net international trade balance. In this sense, the Keynesian approach to final demand can be integrated with Marx's models of simple and expanded reproduction, and with Piero Sraffa's studies originating in the Cambridge current (Sunkel and Paz 1970, Pasinetti 1985).

Latin American structuralist political economy, especially through the development planning efforts of ECLAC-ILPES during the 1950s and 1960s, made abundant use of input-output matrices, both for their economic plans and projections and for the preparation of national accounts.

Theories of value and distribution oriented to explain market prices

Concerning this second topic, we will suggest in this introductory synthesis the existence of three main conceptions on the functioning of the market and the formation of prices. Two have predominated and been debated at length in the academic life of the great Western hegemonic centers. The third can be deduced or derived from the worldview and political economy developed by the L.A.S. In this section, we only intend, in a very schematic and summarized way, to mention some essential features that allow us to differentiate at least these three theoretical positions. One of them is the Latin American structuralist approach.

Classics and Marx

For these theoretical schools of thought the value of commodities is measured in units of labor. For Adam Smith, it is about commanded labor, which implies struggles and negotiations in labor markets between capitalists and workers that will affect the distribution of income. For Ricardo and Marx, it is the labor contained in the goods produced. In Marx's approach (Volume I of Capital) the valorization of commodities takes place in the back room of the market during the production process, while in the sphere of circulation, it is assumed that equilibrium conditions are in force that led to the exchange of equivalents under the "law of value". It is the free competition of capital that determines an average rate of profit for the whole system. Many of the features of Ricardian economics were transferred to Marx's labor theory of value.

For the classics and Marx, social classes are defined by their position in the structure of the property and in the functional distribution of income that results therefrom: owners who receive rents, workers who receive wages, financiers who receive interest, and entrepreneurs who receive profits. From this derives the "essential" social structure of the capitalist order. Marx dichotomized these social classes, distinguishing between income derived from personal labor and income derived from property. In this way, he was able to put forward with greater simplicity his theory of surplus value on which he based his notions of exploitation exercised by the owner of capital over the worker.

In the background of Marx's ideas, there are obvious conflicts of power, domination, and class struggle that form his philosophy of history. But as far as the economic theory itself formulated in his seminal work Capital is concerned, the starting point is the general equilibrium conditions in which his law of value is framed (exchange of equivalents within competitive markets). Thus, in Marx's approach, capitalist markets of final products are excluded as scenarios of exploitation. However, we know that, with increasing frequency, there are specifically mercantile and financial modalities of exploitation that are a clear object of study for the L.A.S.

Original neoclassicals

For this theoretical school, the economic value of goods is a measure of utility and scarcity. It was expressed mathematically for perfect markets in partial equilibrium (Marshall) or general equilibrium (Walras). This interpretation of value and distribution took as its starting point the individualistic and utilitarian metaphysics of marginal calculus and considered the functional distribution of income in the framework of a theory where the remunerations to productive factors express their marginal productivities. It is, once again, the old "invisible hand of the market" translated into the mathematical language of marginal calculus under extremely unrealistic assumptions that eliminate the complex asymmetries and power struggles typical of real markets. The neoclassical distribution theory that associates marginal productivities with factor remunerations requires those simplifying assumptions inherent in the notion of perfect competition, or pure competition that hides the dynamics of power and domination.

Latin American Structuralism and its Theory of Markets

For L.A.S the "social substance" underlying price formation is power, and this statement could be considered the defining feature of the theories of value and distribution of L.A.S This includes not only the growing productive power deriving from technical change but also the other forms of power held by actors occupying a dominant position in the different dimensions of the social structure in the national states ascribed to the logic of capitalism. At the level of Latin America as a whole, this reading of the issue is framed within the center-periphery system of international relations.

The notion of economic value is understood as the power exercised in markets that are quantified through price systems. These markets are not abstract and ahistorical formulations but correspond to historically determined social structures from which this power emanates. The magnitudes of economic value are measured in units of the general purchasing power exercised in the markets (monetary flows of income or capital divided by price indexes).

The notion of economic power in L.A.S includes two differentiable ideas, on one side, the different strata of productive power (or productivity) on whose growth depend both economic development and productivity gains (fruits of technical change) and, on the other side, the exercise of general purchasing power operating in the markets, especially, today, in the international markets.

From a theoretical point of view, perhaps L.A.S could be defined as an economic theory of power since the behavior of markets and prices is conceived as a consequence of the different power games (causally privileging the central role of productive power) arising from the competing social forces.

Raúl Prebisch (1981, 75) made a clear distinction between the forms of economic power, social power (or cultural power), trade union power, and the bureaucratic-political power that is concentrated in the hands of the State. All these forms of power only distribute and redistribute the general productive power and its dynamics of growth both on a national and international scale. Consequently, "productive power" is the dominant name of the capitalist game in the long run.

Prebisch associated this dynamic with the distributive struggle that ends up translating into changes in the structure of relative prices, which in turn jointly determine the price level. In this sense, the inflationary process is also an expression of the social and political struggles that take place in the distributive sphere.

Given the positions and power relations that emerge from the social structure, increases in labor productivity can be socially distributed in multiple ways (profits, wages, rents, tax revenues, lower prices of certain goods, etc.), giving rise to different structures of relative prices of final products, but the nuclear and **primordial phenomenon, the "trigger" of the process, concerns productive structures**. Then come the forms of appropriation of productivity gains. These depend on the dynamics of social structures and are crucial in the theory of value, markets, and prices elaborated by L.A.S.

Under conditions of economic development, those productivity gains that increase corporate profit are what Prebisch calls economic surplus (Prebisch 1949 and 1981). Consequently, the structuralist notion of surplus differs from the approach of Ricardo and Marx and is close to the ideas of Schumpeter (1912).

The process of relative price formation takes place through the different value-adding chains in the different productive branches led by social actors directly or indirectly involved in these transactions. At the territorial level between regions or subnational states, value-adding chains also quantify these power relations (Rofman 1999, 2000). For L.A.S there is no necessary and direct causal connection between market prices and labor-value or utility-value theories considered in the abstract and without reference to positions of power or technological levels emanating from historically determined social structures (Prebisch 1948, 1981, Furtado 1978, Sunkel 1970, Di Filippo 2009).

3. Latin American structuralism understood as a political economy

A distinction must be made between the notions of political economy and those of economic theory. We conceive of political economy as a discipline supporting the legislator and the statesman (Adam Smith 1999: 539), while economic theory includes, first, an underlying value-laden vision, and second, the theory itself. The latter is a system of hypotheses about the behavior of reality that can be verified with the help of the scientific method. This notion of political economy originally formulated by Adam Smith - different from that of the rest of the classical economists and Marx, who make it synonymous with economic science - is very appropriate to show the type of tasks that are proper to an intergovernmental organization such as ECLAC. According to Adam Smith's characterization, this would correspond to the field of political economy and only tacitly or tangentially to structuralist economic theory.

Latin American structuralist political economy admits clear distinctions between the role of the state as the creator of formal institutions and the role of the government as a policy maker, both of which are essential. L.A.S has elaborated development strategies in which the regulatory and fiscal policies of governments occupy a central place, through which the important transition from functional distribution to personal or family income distribution, on which the composition of the final demand for consumer goods depends to a great extent, is considered. State institutions and their policies are also essential in the territorial distribution of income among subregions. At the same time, business culture and behavior (e.g., "creativity" versus "rentiers") strongly influence the magnitude and composition of the demand for investment goods.

4. *Latin American structuralism as an economic development strategy*

The L.A.S took as its starting point the previous historical-structural diagnosis that referred to the importance of export activities of primary products, from which many common characteristics of Latin American development derive. It is industrialist-developmental and integrationist because it set itself the objective of promoting the industrialization of Latin American countries considered jointly, as a basic condition for assimilating technical progress and initiating an autonomous process of economic development aimed at overcoming their peripheral position.

There is no doubt that the developmental proposal of the L.A.S finds coincidences and similarities with Friedrich List's National System of

Political Economy. The latter, in turn, was inspired by the industrialist and protectionist ideas of the American Alexander Hamilton, not only a "father of the American fatherland" but also the founder of the industrialist thinking promoted by that country[4].

These industrialist-protectionist-integrationist schools of thought were not the result of "desktop" academic inspirations, but a projection of analogous historical situations on the part of countries or regions that sought (and succeeded in achieving!) their paths of economic development. They are part of the long international political-economic confrontations between the free trade and protectionist currents that have been confronting each other throughout the history of capitalism.

In its founding proposals, ECLAC's political economy did no more than accompany industrialist, protectionist, and integrationist trends that had previously emerged in the governments of the most advanced Latin American countries; in particular, the industrialization experiences promoted in Argentina since the beginning of the 20th century and accentuated during the government of Juan Perón, those recorded in Brazil during the government of Getulio Vargas or those of the radical governments in Chile, are relevant examples of these historical trends, of which ECLAC was an interpreter.

In the sixties, faced with the discouragement of Latin American industrialization in progress, structural reforms were proposed (agrarian and tax reforms) with productivity and distributivity significance to expand national markets; indicative development planning was promoted

[4] A Latin American structuralist author who explicitly explored these and other sources was Aldo Ferrer (1996, 2000) in his two volumes on the History of Globalization. Aldo Ferrer, a disciple of Prebisch at the University of Buenos Aires, expressed very clearly in his book "The Argentine Economy" the fundamental axes of the structuralist-developmental political economy of the L.A.S, alluding to the "preconditions of the integrated industrial economy". Ferrer stated in this sense, "These preconditions refer to three fundamental fields: the orientation of economic policy, the role of social forces in the development process, and finally the political bases of development" (Ferrer 1963, 243). He later condensed similar ideas in his notion of "national density". This book reached wide circulation giving rise to numerous translations and reeditions, the last of which was elaborated with the collaboration of Marcelo Rougier (Ferrer and Rougier 2012). Thus the L.A.S can also be examined as an interpretation of the international economy on a global scale (Di Filippo and Ahumada 2013)

as a requirement to take advantage of international aid (not yet subject to the much stricter conditionalities of today's financialism).

Within this set of actions, the first post-war Latin American institutions were created at the behest of ECLAC to advance towards regional integration, giving concrete expression to the aforementioned Latin Americanism that characterized the proposals of the L.A.S. However, Latin American integration was not always present in the interests and ideologies of Latin America's ruling classes. The mono-producer and mono-exporter character of its economic structures conspired against the productive diversification required for a sustained and growing reciprocal exchange among Latin American countries. Therefore, there was, and still is, a potential for reciprocal causation of a virtuous nature that has been frustrated by pre-existing interests: the promotion of the industrialization process on a Latin American scale proposed by the L.A.S. thus became a precondition for regional integration, and this, in turn, an essential stimulus for the deepening of industrial development.

The powerful oligarchies that controlled and still control primary export activities in Latin America, in collusion with related external interests of the hegemonic centers of the day, systematically fought against the industrialist efforts that had begun at different historical moments in the 20th and 21st centuries. The institutionalized inertia of a rentier-owner ruling class, always ready to evade tax obligations and flee capital abroad, ended up predominating over the incipient industrialist bourgeoisie that was trying to be born throughout the 20th century. Thus, the peripheral condition was maintained, and characterized, among other features, by the export of primary products, dependence, economic vulnerability, structural heterogeneity, and distributive concentration.

During the period 1945-1975, while ECLAC was formulating its industrialist initiatives, Keynesianism was the dominant political economy in Europe and the United States. Based on its macroeconomic foundations, European reconstruction was made possible and state intervention in developed capitalist economies was legitimized (Di Filippo 2013).

Since the mid-1970s (after the assassination of J.F. Kennedy), the decline of Keynesianism and welfare states in the hegemonic centers also coincided with a certain loss of influence of ECLAC's industrialist-

"developmentalist" proposals. Situations of "stagflation" arose in the hegemonic centers in the face of which the prescriptions of Keynesianism proved ineffective. The double-digit inflation of the 1970s, unprecedented in the centers, strengthened monetarist policies (Milton Friedman) and favored the interests of the monetary-financial powers to the detriment of the fiscal policies and regulations that had prevailed up to that time. The declaration of the inconvertibility of the dollar (1970) invested the United States with the powers of seigniorage and further consolidated the "monetarist and financialist" turn of its current economic policy.

Conclusions: Latin American structuralism in the 21st century: obsolete or current?

Given the objectives of this presentation, one might ask: Have the profound historical changes that took place in the last quarter of the 20th century and so far this century rendered the L.A.S. approaches obsolete? Is this interpretative current still a source of inspiration for the major Latin American development strategies? Can the countries that makeup today's peripheral capitalism benefit from the lessons learned from Latin American structuralism?

The answer outlined here defends the validity and validity of the L.A.S. The foundation of all its reflections is the expansion of productive power based on the assimilation of technical change and the expectation of being able to internalize it and generate it autonomously. After the hegemony of the two great Western centers (Great Britain and the United States), Asian countries are now emerging (China in particular) which, following the same formula (control of technical progress and expansion of national productive power) are beginning to take the lead. Unfortunately, however, the primary-exporting, peripheral, and dependent position of Latin America is maintained (especially in the case of South America), responding to historical traits that have not been modified. Therefore, the lessons derived from the L.A.S. are still relevant and valid, but under new circumstances and mechanisms that need to be taken into consideration.

Armando Di Filippo

Anticipated conclusions

The understanding of capitalism, the system that has dominated the Western world for the last two hundred and fifty years, rests on two central forms of rationality: the technical rationality of production and the instrumental rationality of the market. Just as King Midas turned everything he touched into gold, so too capitalism has turned everything it has touched into commodities, and increasingly encompasses more and more areas of human life which, especially in the West, we call civilized.

What capitalism succeeded in achieving was to place the technical rationality derived from scientific knowledge at the service of the instrumental rationality of capital. Technical change aimed at achieving productive goals had originally been rescued by Adam Smith when, in "The Wealth of Nations", he used his famous example of the pin factory to explain the productivity increases derived from the technical division of labor. Almost a century later, and after the British Industrial Revolution, Marx and Engels, through the "Communist Manifesto", admiringly delved into the astonishing transforming capacity of capitalism associated with the productive power of human labor. Finally, entrepreneurial creativity as a source of growing productive power was highlighted at the beginning of the 20th century in the idea of the innovative entrepreneur put forward by Schumpeter in his Theory of Economic Development (see Chapter I).

The two great industrial revolutions: the British revolution at the end of the 18th century and the American revolution at the end of the 19th century produced enormous qualitative advances in the productivity of workers as a result of the new technical processes.

The originality of the formulations of the Latin American Raúl Prebisch (founder of Latin American historical structuralism) consisted in having examined the impact of these changes on societies which, like

Latin America, had not participated in the gestation of those revolutions (see chapters II and III, in addition to the whole of the second part) but were the counterpart and complement of the productive hegemony of the centers. The elaboration and development of these ideas led him forty years later to write his last book (1981) in which he deepened his notions on what he called peripheral capitalism. Peripheral capitalism and central capitalism constitute a single interdependent system in which centers and peripheries oppose and presuppose each other in a dialectic that Latin American structuralism, first, and dependency theorists, later, developed in a series of studies that ended up building a true Latin American School of development.

As is well known, the instrumental rationality of capitalism is expressed quantitatively through the markets, where prices and quantities of goods are traded on one side. On the other side, the qualitative aspect of the traded goods is also taken into account with a microeconomic business criterion which is instrumentally rational: to produce and offer material or non-material objects which are in demand in the market in order to profit from their sale. The composition and dynamics of this demand is an expression of the distribution of purchasing power among the actors, individuals and firms, who can play the market game. The market responds to relative scarcities, and these in turn are measured by the play of quantities demanded and supplied, both at the level of specific products, sectors or branches and at the level of economic systems considered as a whole (see Part I).

The intimate dynamics of markets was examined by Latin American structuralism derived from Prebisch's approach, seeking support in the notion of power in its different dimensions (see chapter XII). Taking this notion as a source of inspiration, the present paper has rethought concepts that are probably useful for understanding capitalism in the twenty-first century.

Throughout the content of the chapters selected for this book, an attempt has been made to deepen and generalize the notion of power by distinguishing between its economic, political, cultural and biological-environmental dimensions.

The economic power that drives capitalism is capital, understood as the general purchasing power capable of acquiring commercially all the material or immaterial, public or private, national or international conditions required to generate productive power, to produce the product and try to sell it. In macroeconomic terms, the composition of this product must respond to aggregate demand, the only way to achieve its realization (to sell it) in order to recover with profit the purchasing power invested. This is the reproductive logic of capital capable of generating and managing the levels of relative scarcity that directly determine the prices of the goods demanded by those social actors who can pay for them (chapter I).

The political power of the nation-states is the other component required by capital, First by setting the formal rules that regulate society as a whole and, Second, by controlling and administering coercion or threatening to use it in the event that other political forces attempt to change those rules. In this legalized control and administration of coercion is ultimately the crude truth of political power actually exercised. We can call the habitual exercise of established political power political domination (Max Weber 1922) (see the fourth part of the book, chapters XIV, XV and XVI).

Cultural power includes mechanisms and values. The mechanisms of cultural power are the technologies that spread information, communication and knowledge (ICT). Through them (e.g., artificial intelligence generating algorithms) those who control them (e.g., large transnational corporations such as Meta, Apple, Huawei, Google, etc.) are occupying the dominant positions of the social order on a planetary scale. This growing domination has profound political and economic projections, which are transforming the very nature of capitalism and democracy as they were defined in their original versions. On the other hand, the values sustained by cultural power, even the most ancestral ones rooted in the language, memory and institutions of the peoples, are being reshaped by these mechanisms. As will be seen below, this process is already resulting in the rapid discrediting of the previously established dominant principles of social ethics

Biological-environmental power, finally, has been behind all the aforementioned powers; behind their instrumental mechanisms and their legitimizing contents. Until very recently, this power of the biosphere resisted the overwhelming pressure of capitalism. But the very serious environmental crises that we are increasingly suffering in the 21st century remind us that all other human powers are subordinated to this one, which ultimately comes from Mother Nature and, for the believers of the great monotheistic religions, finds its origin in a transcendent and eternal intelligence (Francisco 2015).

In this paper we have interpreted these processes from the point of view of political economy or, if we prefer, from the political economy of power. The thesis defended here is that, ultimately, the dynamics of markets and the distribution of real income respond to the interactive play of these four powers. Therefore, from a theoretical point of view, economic value, understood as the "social substance" that underlies (and ends up ordering) the prices, quantities and qualities of traded goods, expresses the impact derived from this interactive game. The measure of this impact on the markets is expressed precisely in the way in which the prices, quantities and qualities of the goods actually traded can be modified.

A complementary proof of the active presence of these four powers lies in the fact that if we omit the impact of any one of them, we will not be able to understand the reasons that today, in the 21st century, determine the dynamics and perspectives of world markets. In a more detailed analysis, we could detect a permanent retroactive move on the part of the logic of capital, which in turn impacts on the modus operandi of these powers. The current disciplinary compartmentalization in the social sciences conspires against the understanding and study of these multidimensional processes (see Chapter XII).

Therefore, when we take as a starting point the theories of economic value that the great economic schools of the past (classical, historicist, Marxist, institutionalist, neoclassical, Keynesian, etc.) have bequeathed us in order to understand the functioning of capitalism, we lack a sufficiently broad reading to understand and forecast the future of the world economy, and much less can we understand the form these processes take in the Latin American periphery (see chapters X and XI). This statement does not deny that, as these theories of value established, commodities are products, direct or indirect, of human labor, addressed to potential demanders endowed with the purchasing power without which they could not exercise their effective demand (Adam Smith 1776, John Maynard Keynes 1936). However, artificial intelligence is already determining that commodities are more and more "indirect" products of human labor... and of the human mind itself.

Nor should we forget the multidimensional character (economic, political and cultural) of nationalist and historicist approaches such as the National System of Political Economy (F. List 1841) or those of the American School (Alexander Hamilton, Henry Carey). The same could be said of American institutionalism (Thorstein Veblen, John Commons). These currents of thought drew on the experience of crucial historical processes for the economic development of the West, which led to the formation of great industrial powers such as the United States and Germany.

The theoretical currents mentioned in the previous paragraph were industrialist, protectionist and integrationist, opposing the liberal dogmas of free exchange formulated by classical and neoclassical economists.

The integrationism of the United States and Germany eventually resulted in the unification of each of these great powers into a single country. In Germany the task was undertaken by Chancellor Bismarck, and in the United States by Abraham Lincoln after the Civil War. Latin American structuralism has also been, and still is, integrationist. This integrationist attitude of Latin America preached by the L.A.S (Latin American Structuralism) must be understood and reconsidered even more forcefully in this era of globalized capitalism (see chapter X).

These currents of thought have contributed to the understanding of the functioning of markets in the centuries prior to the present. However, the economic science that ended up dominating the Western academic landscape was the one that was functional to the main hegemonic centers of capitalism at the end of the 19th and beginning of the 20th centuries. This science emanated mainly from the neoclassical liberal movement (Menger, Walras, Jevons, Marshall, etc.): abstract, ahistorical, individualistic and utilitarian. For it, the starting point for the study of markets was a situation of stable general equilibrium, under conditions of "perfect competition", where the goods traded were called "economic goods" characterized by their "utility and scarcity".

In the previous paragraph, the words "utility and scarcity" are in quotation marks because their actual effective meanings (different from what the manuals tell us) respond to the instrumental rationality of capital and the systemic logic of capitalism. The utility and scarcity of goods are socially determined according to the distribution of the powers actually operating in society. In terms of social ethics, we are in the field of distributive justice. Under the instrumental rationality of capitalism, the more concentrated this distribution is, the less social attention will be paid to the satisfaction of objective needs that are inherent to human nature[5]. In sum, distributive justice tends to be disregarded or completely ignored not only in academic theory but also in the concrete praxis of capitalist rationality in the 21st century.

Capitalist rationality is opposed also to the liberal democratic reason legitimized since the French revolution ("liberty, equality, fraternity") or to the principles of democratic government ("of the people, by the people and for the people"), inspired by Abraham Lincoln in his republican efforts to promote freedom seen as liberation from the domination suffered by the slaves and also as liberation of the young nation from the ties that subordinated it to its mother country.

The capitalist system operates as a self-expanding cybernetic mechanism founded on the instrumental rationality of capital. Its modus operandi is totally self-referential and tends permanently to control and colonize for its own benefit the political, cultural, and biological-environmental logics. Freed to the economic powers that confront each other in the markets, it tends inexorably to generate monopolistic positions incompatible with democracy (see Part Four).

The voices that predicted the end of capitalism have been wrong many times throughout the 19th and 20th centuries and, in the end, capitalism has continued to expand and deepen its dominance, now on a planetary scale. However, this century has seen the intensification or deepening of at least two new historical circumstances that are changing the "playing field": on the one hand, the emergence of information, communication and knowledge technologies (ICT), and, on the other hand, the worsening of the biological-environmental crisis on a planetary scale. These factors are generating a definitive and irreversible transformational impact that is unprecedented in human history. In particular, they are profoundly affecting the logic of markets in terms of prices, quantities and qualities of traded goods. Hence the need to formulate new multidimensional theories of economic value that explain this new performance and allow the logic of democracy to be introduced head-on into the intimate game of the market.

The planetary impact of these mutations leads to a new ethical rethinking that cannot be directly deduced from the moral precepts of the past. To use an analogy that equates social systems to games. It is

---

[5] Hinkelammert and Jiménez, Economía vida humana y bien común, Reflexiones sobre Economía Crítica. Costa Rica, January 2013. Reflections on Critical Economics.

a new "game", which gives rise to new players (both those who "win" and those who "lose"), operating with new types of moves, leading to the elaboration of new rules.

The current (June 2021) pandemic affecting us on a planetary scale is naturally framed in the ways in which the biological-environmental power is responding to the predatory presence of human beings. Obviously, the author cannot establish any correlation or causal link between the environmental crisis on the one side and the pandemic on the other, but there is no doubt about the planetary scope of this plague and the need to address it jointly in order to avoid a multidimensional collapse of human civilization.

The pandemic has only accelerated historical processes that were latent. We are in a deep epochal change whose outcome we do not know, but which may lead us to a terminal apocalypse or to a new civilizational awakening. A minimum sense of caution and self- preservation requires an ethic that tends to preserve the survival of the human species in the light of the objective impacts that, in the economic, political, cultural and biological-environmental spheres, are deriving from the uncontrolled rationality of capital and the systemic logic of capitalism, supported by the values of utilitarian individualism (see chapter XVII).

This ethics of the survival of the species is not opposed to, but neither is it directly deduced from, transcendent values of a metaphysical nature such as those manifested through the great religions that are the origin of Western civilizations. In the same way, the ethics that the great Western philosophers (Aristotle, Thomas Aquinas, Spinoza, Kant, etc.) have linked to us is composed of principles and precepts for the behavior of human beings who were mostly born in pre- or proto-capitalist societies. It is an ethics that is less and less useful for regulating the actions of instrumentally rational automatons endowed with legal personality (such as large transnational corporations) and oriented towards maximizing private surplus in the context of today's globalized capitalism. Fundamental human values will have to be reinterpreted to meet the challenges of the algorithms that feed artificial intelligence and increasingly regulate our behavior.

We live in a pragmatic world where scientific reasoning (and, what should be, its incorruptible search for truth) has been captured and colonized by the instrumental rationality of transnational capital, based on the microeconomic criteria of the cost-benefit calculation.

Today more than ever in history, the complexity and interdependence of the powers that shape human societies in the third millennium require an economic science and a political economy that reflects and translates them into its general theorization of markets.

On one side, abstract theories of economic value based on the quantity of labor contained in commodities, as envisioned by the classical economists and Marx himself, are destined to become obsolete as technology continues to impose robotization on the productive process. It was Marx himself who anticipated this unraveling in the Fragment on Machinery, anticipating the future demise of his own theory of economic value[6]. Unfortunately, it is not possible to share the optimism that Marx expressed regarding the future of human society from that moment onward.

The emerging problem of capitalism today is no longer (or not only) the exploited human being but the unnecessary and disposable human being who is marginalized from the system by the algorithms of artificial intelligence that are giving life to robotization. The growing redundancy of the discarded labor force resulting from increasing robotization, by creating unemployment and insufficiencies of effective demand on a global scale, is already beginning to call for new policies such as universal basic income, which are unprecedented in the history of modern capitalism (see chapter I).

But, in addition, (and this was not anticipated by Marx) the worst problem of future societies, whether capitalist or not, could be the subordination of our personal freedoms and convictions to the rules and dictates of artificial intelligence controlled by a few economic and/or political actors, who exhaustively record, predict and then try to manipulate (through big data) even our most intimate reactions and behaviors.

Furthermore, abstract liberal-neoclassical theories of economic value, based on the "sovereign" preferences of individual consumers, cloud us even more. They ignore all the forms of power that permanently shape markets and submit to an unsustainable consumer utilitarianism that leads us to

---

6 "As soon as work in its immediate form has ceased to be a condition for the development of social wealth, just as the non-work of the few has ceased to be a condition for the development of social wealth of the general powers of the human intellect. With this, production based on exchange value collapses, and the process of immediate material production is deprived of the form of pressing necessity and antagonism". Karl Marx (1972), Fundamental Elements for the Critique of Political Economy (Draft), 1857-1858, Volume 2, p. 228, Siglo XXI.

ecological disaster. They have been specially designed to divert attention from the power asymmetries inherent in the capitalist game and to highlight the benefits of the self-regulated market.

Such is the case of the stable general equilibrium model under conditions of "perfect" competition. Later neoclassical academic theory has included forms of "imperfect" competition in which differentiated positions of power in the markets are explicitly admitted, but the theoretical starting point is still the self-regulated market, completely isolated from the political, cultural and biological-environmental dimensions of human societies.

In conclusion, it should be pointed out that these theories, which prevailed throughout the 19th and 20th centuries within the framework of the Nation-States, did not at all take into consideration the biological-environmental dimension that necessarily operates today on a planetary scale and of which the pandemic that is currently attacking us is a fundamental element.

It is these two transcendental historical mutations that force us to consider a theory of economic value based on the notion of power: first, the active emergence of the environmental crisis and, second, globalization based on information, communication and knowledge technologies established, this time, on the planetary scale of capitalism. This is the new ambivalent scenario in process of development that radically challenges us.

The first of these two mutations are the impact, coming from Mother Nature, on the protection of our common home. And the second is the instrument (algorithms, artificial intelligence, robotization, etc.) of technical change as the main weapon to address our planetary problems and/or, alternatively, to plunge us into a "digital dictatorship" at the service of increasingly concentrated powers.

From the point of view of the center-periphery vision formulated by Raúl Prebisch in the middle of the last century, the central idea remains more valid today than ever and is related to a certain philosophy of history that can already be traced back to Aristotle's “Politics” when he says:

> Just as for the arts that have a definite sphere, if they are to fulfill their task completely, it would be necessary for the appropriate instruments to exist, so also the domestic administrator must have appropriate

> instruments. Some of the instruments are inanimate, while others are animate (for example, for the pilot the wheel is inanimate but the lookout is animate, for in the arts he who renders services belongs to the class of instruments); so also, a possession is an instrument for life, and property is a set of instruments, and the slave is an animate possession, and so anyone who renders a service is like an instrument prior to the other instruments. For if each instrument could perform its own task, by receiving an order or by anticipating it, as is told of the statues of Daedalus or of the Tripods of Hephaestus, which, as the poet says, walked in by themselves in the meeting of the gods, in the same way the shuttles would weave by themselves, and the plectrons would play the zither, and the architects would have no need of servants nor the masters of slaves (Aristotle, 2005: 63-64).

This reflection by Aristotle expresses a very long-term hypothesis of social change (it is being fulfilled more than two thousand years after it was put forward). The possibility of rendering the alienated and subordinate forms of human labor unnecessary through the use of information, communication and knowledge technologies is the most profound and enduring feature, capable of irreversibly modifying the structures of domination that are characteristic of the capitalist order.

Algorithms and artificial intelligence are rapidly replacing the functions performed by human labor. We are not talking about a very long-term future horizon, nor about imaginative forms of "socio-fiction", but about processes that are already beginning to take place.

In the utopia that this paragraph suggests, we are compared by Aristotle to the gods of Olympus, but unfortunately our human condition is more similar to that of the Sorcerer's Apprentice, a symphonic poem by Paul Dukas (1897) inspired by Goethe, where the apprentice, in the absence of the sorcerer, tries to enchant a broom to circumvent his cleaning job, and produces a chaos that he cannot control. Walt Disney's artistry created a memorable film version of this musical work (see Fantasia 1940).

Now, alienated and subordinate forms of human labor are inherent to the essence of capitalism as an economic system. Marx made this point very clear and elucidated many of its features. For capitalism to exist, private ownership of the means of production, the existence of markets for products and productive factors, and the competition of workers without other resources who need to sell their potential labor in order to live, were necessary. Max Weber also accepted this characterization. In the long run, in order for this type of capitalism to survive, it was also necessary for profit on a macroeconomic scale to stimulate investment and continue to increase the productive power of human labor.

Today (in the year 2021) the end of capitalism will not arise (or will not arise only) from a social revolution, led with epic conviction by the oppressed classes, but from much more pragmatic causes associated with the operating logic of this system. Moreover, the transformation of capitalism (anticipated by Karl Marx in his fragment on machinery) brings to the fore the need for effective demands in the sense given to that expression first by Adam Smith and then by John Maynard Keynes (see chapter X). This demand comes mainly from wage and salary earners, micro-entrepreneurs, independent professionals and scientists with different degrees of education who also live off the income from their own work. Many of them are rapidly being challenged and replaced in the productive sphere by algorithms that feed artificial intelligence together with automated, artificially intelligent instruments connected to them, which not only perform the physical work itself but also an increasing share of intellectual work.

We are rapidly entering the era of substituted and disposable workers, as Pope Francis has called them.

The planetary scale control of artificial intelligence, exercised either by the large private transnational corporations of the West, or by the authoritarian political powers emerging in the East, makes our lives easier, saves us from thinking (as, for example, the so-called GPS to which we entrust the orientation of our car), and lulls us to sleep, entertaining us with banalities "on demand" such as the electronic games that spread from the social networks.

We are like the frog submerged in the comfort of the warm water of a large pan that the fire is slowly heating. When the temperature exceeds a certain degree, the frog tries to get out, but it is too late and ends up boiled. Perhaps global warming boils us literally and not figuratively, but the artificial intelligence of the planetary robot we are creating is gradually corroding our human dignity and is another way of dehumanizing us.

What is new in this approach? What is new is that a new ethics is required, based on the concept of human nature and the objective needs required for the survival of the species (Hinkelammert).

Human beings are no longer massively subordinated to a transcendent power of an ultra-terrestrial nature, such as that once exercised by the commandments of the great monotheistic religions. Citizens also disbelieve the ideologically interested messages that professional politicians pay for by distributing unfulfillable promises in order to achieve government. As I write these conclusions, I remember that at the end of 2019 several large and medium-sized countries in South America (Chile, Bolivia, Ecuador, Peru, Colombia, etc.) registered unusual social outbursts of protests against neoliberal capitalism. When this pandemic is (hopefully) brought under control, the economic, biological, environmental and political situation will probably be even more serious.

Moreover, within the framework of the culture that complements neoliberal regimes, multiple forms of complicity emerge among the holders of economic and political power, defying all inherited ethical precepts. Thus, citizens have less and less confidence in secular temporal powers that must depend on the morality and honesty of those in power.

Today, an ambivalent panorama emerges. On one side, information, communication and knowledge technologies (components of cultural power because they shape public opinion), which are consolidating and spreading in the 21st century, have given rise to "rebel journalism" (Wikileaks, Panama Papers, etc.) that challenge the established powers, and to interactive social networks (Facebook, Twitter, YouTube, Instagram, etc.) that democratize, but also trivialize to a significant degree, the media mechanisms on which public opinion is based. Even so, the illicit activities and complicities of those who hold economic and political power are now relentlessly coming to light, generating a series of media scandals that is unprecedented in history.

On the other side, the control by transnational capital of the mechanisms of media power that shapes contemporary culture, introduces increasing quotas of sensationalism, exotism, banality, and superficial models of life associated with the logic of utilitarian individualism, and the profit motive, distracting and disturbing the search for personal and civic virtues.

The precepts of professional moralists, whether secular or religious, expressed at the rhetorical level, do not persuade many either.

It may not be too far-fetched to predict that the only "commands" to which everyone will be willing to submit in the near future will be those that spring from fear (Hans Jonas 1995, “The Principle of Responsibility”). More precisely, those that spring from anguish in the face of the growing evidence that our common planetary home is collapsing and must be sustained. Political systems must reflect this ethic that can no longer depend only on ideological currents, nor on traditional moral precepts, but on the transhistorical defense of the human species collectively carried out by human beings themselves as stable inhabitants of this planet. In Weberian terms, the ethics of convictions will have to give way to the ethics of responsibilities[7].

However, this does not mean ignoring or rejecting the ethics of convictions translated into some of the fundamental values of Western culture bequeathed to us by the great philosophers and moralists of the past. Rather, it is a matter of testing these convictions in the sphere of the struggle for power as a foundation of the ethics of responsibilities. In short, responsibilities cannot evade the substratum of convictions. Both are mutually presupposed.

Philosophers and moralists should probably reformulate their ethics of convictions, so that they can be conceptually connected with the ethics of responsibilities that we are delegating to the artificial intelligence-carrying instruments to avoid the risks of the sorcerer's apprentice mentioned above.

The notion of human dignity is key to this argument because of its multidimensional nature, and is related to the economic sphere, but the economic sphere is a condition for the exercise of dignity in the political and cultural spheres. Human rights acquire validity to the extent that they are internalized in the habitual behavior of social actors endowed with power. Article 1 of the Universal Declaration of Human Rights (San Francisco 1948) states: "All human beings are born free and equal in dignity and rights, and, endowed as they are with reason and conscience, should behave towards one another in a spirit of brotherhood and sisterhood”.

The theories of economic value that underlie the logic of markets must express this broad context of powers that today influence human life. The instrument of value with which we try to measure the dynamics of markets could, perhaps, take as a starting point a universal basic income, a notion supported by different socio-political philosophers,

---

[7] See: (i) Max Weber 1919, Politics as a Vocation); (ii) Jonas Hans (1995), “The Principle of Responsibility”.

which includes but goes beyond the minimum subsistence basket that can be acquired with a monetary income.

Here the multidimensionality of the powers we have listed corresponds to the multidimensionality of human nature, which is transhistorical. Following Aristotle, we are intelligent animals interacting in the biological-environmental systems from which we come, because we are instrumentally rational animals we interact in economic systems, and because we are morally rational we interact in cultural systems. Finally, we are political animals, that is, we build political systems from which multidimensional structures of power emerge where we act as citizens. In the Greco-Latin republican tradition, our struggle for liberty and equality consists in our subtraction from the forms of domination that emerge from the unjust systems in which we live our lives.

The development of capitalism, supported by the successive technological revolutions of the last two hundred and fifty years, is reaching its culmination. It is extracting every last drop of its instrumental rationality of seeking profit through the expansion of the productive power of human labor. Each increase in this productivity led to the replacement of living labor by new instruments up to the point of artificial intelligence, creating the technical conditions of possibility to make human beings unnecessary in the sphere of direct production.

What is new and disconcerting is that, in fact, machines now produce "ideas", can "think" (identify, classify, select, remember, learn (modify past behaviors and act with increasing margins of freedom) and, if programmed to do so, can also decide and act. They can do so with greater efficiency, speed and precision than humans. However, these entities have no impulses of their own, no moral principles, no feelings and no qualities of their own. They suffer neither physically nor psychically, they neither love nor hate.

They don't feel regret or remorse. And increasingly they will be endowed with the ability to decide for us, both in peace and in war. The obvious and immediate question is the question of the moral sanity of the programmers. The power to program these thinking entities today rests with transnational corporations (Huawei, Apple, Microsoft, Meta Google, etc.) and with some hegemonic powers with growing digital power (suffice it to mention the United States and China).

In the sphere of the political economy of development to which this book refers, very soon the direct producers of the vast majority of goods and services traded in the markets will be artificially intelligent entities.

But this will mean, for reasons already explained, the end of the capitalist system as we know it. The sphere of technology is that of the human-thing relationship, but it turns out that now an increasing part of these "things" will be "thinking" entities.

What will be the results of this unprecedented technical change in human history? If we fail to subordinate the sphere of politics and economics to the sphere of ethics, as Aristotle wanted, then who will defend distributive justice? Who will defend human rights? What will become of the peripheral regions? In short, the great issue will be that of the ethics of the responsibility of the dominant actors who manage to control the levers of power.

For now, 99% of the world's population is part of the frogs slumbering in warm numbness, while the underlying fire increases the heat of the planetary cauldron. Maybe the current pandemic will wake us up and we will go out to fight for our lives.

Part One

Development: content and evolution of the concept

Chapter I

Development, capitalism and social ethics[8]

The notion of economic development

In its origins, the notion of development was primarily economic in nature and was associated with the emergence of capitalism. This economic system gave rise to industrial revolutions that systematically increased the productive power of human labor. Among the scholars of capitalism who delved into this notion of development were the classical economists (especially Adam Smith) and Karl Marx. Also within the neoclassical trend of economic thought, the contribution of Joseph Schumpeter should be noted, who rescued the notions of entrepreneurial innovation as an essential feature of the creative destruction inherent in economic development. Briefly, development in this economic perspective referred to the dynamic nature of capitalism and its growing productive power.

Since the end of World War II, the concept of development has been preached mainly in its economic dimension, as a response to the needs of the reconstruction of Europe devastated by the war, and to the conditions of poverty and social inequality prevailing in vast regions of the planet that joined the UN after the decolonization process.

The product per capita (presumed indicator of living conditions) and the product per worker (presumed indicator of the productive power of

[8] Unpublished work, first publication.

human labor) were compiled and examined in their average magnitudes as indices of improvements in economic conditions.

However, alternative visions soon began to emerge that questioned, on the one hand, the distributive inequalities, above all within the poorest nations, but also in the richest ones; on the other hand, the one-dimensional character of the purely or exclusively economic indicators used to measure development was also questioned.

In Latin America, the first type of issue (distributive inequality) was highlighted early on by ECLAC in its studies on the concentration of productive power on a global scale and the distribution of its results in Latin American development. This led to diagnoses and policies aimed at distinguishing between the conditions of the hegemonic developed countries (centers) and those of the underdeveloped countries and regions (peripheries).

The second type of issue (integral human development) was addressed multidimensionally by various sectoral agencies (FAO, UNESCO, UNICEF, ILO, WHO) of the UN on the basis of the Universal Declaration of Human Rights and other subsequent charters of similar orientation. Since the 1990s, the United Nations Development Program (UNDP) has popularized the notion of human development and published periodic reports on the subject, which have continued to date.

Also, during the 1960s, it became increasingly clear that what is humanly significant for development is what people can become and do, and not the amount of goods they can possess. All these analytical perspectives were consecrating the need for multidimensional diagnosis and policies (not only referring to economic perspectives, but also to political and cultural ones).

Therefore, it was associated with those human dimensions that are universal and shared by all men of all times. The pioneering ideas of the Pakistani Mahbub Ul Haq (who was the early formulator of the human development indexes) were taken up by the Bengali economist Amartya Sen[9].

---

[9] In particular, see: (1997) On ethics and economics. Madrid: Alianza Universidad; (2000). Development and freedom. Buenos Aires: Planeta; (2010). The idea of justice. Madrid: Taurus.

The concept of human nature in this book is understood as a scientific and not a metaphysical notion. Without rejecting the transcendent metaphysical vision, the academic perspective proposed here refers to those universal contents of the notion of human being, compatible with the specific differences that singularize each subject. The human being has defining features that are permanently improved and deepened by scientific knowledge. However, its essential features are maintained in a transhistorical mode.

The multidimensionality of human beings (biological entities, endowed with instrumental and moral rationality, capable of self-organization in concrete social subsystems), requires, therefore, a multidisciplinary examination involving economic, political and cultural perspectives (and today we add the biological- environmental ones) that determine human life.

The notion of economic development as a desirable objective deliberately assumed by public policies and systematically analyzed in the academic sphere is only one aspect of the theme of development that took shape after World War II. In a broader historical perspective, we can speak of economic development processes linked to the emergence of the British Industrial Revolution, which gave capitalism its contemporary technological dynamic.

If we explore the origins of the topic of economic development, what we are doing is tracing the origins of capitalism. It is only by addressing the issue of capitalism that we are able to give the issue of economic development its proper historical context.

Finally, the use of the notion of development in Western literature originally focused on the economic dimension of the concept and was associated with the notion of capitalism, that is, with the economic system that, after several centuries of gestation, from the modern era onwards, was based on the technological foundations of the British Industrial Revolution since the end of the 18th century.

The starting point for the study of capitalism and, consequently, of economic development is the studies of the classical economists and, in particular, the so-called "father of political economy", Adam Smith, who associated the growth of the social product with technical progress, linked to the technical division of labor in the manufacturing workshops.

The main classical economists (Adam Smith, David Ricardo, Robert Malthus) unveiled the structural features of capitalism, and the economic foundations of the class structure inherent to it. They also raised the main problems of economic value, underlying the market prices that weight the social product.

Concrete human labor produces concrete goods, and the relation between the amount of product generated (Q) and the amount of labor required to generate it (T) is called productiveness (or productive power) of labor (Q/T), a basic indicator of the phenomenon we have called economic development. When the average productivity of work is considered at the macroeconomic level, weighted by relative market prices, the counterpart of this increase in the productive power of societies is the increase in the average purchasing power of the population. If we call (N) the total population, we can reach another indicator (Q/N) which would be the quantity of goods and services that can be acquired on average per person. If Q is expressed in physical units, we are in the presence of technical and not economic measures of development, since the measurements of the social product pass through market valuations weighted by relative prices. A deeper understanding of these economic measures brings us back to the theory that studies the features of capitalism.

Apart from the economistic view implied by the above considerations, another enormous shortcoming of these measurements is that they are averages. Therefore, the notion of distribution (or sharing) of the social product is left out. If we introduce the notion of distribution of the social product, not all product growth implies economic development, since the study of distribution "infiltrates" (implicitly or explicitly) the study of distributive justice, opening the door to considerations of a much broader ethical and social nature.

The meaning of the distribution of the social product refers us to a theory of justice. The first of these theories that has long endured in the history of Western economic and political thought is the Aristotelian distinction between distributive justice and commutative justice.

This and later approaches to the issue of distributive justice (the most important in the second half of the 20th century was put forward by John

Rawls in his "Theory of Justice") have emerged with great force in the 21st century, overcoming the limits of Rawls' approach and raising the multidimensional problems of equal civil, political, economic, social and cultural rights.

Moreover, the notions of growth in the productive capacity of labor and growth in the purchasing power of the total population refer us to a purely quantitative and economistic version of growth, but are absolutely insufficient if we wish to penetrate into an understanding of the impact of the notion of economic development on human societies as a whole. For this deeper understanding, it is necessary to examine the historical and structural conditions that gave rise to the emergence of capitalism as the dominant system in the contemporary era of the West.

Indeed, the merely Empiricist-Economic approach to capitalist development is clearly reductionist and does not allow us to penetrate into the more multidimensional visions of the subject of development. It does not take into consideration the profound social transformations that have come with the arrival of capitalism: changes in the structuring of social classes and the formation of an industrial proletariat, processes of urbanization and metropolization, transformation of family organization, separation between the place of work and the place of personal residence, demographic transition, increase in the literacy process, etc. The study of the social impacts of capitalism is today an important part of social studies in general and sociological studies in particular.

As we know, the arrival of the contemporary era at the end of the 18th century was accompanied not only by the British Industrial Revolution (the technological basis of capitalism from that date onwards) but also by the French (1789) and American (1776) political revolutions, which introduced the republican values and principles of democracy and human rights, which still predominate in Western culture. Taken as a whole, the capitalist economic system and the democratic political system are, respectively, expressions of economic liberalism (Adam Smith) and political liberalism (Locke, Rousseau, etc.), which had a simultaneous birth in the history of the West.

Adam Smith, considered not only the father of economic liberalism, but also the founder of the classical theoretical current in economic science, was the first to establish the connections between the technical and social division of labor, the growth of labor productivity and the expansion of national and international markets.

Also, when Marx spoke of the development of the productive forces under the command of the capital ("Capital" is precisely the name of his main work), he gave a central role (as a starting point) to the Industrial Revolution, and in a broader or more general way to the development of the productive forces within the capitalist mode of production. The same was done by non- Marxist authors such as Werner Sombart, Max Weber, and Joseph Schumpeter, all linked to German historicism. Capitalism is the historical structural framework in which economic development has taken place, understood in a restricted sense as the systematic and secular expansion of the productive power of human labor. In addition to the European historicist school, there is another current of economic thought that has deepened the notion of development within the framework of the study of the capitalist system: American institutionalism (for example, Thorstein Veblen and John Commons).

The concept of economic development acquired special political and academic relevance at the end of the Second World War of the 20th century, with the process of decolonization accompanied and promoted by the founding of the United Nations Organization (1945). The theme of underdevelopment then emerged, i.e., the study of the situations of poverty and deprivation of nations that were abandoning their colonial status and entering the process of political independence. This historical process was followed by the study of development and underdevelopment as relatively autonomous disciplines of economic science. It was at that time that the contributions of Latin American structuralism (composed of authors such as Raúl Prebisch, Celso Furtado, Osvaldo Sunkel, Anibal Pinto and Aldo Ferrer) took place. This school of thought, established under the auspices of ECLAC-UN to study the specific features of development and underdevelopment under the conditions of peripheral capitalism, formulated an important historical perspective for the interpretation of Latin American societies from the very moment of their conquest and colonization by the Iberian powers.

Underlying the principles and values of the UN was always the defense of democracy and human rights. Other Latin American sociologists of the time, such as José Medina Echavarría and Gino Germani, also highlighted the issue of democracy in its interaction with capitalism, in the modalities that these systems assumed in Latin America. In his last book, Raúl Prebisch, the founder of the structuralist approach that originated in ECLAC, once again highlighted the historical links between the peripheral forms of capitalism and the obstacles to the firm development of democratic institutions in Latin America (see the second part of this book).

Ethics and capitalism

The birth of economics as a science coincided with the emergence of a new vision of the world, that of economic liberalism, which attempts to demonstrate the existence of a significant connection between the selfish motives of people's behavior and the favorable results that this behavior generates on the general and overall well-being of those same people.

Pre-modern Western ethical principles with Greco-Latin roots were built on the notions of good and evil, virtue and vice, duties and dignities, justice and the common good. In particular, altruistic personal motivations were considered "good", and selfish and hedonistic ones were perceived as "bad". On a social scale, these were the foundations of the common good. However, the advent of economic liberalism was based on the pragmatic recognition that most human beings act selfishly in the sphere of markets and are more concerned with the maximum possible satisfaction of their desires than with the virtuous nature of their behavior.

The paradoxical element, if you will, of classical liberalism from the ethical point of view was the notion, somewhat unusual up to that time, that the pursuit of profit and its unlimited increase was a source of social abundance. This result derived from the logic of competition through the market mechanism.

The historical expression of this economic logic was the emergence of capitalism, a market economic system founded on a Technological Revolution which, from the last quarter of the 18th century, began a sustained process of productive expansion of human labor.

The expression capitalism refers to an economic system based on the power of the capitalist, a person who has sufficient acquisitive power to control not only the commodities, but also the factors required (natural resources, labor and technology) to produce them. The capitalist aims to increase his economic power in an indefinite sequence. His initial instrument is the possession of money, which by acquiring productive factors is converted first into productive power and then into commodities-products; the sale of these products allows him to recover his money with profits, in an indefinite process where the final goal is to continually increase capital.

The Aristotelian-Thomistic version of ethics that predominated in Western Europe for most of the pre-modern period presumed a congruence between the morality of the personal behaviors of individual economic actors and the expected overall results of the economic process. There was a correlation between the virtuous behavior of people and the achievement of the common good. For example, loaning money with high rate of interest was considered usury, which was ethically wrong both on a personal and social level, and the pursuit of unlimited profit was considered a perversion of the logic of exchange. Aristotle had differentiated between the notions of natural Chrematistics, where exchange had as its objective the satisfaction of the needs of the contracting parties, and lucrative Chrematistics, where the ethically reprehensible objective was the pursuit of unlimited profit.

But in a world of scarcity and poverty, the ideologues of liberalism proposed that, from an Eco-economic point of view, the increased production of wealth was a good result in the general interest, even if it was based on individual personal behavior whose motives were considered bad by traditionally accepted ethics. The magic or invisible hand of the market made it possible for people who enriched themselves beyond all limits (conduct considered bad by traditional ethics) on an individual scale to achieve a result (considered good by emerging ethics) that created wealth and increased the economic well-being of all.

This generated new moral attitudes that fostered the development of capitalism, and new ethical justifications, congruent with an economic science based on quantitative criteria that were measurable by market prices.

The classical ethics of Greco-Latin roots, conceived and applied to personal behaviors and, by extension, to their social results, whose most generalized expression in the Western world consisted of pursuing good and rejecting evil, had to confront the new individualistic and utilitarian ethics according to which, through selfish but efficient behavior on an individual scale, the market mechanism promised to overcome the pain of scarcity and enjoy the pleasure of abundance.

The drivers of this process, members of the nascent industrial bourgeoisie, owners of productive capital, imposed a code of selfish behavior that was legitimized through the market. The purchasing power of capital applied to production and based on the control of technological power proved capable of generating an indefinite expansion of the wealth of nations. This is precisely the title of the book by Adam Smith, economist and moral philosopher considered the founding father of economic science, which emerged as an autonomous discipline in this historical period.

In his foundational book "The Wealth of Nations", Adam Smith clearly enunciates that mutation by virtue of which individualistic and selfish behavior applied to market operations gives rise to an expansion of general welfare, to the extent that such welfare is measured or associated with the increasing expansion of productive capacity per capita. It is not by the benevolence of the butcher or the baker that we obtain the products of consumption, Smith will say, but by appealing to their selfish self-interest that we get them to supply us with the goods we need.

The different ethical formulations that subsequently emerged show that the development of the institutions of capitalism can be based on different positions (perhaps we should say justifications or legitimations) in the field of morality and ethics. This process is far from being finished.

Examining the historical facts, the German sociologist Max Weber, wrote studies published in the early twentieth century, that linked the birth of capitalism to the emergence of a formal rationality based on economic calculation, which could be taken to its ultimate consequences when the institutions of capitalism made it possible to convert all the conditions and resources required by the production process, and not just some inputs and final products, into commodities with a calculable price. Capitalism turned the labor capacity of human beings, natural resources, technological knowledge, etc. into commodities, expressing them in units of economic value through the use of money, unit of measure and means of circulation.

This process of expansion of the so-called formal rationality was accompanied by a so-called material rationality which, according to Weber's terminology, was expressed in the Calvinist ethic, endowed with what we could call an asceticism applied to the production of wealth. Protestant ethics, and Calvinism in particular, thus emerge as an alternative to Catholic ethics, creating conditions capable of legitimizing the development of capitalism by making it possible to reconcile in principle the mechanisms of the market with some of the old notions of virtue on a personal scale, suitably modified.

However, the most generalized and enduring ethical foundation for the legitimization of the capitalist order came from utilitarianism. It was the Englishman Jeremy Bentham (1748-1832) who laid the foundations of this ethical system on which capitalism as an economic system and the academic theory that continues to be the most widespread in the West to this day are based: neoclassical microeconomics.

Utilitarian ethics and neoclassical economics

Utilitarianism tends to identify the notion of happiness with the notion of pleasure. According to Bentham an innate principle of human behavior is to flee from pain and pursue pleasure. But to say that happiness is the pursuit of pleasure is not the same as saying that happiness is the result of a virtuous life. This not only generates a terminological confusion but also a gulf in relation to the foundations of traditional ethics.

Pleasure is the outcome of the satisfaction of individual desires regardless of the virtuous or vicious character of those particular desires and, even of the concrete morality of those who seek such pleasure. John Stuart Mill, a disciple of Bentham, is content to accept that happiness is a desirable thing and it is sufficient that it be desirable to consider it a good.

In short, for utilitarians a good has the quality of satisfying desires, that is why it is a good, that is, why it is something good. The quality of satisfying desires that a good has is the utility of the good, and the satisfaction of desire generates "happiness". Hence the notion of "happiness", in its utilitarian meaning, consists in the satisfaction of desires and not in the cultivation of a life of virtue as had been established in the Aristotelian tradition.

The theory of markets and prices was built on the notions of utility already put forward by Bentham, whose most important feature was the claim of cardinal measurability and interpersonal comparison of magnitudes of utility. Therefore, this ethics admitted its theoretical association with the price system. From these ideas, continued by John Stuart Mill, arose the neoclassical theory of markets and prices, in which the substances of value, measured by the price system, were utility and scarcity, and the measurable matter was marginal utility. The utilitarian theory of welfare was perfected by Wilfredo Pareto, in the framework of the general equilibrium model under perfect competition conditions formalized by Leon Walras.

But utilitarianism, understood as the ethics on which capitalism was based, was part of a broader conception called liberalism, which also included a new vision of the political process, where the ontological foundation of the social order rested on the individual. This was the starting point of the political system, contractually constructed by individuals to preserve themselves from abuses of power coming from themselves in the course of social interactions. This contractualist vision of society had important intellectual supporters, in particular Rousseau. The contractualist vision of the political system implied that authority came from the individuals themselves who agreed on its constitution. The sovereignty of the state no longer came from a divine origin, but was the result of the individual decisions of human beings.

In Locke's case, this system considered private property as a natural right whose origin and legitimacy should be sought in personal labor needed to appropriate the goods of nature and thus contributed to the elaboration of a theory of markets in which prices were considered as a measure of the labor contained in the goods. From this point of view Locke is a predecessor of the labor theories of value held by the classical economists and by Marx. He is also an indirect and remote predecessor of today's so-called libertarian theories that take as their starting point the "ownership of oneself" and of all property lawfully acquired through personal labor.

In the mid-nineteenth century and as a consequence of the excesses of capitalism in the treatment of the working class (during a historical period in which democracy was still far from prevailing in Europe), different forms of "utopian socialism" arose, founded on principles of a cooperative type, those who herald the arrival of the ideas of Karl Marx and his "scientific socialism"

Implicit determinism in Marx's economic theory

In the case of Marx's theory of value there is a technological determinism which fixes the values of commodities in accordance with their content of abstract labor embodied under average technical conditions corresponding to a given era. In the purest model (set forth in volume I of "Capital") the "law of value" operates without restriction, according to which commodities are exchanged in accordance with their content of abstract, social and average labor. In the third volume of the same work, the notion of production prices is introduced, which are also calculated in terms of value but include the premise of the equalization of profit rates as a consequence of the transfer of capital from less profitable processes to more profitable ones. Here we find a mixture between a mechanism originating in the sphere of production (attribution of value to commodities through abstract labor), and another mechanism originating in the sphere of markets (competition between capitals that, seeking to maximize their individual rate of profit, end up generating the equalization of the general rate of profit).

Where do human beings, and, with them, social ethics, come into these processes? Nowhere. Indeed, Marx remarks in the penultimate paragraph of his preface to the first German edition of the first volume of "Capital": "A few words to avoid possible misinterpretations. The capitalists and landowners are not depicted in a rosy light. But people are referred here only as personifications of economic categories, as bearers of certain class relations and class interests. My point of view, which approaches the development of the economic formation of society as a natural-historical process, can less than any other make the individual responsible for relations of which he is socially the product, although subjectively he may be far above them."

In other words, the vision is completely deterministic and the person is a creature of the structures that have conditioned him. The notions of freedom and social responsibility are not taken into account.

In the first quarter of the twentieth century, the Russian Revolution installed a collectivist experiment in centralized planning, inspired by Marx's ideas, and based on the notion that prices could be understood as a measure of the labor content of commodities. The collectivist vision, from an ethical point of view, subsumed the individual in a raison d'état oriented to a transition from class society to communist society. Once again, the idea of the individual was sacrificed to the great political objectives of the construction of communism, and the transition from one stage to the other was to be verified through the dictatorship of the proletariat, legitimized in its excesses by the final outcome, in which the sacrificed generations did so for the benefit of the future generations that would enjoy the communist world. Marx believed that in the classless society human nature would appear again in all its integrity without the alienations that were imposed on it in the class societies.

In the centrally developed economies where the so-called dictatorship of the proletariat operated, considerations of social and human ethics remained, waiting for the process of the dictatorship of the proletariat to bring the world to the promised land of communism proper. At that utopian moment, ethics would emerge in the behavior of effectively free people.

Implicit determinism in neoclassical economic liberalism

On the other side, it is also possible to demonstrate the determinism contained in neoclassical economic theory. Note that classical liberalism was founded on other theoretical bases than Neo-classical liberalism. Unlike the classic theories, according to whom prices measure human labor, the neoclassicals say that prices measure utility and scarcity, marginally determined according to the rational calculus of consumers and producers. Consumers are the starting point of the whole process (consumer sovereignty) and seek to maximize the satisfaction of their individual desires, expressed through their individual preference functions. Although the neoclassicals did not emphasize that point at all, that optimum or maximum depends of course on the general purchasing power possessed, determined at the point where (graphically speaking according to neoclassical formalizations) "the budget line is tangent to the highest indifference curve in consumption, on the basis of which each consumer determines his personal basket". This jargon, intelligible only to those initiated in analytical geometry, inaugurated the widespread use (and sometimes abuse) of mathematical analysis in the study of economic theory.

Producers, on the other hand, based on the marginal preferences of solvent consumers, face a demand curve that allows them to produce under conditions of efficiency, associated with the calculation of marginal costs that determine the quantities produced. In both cases the economic agents lack the power to influence prices significantly on their own, they are in economic lexicon "price-takers", and the premises of the analysis assume the atomicity of these contracting parties ("perfect" competition).

Under conditions and positions of general equilibrium (or partial equilibrium under the “Ceteris paribus” clause) of markets, the agents of the process are mere optimizers of magnitudes, calculated on the basis of the instrumental rationality of an economic man. In this sense, it is apparently free individuals (consumer sovereignty) who determine the logic of markets and prices through their behavior.

But only apparently, because the premises of perfect competition mean that the only "freedom" of economic man (characterized by John Stuart Mill) consists in moving towards positions of optimum, according to his consumption preferences or technological alternatives. The mechanism is deterministic, because the premises of the model of "perfect" competition and the behavior of "economic man" mathematically predetermine the results of market functioning.

The two substantive elements that really ultimately determine prices are not materially considered by neoclassical economic theory. The theory does not deepen further into the field to determine the content of consumers' preferences nor to determine the real income that determines their purchasing power. The subject of consumer preferences is not something that, according to the positivist view of neoclassical economics, is a subject for the theory, but only for the desires of the sovereign consumer. In the same way, the magnitude of personal consumable income is part of the distribution of real income which, according to the neoclassicals, is not a matter for economic science either. On the other side, the minimum essential needs that every human being must satisfy, and which the classical economists (and also Marx) had considered under the notion of subsistence wages, disappear from the neoclassical theoretical space. Therefore, social ethics is out of the question since it is impossible to determine either the distributive justice associated with these behaviors, or to evaluate the nature or motivations of individual behaviors expressed in the market. Utilitarianism remains as an ethical background according to which the total utility of goods is always positive, which constitutes a good basis for the excesses of a consumerist psychology.

The process, mathematically formulated by the neoclassicals, leading to the stable equilibrium of markets is inexorable. It is totally predetermined by the premises of the analysis, and the only rationality that is presumed in the contracting parties is of an instrumental nature associated with the notion of efficiency. It consists in optimizing the ends (producers' profit or consumers' welfare) for a given endowment of means. But ethics does not enter into the analysis, or rather, the only one that "can enter" is utilitarian ethics in its most individualistic and consumerist version, because preferences are evaluated by levels of personal satisfaction and not by good or bad content, altruistic or selfish, fair or unfair of the decisions of the individuals. This instrumental rationality is perfectly isolated from the realms of politics and culture. Moreover, the neoclassical notion of "economic men" assumes that they communicate with each other only through markets, and their "human" nature is devoid of any other dimension, not only ethical, but also cultural, ludic or political.

When neoclassical theory, starting in the first third of the 20th century, had no choice but to admit, reluctantly, that perfect competition does not exist and that markets are affected by asymmetries of economic power, political power or cultural power, this admission brought up the notion of market "imperfections". In other words, "deviations" from the premises of perfect competition were examined. Even so, the academic microeconomic theory that is still mostly taught today in the United States and Latin America continues to consider the mechanism of more or less pure or perfect competition as the starting point for the study of resource allocation. Once this article of faith has been established, neoclassical economic theory studies some of the asymmetries of power in markets under the label of "market imperfections" (monopoly, oligopoly, game theory, monopolistic competition). Under these imperfections, which are obviously not such, but rather the real conditions in today's global markets, the issue of the responsibility of the most powerful actors emerges, for example, in recent reflections on corporate social responsibility.

An important conclusion arises from this in the sphere of economic ethics. Only by recognizing the real asymmetries of power that operate through markets is it possible to raise the issues of commutative and distributive justice that are inherent to social ethics.

State and public policies in the capitalism

In the neoclassical theoretical vision and in the concrete historical practice of capitalism, after the emergence of the Soviet regime, the image of the state was that of the executioner of the "free" economy. Thus, the paradigms of the theory of perfect competition became not only an allegedly scientific instrument to understand the logic of capitalist markets, but also a powerful ideological instrument to confront the excesses of government regulation. From an ethical point of view, here too we were confronted with a determinism where human freedom and creativity were annulled, or rather, put at the service of the construction of a utopia: the communist society where class society would have been definitively overcome.

In the 1930s, the idea of the invisible hand and the self-regulation of markets entered into a deep crisis. The Great Depression of the 1930s demonstrated that micro-economic behavior based on the postulates of competition could not rescue the capitalist economy from a recessionary paralysis where economic activity levels plummeted and unemployment reached dramatic proportions. At that historical moment, the theoretical message of the English economist John Maynard Keynes had a strong impact on the dynamics and logic of both capitalism and democracy.

Keynesian economics legitimized the role of the state as an economic agent. The liberal democratic state ceased to be the executioner of capitalism, as in the Soviet Union, and became its eventual savior. Another macroeconomics emerged as a new and well-established branch of economic science, and recalcitrant liberalism based on the self-regulation of markets gave way to the legitimacy of the State's public, fiscal, monetary and exchange rate policies.

Keynesianism was born to save capitalism, not to bring it down, and it promoted the emergence of a consumerist ethic, since the dynamics of the capitalist system suffered cyclical declines in the demand for consumer goods, which had to be stimulated in both the short and long term. In the short term, fiscal and monetary policy could help to alleviate recessionary situations with a low utilization of installed capacity, and, in the long term, the accumulation of capital, exacerbated advertising, consumer manipulation, and the accelerated obsolescence of goods became mechanisms for stimulating the effective demand that kept the capitalist machine in operation. The results of these strategies have not only promoted consumerism, but also wastefulness, "charged to the account" of the human environment and the stability of the biosphere.

This role of the state as the necessary regulator and stabilizer of capitalism, after the end of World War II, was also transferred to political systems. The process of decolonization and the founding of the United Nations created a space for action in the field of development policies. After two catastrophic wars and an unprecedented economic crisis in the history of capitalism, the subject of ethics, which had been eclipsed from the scene in the first half of the 20th century, reappeared. The dignity of human beings was emphatically and explicitly recognized in the Universal Declaration of Human Rights.

Regulated or mixed-economy capitalism and the emerging social democracies showed a face of the regulatory and welfare state, very different from the oppressive and authoritarian state of the Soviet world. A very important theme of this historical stage is that of the consolidation of democracy in Western Europe. In this post-war historical moment, European society suffered several risks. Firstly, the risk of being absorbed by communist ideology, and secondly, the risk of political fragmentation and irrelevance in a world where the hegemonic powers presented an enormous scale in terms of geography and demography.

The European reaction to these risks, led to a large extent by neo-Thomist Christian-social visions (such as those inspired by the ideas of Jacques Maritain), was to advance along the paths of democratization and integration. Europe was finally democratized. For the first time in a generalized way, parliamentary democracies were installed to remain. The democratization and integration of Western Europe fed back on each other, giving rise to a great economic and political experiment that has culminated in the European Union.

The ethics of regulated capitalism in developed economies

The ethics of regulated capitalism in the economic sphere and of social democracies in the political sphere, was a compromise between the notions of individualism and utilitarianism that are at the essence of the capitalist behaviors, on one side, and the notions of economic, social and cultural rights that are at the core of the political behaviors of social democracy, on the other side.

As these economic and political processes took hold, new ethical positions emerged to reflect them. One of them, very representative of the new ethical visions that this process brought with it, was liberal egalitarianism (John Rawls). The academic impact of Rawls' ideas was enormous, perhaps because he reintroduced a notion, typical of pre-modern social ethics, which the individualism and libertarianism of the first half of the twentieth century had erased from the dictionary: justice.

Rightly understood, John Rawls was first and foremost a political philosopher who tried to preserve the worldview of contractualist liberalism. However, he also claimed to be an egalitarian, and the convergence of these two objectives (freedom and equality) helps to shape his "Theory of Justice". It is useful to outline his main ideas in view of the enormous impact they have had on current studies of ethics and political philosophy.

His theory of goods is a basis for his theory of justice. Primary goods are characterized as the general means required to be able to aspire to or have access to a good life (note the difference between this concept and that of welfare in its utilitarian origin). Rawls distinguishes between two types of primary goods: natural and social. Natural primary goods are health and talents. Social primary goods are basically three: fundamental freedoms, opportunities for access to social positions and the socio-economic advantages linked to these positions.

His theory of justice is aimed at achieving a fair distribution of social goods. According to Rawls, the normative principles for such a task are twofold: 1) Each person must have an equal right to the most extensive scheme of basic freedoms that is compatible with a similar scheme of freedoms for others. 2) Social and economic inequalities are to be shaped in such a way that: a) they are reasonably expected to be advantageous to all, b) they are linked to jobs and positions that are affordable to all, and c) they are linked to jobs and positions that are affordable to all, and d) they are not only advantageous to all, but also to all. This minimal reference to Rawls' theory of justice is not sufficient to go into it in depth, nor is it the purpose of this article to attempt to do so.

However, a central feature of Rawls' vision is to have achieved a convergence between the notions of freedom and equality. The first (freedom) considered as a central feature of libertarianism and the second (equality) considered as a central feature of the vision of a shared human nature, which assumes different origins and versions. In a certain sense, the Rawlsian social ethic, compatible with Keynesianism, is the one that best represents, legitimizes and rationalizes the regulated capitalism and social democracy installed in the world from the immediate post-war period until the so-called conservative revolution of the 1980s.

A decisive point of Rawls' ethical vision is his rejection of utilitarianism and his attachment to a Kantian vision of freedom, where what is necessary is to preserve the dignity of each man considered as an end in himself. Another essential point is the enormous importance that Rawls gives to the notion of public goods or social goods in the creation of a just society.

Economic globalization and neoliberalism

Finally, in the last quarter of the twentieth century it was regulated capitalism and social democracy supported by a welfare state that went into crisis in the developed centers. Excessive fiscal spending in the United States, and the heavy tax burden on large corporations led on the one hand to inflationary positions and on the other hand to a discouragement of productive investment. The excess of social benefits tended to produce an increasing share of the public sector and wages in total income, reducing the share of corporate profits. Thus began a process of inflation with recession that was unprecedented in the U.S. economy. In the 1980s this process led to a rejection of Keynesian economics, to an effort to reduce both the size of the state and its intervention in the field of economic life, including spending on public social goods. The arrival in the early 1980s of the governments of Margaret Thatcher in England and Ronald Reagan in the United States ushered in an era known as the Conservative Revolution.

The 1980s witnessed the accelerated spread of information and communication technologies, coinciding with a new vision of political economy in harmony with the principles of the so-called Washington Consensus, which restored the process of resource allocation controlled by large corporations in a context of emerging globalization understood as a growing mobility not only of goods through trade but also of new services associated with the development of ICTs, as well as of technologies and investments linked to foreign direct investment. The same year as the promulgation of the ideas of the Washington Consensus was the year of the fall of the Berlin Wall and the collapse of the centrally planned economies of Central Europe.

Capitalism and liberal representative democracy remained the only systems regulating economic and political processes in the Western world. However, capitalism began to operate on the basis of new technological positions, and resorted to new market strategies and tactics. This process contributed on one side to the concentration and on the other side to the depersonalization of economic power.

From an ethical perspective, this historical inflection at the end of the 20th century generated "restorative" positions of a highly concentrating liberal individualism called neo-liberalism. The foundations of this economic power are "sincere", based no longer on alleged contributions to the general welfare (along utilitarian lines) but simply on the legitimacy and economic and political necessity of a solid private property regime. The economic process that has resulted in the emergence of the Conservative Revolution and the principles of the Washington Consensus in its translation into the sphere of ethics and political philosophy has come to be known as libertarianism. Its main ideologues have been Von Hayek and Robert Nozick. The most extreme positions of this approach have come to be called anarcho-capitalism.

Libertarianism defines human freedom as the ownership of oneself and of all legitimately owned objects. The legitimacy of contractual and market relations depends solely on the will of the contracting parties (who by definition are owners). Libertarianism is concerned with the origin of a legitimate property, and presents different arguments in an attempt to justify it, which we cannot go into in this review. Suffice it to say that, for libertarians, the just price is by definition the one "sovereignly" agreed between two legitimate contracting parties and does not depend on any other consideration related to the issue of justice.

In certain extra-economic moral aspects, libertarianism recognizes the right of a person to do with his or her life as he or she sees fit to take drugs, to commit suicide, to be the object of consensual and voluntary euthanasia, to have sexual relations or establish stable ties with persons of the same sex, to isolate himself or herself from the world, etc. The only limits imposed by this vision are first, not to cede ownership of oneself to another person or persons, second, to accept the need for supervision that young people require until they acquire their full capacity, and, third, to limit the freedom of each individual with respect to criminal actions against the property of others or legitimately acquired goods. These limits apply especially with respect to taxation or expropriation prerogatives on the part of the State, which in the case of anarcho-capitalists is considered theft.

Although this ethic acquires full intelligibility with respect to human beings, its greatest use has been in legal entities, organizations and, above all, large economic corporations. In these, ownership is depersonalized in the form of large limited liability companies or joint stock companies whose share capital is listed on the stock exchange and is easily transferable.

In practice, the globalization process has pitted increasingly weakened nation states in their public policy options against large transnational corporations. These corporations impose transnational legal norms originating in intergovernmental and private agencies with respect to the transnational ownership of investments, services, innovations and industrial brands, etc., which often conflict with the legal norms of the countries in which their investments are based. At a deeper level the issue can be seen as a confrontation between the property rights of transnational corporations totally depersonalized in their responsibility and the human and citizens' rights of the inhabitants of the nations where they locate their investments.

Today's economic world is, more than ever before, a world of business institutions and organizations linked together by an inextricable web of legal commitments of a patrimonial nature. Unlike human persons who are individuals, organizations are legal entities that cannot be considered as human rights protectors because organizations as such lack conscience and will and are merely instrumental. Their rights and obligations are patrimonial and are governed by the norms that regulate contracts (public and private) proper to commutative justice. Even those institutions dedicated to satisfying elementary human rights (social security organizations, schools, hospitals, etc.) must acquire legal personality and are subject to patrimonial norms that are set with a view to the things that are administered there and not to the persons who benefit from those services.

Of course, there are also norms that regulate the rights and duties of individuals, family and penal codes, written and unwritten moral norms, but the distributive justice that is due to individuals is always mediated, in organizations, by multiple "transaction costs" that limit or hinder its practice.

In today's globalized world, institutions regulating commutative justice applicable to organizations, especially transnational economic organizations, tend to predominate over those regulating distributive justice applicable to individuals who are citizens of States. The former is imposing themselves on companies (which lack political citizenship) with great force through the process of globalization of capitalism, while the latter can only operate through national political systems (or eventually supranational ones when several nations join forces to defend their rights).

The process of globalization of capitalism is above all a process of trans-nationalization of enterprises on a global scale, or at least on a supranational scale, with the consequent consolidation of the changes in property rights that are required for the efficient functioning of commutative justice. Consequently, commutative justice applied to the logic of global capitalism pre-dominates distributive justice applicable to democratic political systems.

The challenge is to create a consolidated democratic culture on a Latin American scale, considering pre-existing affinities, especially those linked to the common heritage that still underlies our cultural ethos. The fundamental objective should be to give priority to the fundamental human and citizens' rights of individuals over the economic rights of corporations. This does not mean imposing economic burdens (minimum wages, for example) on enterprises, especially micro, small and medium-sized ones, that they are unable to pay, but rather using the mechanisms of political democracy to consolidate the economic and cultural dimensions of democracy. It also implies the application of corrective measures of a redistributive nature in the face of the enormous asymmetries in economic power that exist, for example, between the large trans nationalized economic groups and the small and medium-sized enterprises that contribute so much to the generation of job opportunities.

The conservative revolution and its economic policies

In 1980, the new economic strategies of the so-called "Conservative Revolution" in the United States ("reaganomics") were unleashed, preceded by the British turnaround under Margaret Thatcher. This date (1980) could also be accepted as a starting point for the worldwide spread of information technologies that enthroned the leading role of transnationals in the world economy and initiated the process of globalization. The transition was thus towards increasingly open economies, guided by the strategies of transnational corporations in the search for competitive advantages.

The new neoliberal theorizing of the 1980s de-emphasized the role of fiscal policies of public spending (and especially social spending) after the high inflation of the 1970s in the United States. The conservative revolution encouraged "monetarist" policies (based primarily on interest rate management) and "supply-side" policies (based on corporate tax cuts) so that private investors would replace public investment and assume a decisive role in the allocation of resources.

Supply-side theories (so called "supply-side" theories) were promoted by authors such as Laffer, who called for a reduction in the tax burden. He argued that this measure would stimulate private investment and economic growth, thus making possible, as a consequence of the growth of the economy, a higher tax collection with lower tax rates.

The neoliberal or libertarian economic position derives from this Conservative Revolution of the 1980s. Its strategy in Latin America is " growth-oriented " (development-oriented in the narrowest and most economy-oriented in terms) and compatible with a recalcitrant " libertarianism " at the level of ethics. It is " growth-oriented ", if one accepts this terminological barbarism, at the level of the economy as a whole, but its libertarianism makes total abstraction of any egalitarian or solidary conception, at the distributive or social level.

Economic neo-liberalism, strongly akin to the postulates of neoclassical economics already examined, rejects the minimum wage because the wage "must be fixed by market forces" and employers will not pay wages above what, in their opinion, the hired worker marginally produces. Therefore, they say that a minimum wage would be "arbitrary" (i.e., not linked to labor productivity). Therefore, if they are forced to accept it, they will not hire additional workers, they will not invest and the economy will not grow, all of which will obviously lead to an increase in unemployment.

This point, developed with wage policy and practices, deserves further consideration. On one side, it is necessary to accept that the survival and development of private enterprise requires average wages that are lower than the corresponding average labor productivities, as the only way to allow profits and reinvestment in the productive branch in question. On the other side, the neo-classicals are also forced to accept that the wage set by the market may not be sufficient to overcome the poverty line of hired workers. However, in such a case, they dissociate themselves from the problem and hand it over to the State, which is responsible for assisting the unemployed or underemployed.

In the concrete neoliberal version of the economic policy propagated by the so-called "conservative revolution" ("reaganomics" and "thatcherism") proposes a reduction in the tax burden, which reduces the state's possibilities to provide unemployment benefits or wage supplements.

The only true and profound solution to the problem of poverty is, for neoliberals, the very accelerated economic growth, and in this sense, (narrow and reductive) they are "developmentalists" or, more precisely, "growth-minded". Of course, this economic growth, thus postulated, depends on the investment of productive capital coming from the entrepreneurs themselves (national and/or transnational). If these, as a whole, decide not to invest productively, they will impede growth and generate unemployment.

In the neoliberal perspective, which grudgingly accepts the existence of the State, the State should be in charge of subsidizing the unemployed in order to lift them out of poverty. But the position frequently held by the business chambers, in terms of fiscal policy, is that a budget deficit derived from "excessive" social spending should be avoided, so that the upper limit of such spending will depend on the tax income of the high- income sectors, starting with that of the businessmen themselves. Businessmen are asking for "clear and stable signals" on taxes, and, in a way, consider that the contributions to the tax coffers, which employers are required to make under the social and labor laws, are also a form of taxation.

The neoliberal vision ignores the issue of poverty, because it does not start from human needs to set a minimum wage, but takes as its starting point the marginal productivity of labor. It should also be noted that, if businessmen decide not to create jobs, the State will probably not be able to do so either, because recessionary conditions will reduce its tax revenues and the possibility of social spending. The main neoliberal arguments are: that poverty can only be overcome through economic growth that ensures full employment of workers with increasing wages; that state subsidies are inefficient and insufficient; that full employment depends on private investment, but that employers will not invest when the minimum legal wage exceeds that compatible with the maximum wage they are willing to pay.

In the most recalcitrant libertarian formulations, there is not even an attempt to determine what this minimum wage should be based on its effective productivity, but rather the argument is based on the employer's discretion regarding the wage he is willing to pay, according to his positions of power in the distributive struggle. In this way, we fall into a self-fulfilling prophecy: the objective indicator that minimum wages are high and that relations are rigid is the existence of unemployment. When businessmen consider that the minimum or average wage is too high, they simply reduce their levels of activity in the country concerned, automatically creating higher levels of unemployment. In the global world, this option is becoming increasingly viable, without detriment to business interests, in view of the growing globalization of investment opportunities in both the productive and financial fields.

In opposition to this vision, it will be suggested here that the correct planning of development, as a necessary mechanism to alleviate or solve the problem of poverty, requires starting from the real existing people interacting in concrete social environments, and taking into consideration their capacities or potentialities, on the one hand, and their needs on the other. This is what is done, for example, by the Social Teaching of the Catholic Church, or by the original Aristotelian visions on which it is based. But we can never arrive at the concept of poverty on the basis of the efficiency conditions of the labor market, or of the individual preferences of "solvent" consumers.

Neoclassical economists, including their contemporary neoliberal expression, accept that poverty exists as a social problem. Obviously they could not deny it, but they derive to the State the obligation to subsidize the poorest (the richest have an increasingly privatized social security). It is clear, however, that the capacity of the State to subsidize via social spending remains within very strict limits given by the budgetary balance and by a tax containment defended at all costs by the business associations.

Over the last thirty years, the rules of the Washington Consensus have helped to consolidate these restrictions on the operational capacity of the state. Therefore, the State does not necessarily have sufficient resources to ensure a minimum standard of living for the entire population. In short, the logic of the market in global capitalism, if it operates without political counterweights, conspires against the logic of distributive justice and democracy.

It is a matter of subordinating the logic of capitalism to the logic of democracy through political means.

The self-regulation of the markets puts corporations as the key player in the capitalist system. The liberal vision of the world according to which, in the pursuit of private interest, companies, through the market mechanism, manage to increase the general welfare, understood as a greater growth of income and wealth per inhabitant, has survived as the foundation of capitalism since the beginning of the contemporary era.

As this mechanism is presumably "automatic", we have already seen that individual responsibilities are diluted, and in particular the responsibilities of the powerful. However, the growth of large global corporations since the late eighties of the twentieth century makes evident their immense power and highlights their growing social responsibility (see chapter XVII in part four of this book).

Part Two

The Latin American School of Development[10] [11]

[10] Paper published in Revista Electrónica Cinta de Moebio year 2007 issue 29: 124-154 www.moebio.uchile.cl/29/difilippo.html.

[11] I would like to dedicate this section to José Besa, former director of the ECLAC Library, who has patiently and rigorously created the ECLAC Room where present and future researchers can directly learn about the sources of Latin American thought on development originated in that institution.

Chapter II

Reference framework

The main objective of this book is to create a frame of reference for a joint analysis of the contributions to Latin American development made by social scientists linked to the United Nations Economic Commission for Latin America and the Caribbean (hereinafter referred to as ECLAC). This objective takes on special significance in the social sciences because ECLAC's diagnoses and recommendations in the field of development gave rise to a unitary and internally coherent vision that constituted an important contribution to Latin American thinking on the subject. In this essay, we refer to this vision as the Latin American School of Development (ELADES).

The decision to situate ECLAC's thinking as the starting point of the ELADES can be criticized by the fact that some Latin American authors, not institutionally linked to this international organization, contributed in advance with comparable perspectives to several of the topics that were later deepened by the ELADES, and because the same thing happened during the evolution of this School, in the period of approximately fifty years described in this review.

However, ECLAC, as a UN agency, fulfilled certain functions without which the central ideas of the ELADES would probably never have been articulated and consolidated with their specific features. The Latin American scope of ECLAC studies and reports made it possible to consider, implicitly or explicitly, Latin America as a unit that could be analyzed jointly.

In addition, during the second part of the 20th century, ECLAC was an irreplaceable and regular source of updated economic and social information on the region as a whole (the English-speaking Caribbean was added later). This made possible and stimulated the preparation of comparative studies between countries and the formulation of interpretative syntheses of regional development, not only within the institution but also in the university and academic sphere in general.

Thirdly, the main social scientists who contributed to this thinking found in ECLAC a long-term historical interpretation of the international order, developed in 1949, from which they formulated their own interpretations. This framing or vision, which came to be known as center-periphery, gave the Latin American region a very strong identity as a joint object of study and reflection.

It should be noted that other United Nations Regional Economic Commissions in Europe, Asia and Africa came into operation at the same time as ECLAC, but none of them produced a unified, academically recognized vision of the regions covered by these agencies that was closely comparable to that originating in ECLAC. The reason for the strong impact of these ideas is not without epistemological interest. The "epistemology" of the ELADES achieved a surprisingly unified vision because the "ontology" (the external reality) of Latin American social processes objectively contained those common patterns and regularities in the economic, political and cultural spheres. All that was needed were keen and sensitive observers to capture and express these basic regularities. Latin America was able to find in its midst exemplary interpreters of its historical reality.

The unified vision of a Latin American society with analogous and therefore comparable historical and institutional features, especially in the economic sphere, which ECLAC was able to formulate in the short term, conferred unity and identity on Latin America as an object of study. Its dynamics of historical change could be periodized by recounting certain "watersheds" drawn from the global international order, which were fundamental factors of regional change. Although the periods of historical change within national societies were not the same, such asynchrony in internal change did not deny the main, external, origin of the main transforming impulses and the permanence in the long term of certain common structural features.

By using these patterns of behavior, inherent to the history and social structures of Latin America, ECLAC developed broad notions or categories that helped to interpret regional history in a comparable way. ECLAC was able to speak of a common historical heritage, and to use its own language, quickly adopted and popularized in various academic studies, regarding the phases or scenarios of "outward growth", "primary- export economies", "import substitution, industrialization", "development from within" or "inward", etc. It was also able to develop hypotheses that encompassed most Latin American nations in terms of foreign trade, productive diversification, typology of exportable products, or, with greater socio-cultural implications, of manor estates, tropical plantations, large estate-minor estate complexes, etc.

What was specifically new about this approach was its ability to articulate many of these categories, some of them pre-existing to the ELADES, in a historical and structural framework that gave them intelligibility and reciprocal articulation, precisely the center- periphery vision, within which successive historical versions of the center-periphery systems could be analyzed.

This book discusses the counterpoints between the economic and socio-political visions of ELADES. Finally, it proposes an integrative framework in the epistemological sphere, in which both Latin American political economy and political sociology of development could be jointly analyzed.

The center-periphery vision as a starting point

The 1949 Economic Survey of Latin America (hereinafter referred to as "the Survey") was conducted under the guidance of Argentine economist Raúl Prebisch.

The Study fundamentally (without quotes) expressed the center-periphery vision. The following stand out in it: a) its global (in the sense of planetary or universal) starting point to historically situate Latin America in a process of economic development b) The strategic position given to the spread of technology resulting from the successive industrial revolutions associated with the planetary expansion of capitalism c) the central importance given to the study of distributive issues both at the international level (between centers and peripheries) and at the national level (within peripheral national societies); d) the structural characterization of the peripheral condition and its historical specificity based on the aforementioned features; e) the need for new economic and social typologies that are specifically Latin American in order to capture organizational and institutional forms that are specific to Latin America; f) the formulation of an industrialist economic strategy, applied to the post-war period, as a decisive way of raising living standards and combating social asymmetries.

In a few opening paragraphs of its introduction[12], the Study anticipates or hints at most of the issues and problems that would give life to ELADES studies and debates.

The realities to be studied were conceived as social systems composed of dynamic agents interacting within technological and institutional structures that condition their behavior. The reality to be examined was history, conceived as intrinsically changing in an open and unpredictable manner. The vision was systemic but was not confused with a holistic vision in the sense that the whole determines the behavior of the parts, nor was it deterministic in the sense that the historical process follows an inexorable course or is predetermined by its "structural logic"

but the study of historical dynamics was conceived as extending from the whole (structures) to the parts (agents) and from the parts to the whole.

This distinction is important because holistic-deterministic visions usually imply philosophies of history that leave no room for individual or group human action. Nor was it confused with an atomistic or individualistic vision, in which micro-social behavior, considered in aggregate, determines

---

[12] The Study develops this vision in eight paragraphs that make up the first section of chapter one. It formulates the following basic propositions. It raises the skewed universal spread of technical progress derived from the English Industrial Revolution. It introduces the terminology of "center and periphery" concerning the unequal world distribution of technical progress and its benefits. It defines the "primary-exporting" and technologically subordinated position of the peripheries in world productive specialization. It highlights the insufficient assimilation of technical progress and its benefits by the majority of the world's population. It highlights the economic and social benefits derived from the non-deliberate process of industrialization by import substitution, and the subsequent deliberate industrializing production strategy. He rejects the idea that the stages of Latin America's development are fulfilled "in the image and likeness" of the development of the centers, and outlines a basic type-logical distinction between the colonial heritage and the capitalist expansion induced from the centers. He alludes to the enormous impact that the reduction of employment in agriculture will have on the Latin American economy as it assimilates the technical progress originating in the centers. And, finally, he promotes the overcoming of "certain pre-capitalist or semi-capitalist modes of production under which a large part of the population still works".

by itself the functioning of the whole (the whole conceived as the sum of its parts). The individual-society counterpoint (or more precisely atomism-holism) was very present in the reasoning of the founding fathers of the school, especially Prebisch[13] and Medina Echavarría.

This consideration explains why the ELADES was a heterodox current that cannot be framed in the predominantly holistic visions of Marxism nor in the predominantly atomistic visions of methodological individualism. The clearest affiliation of the economists of the so-called Latin American structuralism links them, rather, with the so-called institutional or institutionalist economics.

The School's economic approach, unlike the neoclassical tradition in economics that predominated academically, does not put forward a formal model whose scientific criteria rest exclusively on its internal coherence or on its capacity to forecast, as is the case with the epistemological proposal of the neoclassical economic school.

The starting point of the center-periphery vision to study the development process was the British Industrial Revolution, the engine and core of the changes that, in the long term, gave rise to capitalism as a contemporary economic system. From that point historical periodization criteria have been based on successive technological revolutions (the American revolution at the end of the 19th century and the current information technology revolution).

The fact that the vision takes historical realities as its starting point and does not assume " in block" theoretical schemes pre-designed in the academic world of the centers, already possesses a profound epistemological significance because from the outset it seeks to define its own categories of analysis for specific historical processes. The very

[13] "The prevailing social structure in Latin America is a serious obstacle to technical progress and, consequently, to economic and social development. There are three main manifestations of this fact: (a) this structure considerably hinders social mobility, that is, the emergence and ascent of the dynamic elements of society, of men with initiative and drive, capable of assuming risks and responsibilities, both in technology and the economy and in other aspects of collective life; (b) the social structure is largely characterized by privilege in the distribution of wealth and, consequently, of income; privilege weakens or eliminates the incentive to economic activity, to the detriment of the efficient use of men, land and machines; (c) this distributive privilege does not translate into a strong rate of capital accumulation, but into exaggerated modules of consumption in the upper strata of society in contrast with the precarious existence of the popular masses" (Prebisch 1963: 4).

definition of "center-periphery" is a decisive sign of this rethinking. Although the expression had been used by Werner Sombart in the prologue to one of his studies on capitalism, the content that the structuralists conferred on it was totally original.

However, the vision does not start from "zero" because it uses both epistemological approaches and totalizing categories originating in the European social sciences, such as the clearly systemic concepts of capitalism and democracy, but it substantially reformulates them according to the historical realities it studies..

In the original versions of the specifically economic center-periphery vision, the concept of capitalism was accepted as the ideal type of economic systems prevailing both in developed societies and in the post-war international order. Despite starting from this accumulated knowledge on capitalism, its impact on peripheral societies was examined autonomously, risking "open" notions such as "semi-capitalism" as well as "pre-capitalism" to provoke conceptual discussions that would animate the sociological debate of the 1960s and 1970s, and which would later be translated, by Prebisch himself, into his versions of what he called "peripheral capitalism."

The same happened, in the field of Latin American political sociology, with the other major encompassing category characteristic of contemporary Western societies: the concept of democracy. Here too, despite the accumulated knowledge of the category "democracy", both from classical antiquity and modernity, the impact of democratic institutions in peripheral societies had to be re-examined autonomously by the ELADES, giving rise to specific modalities and deviations the ELADES main objective is to promote the development of the Latin American ideal types, which are characteristic of Latin America (populism, bureaucratism, authoritarianism, clientelism, personalism, caudillismo, etc.), energetically rescued in the foundational works of José Medina Echavarría who, together with Prebisch, was the great architect in the formulation of the themes and problems dealt with by the ELD.

The ELADES approach is systemic, moreover, in a more or less strict epistemological expression of the content of this concept. The center-periphery vision studies systems: dynamic totalities whose agents are national states, whose structures are the technological and institutional relations that link these agents in the international order, and whose processes are the mechanisms that are established among the system's agents and explain their asymmetrical relations of power. The emphasis on institutions and technologies is the structural reading of the approach. This reading uncovers different and asymmetrical structures in Latin American societies compared to the societies of the centers of Latin America and the Caribbean..

The approach is systemic, finally, in a more general and "deep" sense, because the agents (national or supranational societies) of this global system can also be treated, in turn, as systems, decomposing them into their own dynamic agents, their own structure (technological and institutional), and their own processes and mechanisms. Consequently, the center-periphery approach from the outset operated at two levels: the global or international and the national or regional.

The center-periphery vision is also multidimensional or multi-disciplinary (economic, social and political). This multidimensionality emerges in such specific issues as, for example, the famous and controversial thesis of the deterioration of the terms of trade, where the causal factors that explain the international prices of primary products (a clearly economic issue) include the weak or non-existent bargaining power of Latin American workers in export activities, strongly influenced not only by the economic but also by the political and cultural structures in which they worked.

Finally, from an ethical perspective, first implicitly and then increasingly explicitly, the vision immediately raises the problems of justice and equity arising from the unequal distribution of resources, and social benefits of technical progress and its fruits. This emphasis on power asymmetries, based on a different positioning in terms of access to technology and dominant institutions, and control of the concrete mechanisms through which this power is exercised, is at the heart of the center-periphery vision with obvious and immediate distributive implications

The first chapter of the Study, mentioned here, constituted the starting point for the contributions, debates and interpretative currents on economic development that were interwoven around ECLAC's activities during the second half of the 20th century. Moreover, the development of the social, cultural and political implications of the approach prompted contributions from other social scientists to generate a body of thought here called ELADES.

In the following chapters we will recapitulate some of the fundamental diagnoses and proposals of ECLAC economists, and their impact on reflections in the social field during the second half of the twentieth century. The selection is obviously arbitrary, but it is intended to illustrate some particularly relevant contributions, while inevitably discarding many others that would have merited mention in this review[14].

[14] Among the names that, for reasons of space, have been omitted, or not sufficiently highlighted in the review, we could include: from Chile to Anibal Pinto, Osvaldo Sunkel, Pedro Sainz and Ricardo Ffrench Davis; from Argentina to Aldo Ferrer, Benjamín Hopenhayn, Alfredo Eric Calcagno, Adolfo Gurrieri and Pedro Paz; from Brazil to Celso Furtado himself ("founding father" together with Prebisch of the ELADES), Helio Jaguaribe, Carlos Lessa, María Concepción Tavares and Antonio Barros de Castro; from Mexico to Juan Noyola; from Uruguay to Octavio Rodríguez; from Peru to Aníbal Quijano. This list could be extended much further and it would still be hopelessly biased and unfair. Hence our exhortation to visit the ECLAC Room prepared by Mr. José Besa, former director of the ECLAC Library.

Chapter III

The post-war historical context

The historical conditions that shaped ECLAC's thinking include factors of a global or planetary nature and factors inherent to the internal dynamics of Latin American societies. The global factors include the post-war situation that gave rise to a new international order marked by a spirit of peace and international cooperation, strongly assumed in the face of the terrible ravages of World War II.

Unlike the first half of the 20th century, which was characterized by two bloody world wars associated with the nationalist and colonialist positions of several great powers, the end of World War II inaugurated a new order that sought to contain the scourge of war and replace it with the mechanism of international negotiations. Likewise, the new spirit of negotiation and peacemaking would include the end of the colonialist logic and a rapid expansion in the number of politically independent nations.

It was in this context that the issues of poverty in the former colonies and, in general, in the peripheral regions, were placed at the center of world forums and were taken up by the developed nations through the founding of the United Nations (UN). In addition to Latin America, the former colonies of Asia, Africa and the non-Latin Caribbean, whose independence began to take place at the end of World War II, joined the UN.

Latin America was clearly a peripheral region with a colonial past, but its decolonization process had taken place early in the 19th century. Its insertion in the international order of that century had been based on the production and export of food and raw materials, required for the development of the Western powers (particularly Great Britain), which, during the 19th century, were deepening their industrial revolution.

Moreover, in terms of intellectual production, Latin America inherited the main features of Western culture. It was the "extreme West", as Alain Rouquié (1989) called it, but the West nonetheless. A feature of this ascription to Western culture came from the pre-modern influences of more than three centuries of Iberian colonization, crystallized in the predominant languages and religion..

The values of Western modernity only began to be institutionalized in Latin America at the beginning of the 19th century. They came first of all from political independence, with the adoption of liberal constitutional charters, emulating the one imposed by the American Revolution of 1776 Secondly, the other feature of the modern West was its insertion into the world capitalist order led by England. But, as is obvious, none of these forms of modernization took place "in the image and likeness" of the processes that took place in Europe and the United States. In Latin America, both historical processes involved the superimposition of liberal ideology (economic and political) on the pre-modern, but clearly Western, values, principles and institutions of the colonial heritage.

Moreover, the complexity of Latin American societies was enhanced by two additional historical facts. First, because of the existence of pre-Hispanic civilizations which, in spite of having assumed, in general, the language and religion of their conquerors, kept latent the fundamental features of their own cultures. And secondly, because of the internment of African (and to a lesser extent Asian) immigrants in conditions of slavery, who also carried their cultural traits. Both ethnic groups kept in their collective memory the sufferings of colonial oppression.

For all these reasons, it is not surprising that in Latin America a current of thought has arisen aimed at trying to explain the reasons for poverty and social inequality, starting from an examination of Latin American economies, but opening it up to the other societal dimensions, taking advantage of the contributions of Western social sciences, but at the same time seeking to highlight regional problems.

The ECLAC was in an exceptional position to attempt this undertaking, interpretative and proactive at the same time, because it was an international organization of the United Nations, founded on the values of tolerance, peace, cooperation and the defense of human rights and freedoms. ECLAC's scope of action included Spanish and Portuguese America, to which was later added the English-speaking Caribbean, mainly decolonized at the end of World War II. In many ways, for the reasons mentioned above, its position was exceptionally favorable to assume the role of spokesperson for Latin America and standard-bearer of the regional identity.

The economists' angle

The asymmetries or structural imbalances of the peripheral economies that were highlighted in the ECLAC reviews already included in the Study were basically two. The first is linked to the peripheral economic structure and its inherent imbalances. The second is linked to the social problems of income distribution and the power relations between the classes involved in the appropriation of the product.

The first structural imbalance, of greater interest to economists, took place at the level of international trade and finance and derived from the peripheral insertion of Latin American economies in world trade. Two versions of this peripheral position are presented here: the nineteenth century and that of the first half of the twentieth century.

The central point consists in the fact that world productive specialization dictated by these centers is such that the fruits of technical progress (productivity gains) are controlled by them, and affect the development dynamics of the peripheral regions, which passively assimilate the waves of technical progress coming from the centers. In the nineteenth century and the first half of the twentieth century, global productive specialization assigned to the peripheries the mission of producing foodstuffs and raw materials exported to the centers in exchange for manufactured goods from the latter, which were required to meet the consumption and investment demands of the peripheral regions.

Two of the main consequences of this systemic dynamic on a global scale were, first, the tendency of the peripheries to suffer deficit positions in the world trade balance, and, second, the tendency for the terms of trade of peripheral primary products to deteriorate vis-à-vis centrally located manufactures.

On the side of international demand for Latin American primary products, two basic starting points were used to explain these asymmetries. On one side, the so-called "Engel's laws" (in reference to the German economist and statistician Ernst Engel [1821-1896]) showed that household and personal spending was structured in consumption baskets that grew asymmetrically as per capita income increased. Indeed, there was a reduction, in relative terms to total expenditure, in the consumption of food and other scarcely processed products, in favor of an increase in the manufacturing and services component. On the other side, it was based on the propositions that Prebisch himself had formulated on industrial technical processes and their cost structures, regarding the decreasing share of primary products in the final value of manufactured goods produced by the central economies as labor productivity grew as a result of the introduction of technical progress.

As a consequence of this dual order of factors, world demand for manufacturing companies was, both nationally and internationally, much more dynamic than the demand for primary products. Thus, peripheral countries that imported the former and exported the latter would generate chronically deficit trade balances. According to ECLAC's interpretation, this would lead to an equally chronic tendency to become debtor economies.

On the side of the international supply of Latin American primary products, the second structural imbalance, which would open up space for socio-political analysis, was observed at the level of employment and influenced the capacity of workers to capture a fair or equitable fraction of the increases in labor productivity. At the global level, the main employment-absorbing activities were industry and services associated with the industrial presence. But the peripheral economies, under conditions of free and unprotected trade such as those prevailing in the second half of the 19th century, specialized only in primary production and low-productivity handicraft activities, oriented to local markets and, rather, linked to subsistence and self- consumption economies. Consequently, there was a structural surplus of labor force, which was expressed not so much in open unemployment as in different forms of underemployment.

The explicit approach of this second unbalancing trend of a structural nature was, in the long run, the main way in which ECLAC's diagnoses were connected with the efforts of other related scientists to interpret the social development of Latin America. These social aspects alluded to the capacity of peripheral economies to generate enough jobs in view of their particular insertion in the world economy, and also referred to the bargaining power of workers employed in these economies to achieve wage increases in line with productivity increases linked to the exogenous introduction of technical progress. Therefore, when technical progress in primary export activities increased productivity gains, these did not translate into parallel increases in wages, but rather into increases in corporate profits and/or reductions in export prices.

These two imbalances (international trade and employment) had become evident as the so-called "outward growth model" (based on the mono-production and mono-export of primary products) deepened and were derived from the asymmetrical nature of peripheral development. This was the first step in ECLAC's industrialist proposal: to highlight the long-term structural unfeasibility inherent in the outward growth process (or "model"). However, it should be highlighted that ECLAC's ideas, written in the late 1940s, were an a posteriori ratification (or "rationalization") of the industrialist strategies that were already being applied in several of the medium and large countries in the region.

Both structural imbalances were empirically verifiable, and made economic growth based solely (or mainly) on the export of primary products unviable. This mono-export was the policy recommendation underlying the conventional version of the theory of comparative advantages of neoclassical microeconomics. Instead of moving towards the ahistorical general equilibrium of "perfect competition" of the neoclassical textbooks, the center-periphery dynamics, historically founded, predicted that the application of the theory of static comparative advantages would lead to an inexorable structural imbalance. This meant denying or refuting the alleged trend towards the equalization of wage levels in the world, predicted on the basis of the assumptions included in the neoclassical models in vogue, referring to the theory of comparative advantages in international trade.

Hence the need to promote industrialization, firmly postulated by ECLAC economists in the 1950s as the only way to overcome both types of imbalances. The industrialist proposal was at the core of the strategy formulated and pursued by the ELADES.

Another diagnostic derivation of these same ideas, of enormous importance for the later social approaches of ECLAC, but already present since the 1950s, was the thesis of the deterioration in the terms of trade (DTT) of primary products with respect to manufactures. This thesis was a challenge both to the Walrasian theory of prices derived from the study of an ideal model of perfect competition, and to the theory of comparative advantages based on this model, which predominated in the Western academic world.

It is interesting to note that, in the DTI thesis, the simultaneous effects of the two structural imbalances mentioned (foreign trade and employment) converge as a consequence of the sluggish world demand for primary products and the limited bargaining power of peripheral workers within the framework of the labor institutions in force in export activities. Thus, real prices of primary products tended to fall for reasons that can be empirically verified.

By contrast, in manufacturing activities in the central regions (and here the interpretation of the center-periphery approach reached a planetary perspective), increases in labor productivity translated into proportional increases in wages and salaries, as well as in property income, leaving the international prices of manufactured goods unchanged

In the industrial centers, the appropriation of the fruits of technical progress was not transferred, via lower prices, to the peripheral regions with which they traded. Obviously, in this case too, the explanation lay - and continues to lie - in the more egalitarian and dynamic social structure of the developed countries, and in the greater bargaining power of their workers[15] [16].

---

[15] This explanation is consistent with some developed later by the French regulationist school in relation to the European Fordist regime. A central concern of this school of thought has been the issue of productivity gains; however, none of its main authors acknowledged to the ELADES, or to Prebisch in particular, the much earlier contributions made on this subject.

[16] After long and bitter debates between the neoclassical economists of the centers and the "structuralists" of Latin America, the veracity of the thesis of the deterioration of the terms of trade became a fundamentally empirical question, and it was the latter who emerged victorious in the controversy. In fact, the data subsequently demonstrated the tendency for the simple real terms of trade (relative prices) of raw materials to deteriorate with respect to manufactures. Regarding the double factor terms of trade (which sought to compare changes in producers' productivity (and income) with changes in product prices), the measurement difficulties were greater, but evidence was also accumulated that tended to verify the hypotheses of deterioration formulated by Prebisch, the main inspirer of ECLAC's ideas in this period (Di Filippo 1987).

The angle of ECLAC sociologists and political scientists

It was also left open the possibility of examining the issues of equity in the distribution of the benefits of technical progress as a necessary condition for the broadening and deepening of the process of democratization, based on the anticipated economic imbalances.

This strengthening of democratic processes was evident in Western Europe from the 1950s onwards, stimulated by the emergence of the European Economic Community and by the process of decolonization driven by the principles of the Charter of Nations, the Universal Declaration of Human Rights and other similar declarations, which had a decisive impact on the post-war world. ECLAC, given its membership in the UN, could not be unaffected by this influence.

Capitalism and social structure

The first in-depth approach to the subject of social development, within the work of the time prepared by ECLAC, was addressed by José Medina Echavarría in a series of essays written in the mid-1950s and finally published in 1959 under the title *Social Aspects of Economic Development*[317].

In these papers Medina first accepts the need for Latin American industrialization based on what he calls "the methods of Western industrialism"; second, he introduces the concept of capitalism and social

[17] In Medina's own preface to the 1973 reprint of this work, it is noted: "I begin by highlighting two facts that seem to me to be significant or at least worthy of some attention. One -the most important without a doubt- is that which concerns the dates on which these works were published. The first dates from August 1955, which means, after adding the time consumed in the preparatory tasks and not only those of thought, that ECLAC was energetically ahead of other organizations in the task of confronting and taking into consideration the social side of economic development, as recognized by Flacso itself in the brief preface to the aforementioned edition and later admitted in other statements by its own and by outsiders. The second fact to be emphasized concerns the cautiousness with which these first contributions appeared, a caution that today could be considered excessive and which was revealed by the very term " side", a notoriously preferred term at the time. It can now be stated without embarrassment that such caution or caution was due to the tactical need to penetrate into what appeared to be the closed preserve of economists". José Medina Echavarría. 1973. Social Dimensions of Economic Development, ECLAC, XXV Anniversary Commemorative Series, Santiago, February, page xi.

structure, thus strengthening the reference to an ideal type that had been fleetingly mentioned by Prebisch in the first chapter of the Study. He does so by applying the Weberian vision to the Latin American reality: "Everything that, with different twists and turns, was said about economic activity in its relations with human characters and motivations, and with the uses, traditions and customs of a society, was equivalent to posing in reverse, and sometimes purely descriptive form, the theme that made Weberian research classic with reference to capitalism. What are the social conditions that make the functioning of this system possible? Reiterating the same question from the point of view of today's economic development is to continue a tradition of rigorous conceptual precision".

Medina also introduces the central and multidisciplinary concept of institutions, including in them "the moral and social structures" of Latin America, thus contributing to open the theoretical and analytical field of the ELADES[18].

Contributions to ELD not linked to ECLAC's institutional framework

Among the most important contributions to the ELADES not directly linked to the ECLAC institutional framework are the works of Sergio Bagú (1949 and 1952), an Argentine historian, who contributed early on to formulating the historical bases of the so-called "dependency" current in Latin America, to which we will refer in future sections of this review.

---

[18] "Economic development is a process of induced change that forces us to ask not only about the primary or desired effects, but also about the secondary or unforeseen ones. Or, as we said earlier, economic change has repercussions, whether we like it or not, on the other institutions that make up the social structure. Are these repercussions foreseeable? In order not to insist on these abstract approaches, which will have to be repeated later, the more concrete problem regarding the situation of the underdeveloped countries has been seen in various ways, but one of the most direct and plastic formulas is formulated as follows: it is necessary that these countries succeed in modernizing with the methods of Western industrialism, without having to pay the price paid by the nations of the West for their industrial revolution. In other words, "industrialization should not destroy the moral and social structure of the newcomers, as was the case in the old industrial countries" (E. Heimann). "This is the idea that, in one form or another, presides over the concern for the social effects of economic development" (Medina 1973: 12 and 13).

Sergio Bagú was the first to categorically reject the mechanical and uncritical transplantation of European categories of analysis to the understanding of Latin American development. He rejected above all the idea of a feudal Latin America, popularized by some Marxist authors (Puigróss 1940) and established the term colonial-capitalism to refer to the modalities of structuring the export zones of raw materials since the colonial period: "The economy that the Iberian metropolis organized in America was of an unquestionably colonial nature, in function of the central-western European market. The purpose that animated the Portuguese-Hispanic producers in the new continent had the same character" (...) "It was not feudalism that appeared in America in the period we are studying, but colonial capitalism.

There was no servitude on a vast scale, but slavery with multiple nuances, often hidden under complex and misleading legal formulations" (...) "Ibero-America was born to integrate the cycle of nascent capitalism, not to prolong the agonizing feudal cycle" (Bagu 1993: 85-86).

Chapter IV

The turbulence of the sixties

The most serious problems of social inequality suffered by Latin America were rooted in rural areas, associated with the existence of traditional ranches and large estate complexes that still housed in the early sixties of the twentieth century about half of the Latin American population of Andean, Central American and/or Caribbean nations.

The Bolivian Revolution of the early 1950s had been a first warning of the unsustainable rural social inequality in Latin America. The second major warning was the Cuban Revolution in the late 1950s. Other social upheavals in Central America and the Caribbean increased social turbulence in rural areas of Latin America. On the other hand, the accelerated rural-urban migrations at the beginning of the 1960s also transferred social tensions to the suburbs and slums of the big cities, with the creation of emergency neighborhoods forming belts of poverty and indigence (slums, shantytowns, callampas, favelas, etc.).

The Democratic administration in the United States, led by J. F. Kennedy, tried to separate the very serious tensions of the East-West conflict (the episode of the Cuban missiles installed in the Soviet Union) from the need to promote better conditions for democratic development in Latin America. The Alliance for Progress (ALPRO), was a bet in favor of a democratic transformation, promoting technically and financially a series of structural reforms in the sphere of agrarian property, the tax system, and the formulation of economic plans elaborated by Planning Ministries oriented to accelerate the economic growth of Latin America.

In ECLAC's official internal approaches, the sensitive and debatable concept of development planning emerged. Given the resentments of the East-West struggle, the mere term "planning" aroused mistrust and visceral rejection. ECLAC had contributed to the dissemination of democratic planning (or programming) methods through the Latin American Institute for Economic and Social Planning (ILPES) incorporated into the ECLAC system. But the planning concept considered here was useful for industrial development under conditions of foreign exchange scarcity, within the framework of an import substitution industrialization strategy.

These intentions and projects, which originated in the Democratic administration of the US government, were overtaken by historical dynamics. After the assassination of President Kennedy, the initiative was replaced, de facto, by pragmatic mechanisms that did not oppose the installation of "reliable" dictatorships in the face of the anti-communist apprehensions of the U.S. government.

Even so, social turbulence in rural and urban areas continued with increasing violence, different guerrilla groups emerged, and social scientists felt the profound responsibility and enormous tension of doing social science in a convulsive scenario in which extreme and polarized positions were directly or indirectly fueled by East-West struggles.

ECLAC's developmental-integrationist program

In the early 1960s, Prebisch wrote and published "Hacia una dinámica del desarrollo latinoamericano" (Towards a Dynamic of Latin American Development) (1963). In that work he outlined the main structural factors which, in his opinion, prevented the equitable, dynamic and autonomous development of Latin America. Among them he examined the problems of over-consumption by high-income groups, excessive population growth, and the restrictions derived from the unjust and inefficient agrarian structure.

The study directed and written by Prebisch penetrates resolutely into the role of the social structure, highlighting the distributive privileges that hindered social mobility on one part and the proper deployment of incentives for economic activity on the other.

Prebisch's examination of structural obstacles includes not only internal factors, but also external ones, related to the external "strangulation" (or "asphyxiation") of development due to the lack of sufficient international means of payment, associated with the end of the "easy" stage of import substitution, the growing presence of transnational companies oriented to the domestic market, and the insufficient capacity to import due to the slow growth of primary exports.

During this decade, ECLAC recommended, first, the structural reforms already mentioned, which had a great impact on the social area; second, the promotion of the competitiveness required to achieve the expansion of industrial exports to the world market (which refutes the allegedly recalcitrant protectionist ideology generally attributed to it); third, Latin American integration, as a way to take advantage of economies of scale and specialization, favored by the expansion of markets[19].

ECLAC's program was certainly not an abstract inspiration without precedent in the economic history of the West, since the strategy had already been successful in the experiences that led to the development of two first-rate powers that emerged on the world economic scene during the 19th and 20th centuries: the United States and Germany. The works of Alexander Hamilton, Frederick List and Henry Carey, among others, give an insight into the ideas that guided these important historical processes. For structuralism, the development process should be approached, at least on a South American scale, with a long-term horizon. Hence the need for an integrationist strategy that, at least to date, we have seen, has not been successful. The most distinctive and profoundly transforming feature of the Alliance for Progress (ALPRO) in the case of Chile was to enable agrarian reform to pave the way for that essential transformation aimed at putting an end to the ancestral hegemony of rentier landowners - not only farmers, but also miners- installed since the Iberian conquest and colonization. From the perspective of the center-periphery system of international relations, this transcendental reform was a prerequisite for the promotion of industrial development and required the "permission" (consent, tolerance, flexibility) of the main hegemonic center. And the ALPRO led by John F.

---

[19] Incidentally, the idea of economies of scale and specialization, which ECLAC put forward in the mid-1960s, would be reluctantly incorporated much later by international economics textbooks in the developed world, because it was incompatible with the pre-mixed rules of the neoclassical model of perfect competition and because it required a theory of monopolistic competition that called into question the very foundations of the neoclassical theory of comparative advantage.

Kennedy accepted this shared challenge proposed by Latin American structuralism from ECLAC. The challenge implied aspiring to make the transition from a colonial and/or neocolonial heritage that was still very important in rural areas to a peripheral capitalism that did not yet fully exist. This transition was a first condition for generating capitalist structures in the Latin American economies from which the great industrialist strategy could be proposed. The expressions "capitalism", "pre-capitalism" and "semi-capitalism" were used repeatedly by Raúl Prebisch in different sections of the first part of the 1949 Economic Survey of Latin America, the first of a long series of annual reports prepared by ECLAC that have continued to the present day. Capitalism presupposes the existence of a capitalist, innovative and entrepreneurial business class oriented towards profit and capital accumulation, as opposed to the figure of the landowner or the rentier mining landowner, typical of neocolonial Latin American rural societies. Rural farms were compartments or micro-worlds where the peasantry was subjected to subsistence self-consumption regimes that were highly excluded from national market circuits. at the end of the 1950s and beginning of the 1960s, the rural social structures of all Latin American countries contained the highest percentage of their total populations and still showed significant pre-capitalist and semi-capitalist traits. Even in Argentina, where the late incorporation into the world market generated an extraordinary impulse to the growth of that country at the end of the 19th century, there were still large areas of its national rural territory where those hybrid traits predominated. Chile was perhaps the only South American country where these revolutionary transformations, agrarian reform and "chileanization" of mineral wealth were attempted by the State with a declaredly developmentalist intention.

In short, in the second half of the 20th century, the old traditional structures inherited from the colonial phase and sustained throughout the 19th century were dismantled, but it was not possible to create the national and international target conditions to attempt an autonomous and sustained industrial development on a Latin American scale. At the core of the developmentalist ideal formulated by Latin American structuralist thought, the diagnostic point was the historically confirmed verification of the concentration of technical progress and its fruits in the development of the world economy, with its obvious repercussions on the Latin American process. This concentrating process was verified both in the hegemonic centers with respect to the vast global periphery on an international scale, and within the Latin American periphery itself in relation to the national or local social segments favored by the functioning of peripheral capitalism.

ALPRO was a project of a Democratic government in the United States that made a great effort to open an alternative reformist path, on a hemispheric scale, in the face of the advance of the radical leftist ideas promoted by the Cuban Revolution. This project went against the grain of the traditional imperial ideologies that encouraged, and continued to feed the expansionism and "exceptionalism" of the United States, in the interpretation of the Monroe Doctrine summarized in the phrase "America for the Americans" (which in the line of the American imperialist right was read as "Latin America for the Americans").

The ultimate objective pursued by ALPRO was eliminated outright after the virtual coup d'état, which essentially meant the assassination of the Kennedy brothers and Martin Luther King.

The structuralist worldview, from which the developmentalist strategy promoted by ECLAC emerged, was not "hemispheric" nor did it promote an alliance of "The Americas" as John F. Kennedy intended, but was Latin Americanist, related to the ideals of Simón Bolívar and oriented in the direction of the search for political unity of the countries located south of the Rio Grande. After the collapse of the ALPRO, these Latin Americanist aspirations were also eliminated during the 1970s with the military dictatorships stimulated by the United States under the Nixon administration and its Secretary of State Henry Kissinger.

These military governments swept away not only Marxist ideology but also all traces of social democracy in most of the large and medium-sized countries of South America. It was only in the 1980s that a process of return to democratic civilian governments began.

The concept of structural heterogeneity

Parallel to these approaches, since the mid-1960s ECLAC developed its diagnoses of the so-called structural heterogeneity and accentuated its criticisms of the inequitable personal and family income distribution prevailing in the region. Structural heterogeneity was characterized from two perspectives, one "techno-economic", which highlighted the abysmal differences in labor productivity that existed even within the same economic sectors, and the other "social", which emphasized the archaic social relations and institutions of colonial or nineteenth-century origin that were intertwined with more modern ones based on complex positions and power relations.

The decisive contribution to the concept made by José Medina Echavarría is worth mentioning. Although Medina did not use textually the expression structural heterogeneity, he gave a very precise definition of its features, which expressed a more complex and historically sustained version of the dualist vision in the social sciences. However, the dualist reminiscences are historically framed by Medina in a process of dynamic transition, which will relate him, on one side, to the concept of dynamic insufficiency in Prebisch and, on the other, to the works of Aníbal Pinto and Celso Furtado, which are more based on the technological contrasts of the productive structure[20].

The concept of structural heterogeneity is central to the ELADES conceptualizations. In its techno-economic version, it expresses a stratification of labor productivities in which there is a stratum with such low levels of labor productivity that it prevents the generation of any surplus and therefore any option of capital accumulation originating in that stratum. This lower stratum of labor productivity included (especially in the fifties and sixties) a high percentage of the Latin

---

[20] In Furtado's first formulations, structural heterogeneity was characterized essentially as a problem of technological heterogeneity projected onto economic structures. In the approaches of Anibal Pinto -who decisively enriched the contents of the concept- it was raised in its complex historical roots. As already mentioned, this concept benefited from the solid critical position of Medina Echavarría, regarding the simplistic and dichotomous versions of dualism. Raul Prebisch would later deepen this concept in the final phase (1980s) of his reflections, related to "peripheral capitalism". On the side of the dualist influences, in the traditionalism/modernity dichotomy, it is worth remembering Gino Germani's (1962) concept of asynchrony in change. Later versions of Aníbal Pinto and Armando Di Filippo on the concept of heterogeneity (some of them written in co-authorship: 1974 and 1979), rescue other institutional elements that go beyond technological and productivity aspects, and revive the concept with the typological proposals of colonial economies and export economies elaborated by the ELADES since the 1950s.

American population. This feature, seen from the perspective of development, was an objective limit, derived from the productive structures, to the growth of the living standards of the population incorporated in it. From this rather techno-economic version resulted, in part, the concept of dynamic insufficiency suggested by Prebisch, according to which the levels of capital accumulation and the increase in labor productivity were not sufficient to "rescue" the labor force located at the "bottom" of the stratification of productivities. Therefore, structuralist economists found here an objective, empirically verifiable basis for suggesting strategies to increase the rate of accumulation, even changing the consumerist cultural patterns that, according to Aníbal Pinto, turned the consumption of the economic elites into a "caricature of the affluent society" that flourished in the centers, and distracted resources towards superfluous activities that underlay the dynamic insufficiency of the system.

In its "social" version, the concept of structural heterogeneity was redefined in a way that criticized the merely statistic character of the previous stratifications, which did not take into consideration the class structures and institutional mechanisms that kept such a large part of the population in subsistence conditions. The definition of the lower stratum as subsistence (Celso Furtado used this expression, as did Pinto and Di Filippo (1979) in one of their joint works where, from a historical-structural perspective, the issue of poverty was explicitly considered, obviously linked to the subsistence stratum), this treatment opens the game to other sociological, anthropological or even sociopolitical visions of this stratum. Among structuralist economists, this "social" version of structural heterogeneity received particular attention from Di Filippo (1981). Subsistence is a concept associated with the definition of certain minimum parameters for the satisfaction of human needs. This implies a more qualitative characterization of the concrete ways of life of a part of the population and, specifically, of the forms of production and life in which they were habitually involved. This more "social" definition of structural heterogeneity transcends (although it may include) empirical measurements in the stratification of productivities and requires characterizing, at least, the property, labor and exchange relations in which the people located there are inserted. The subject is not defined then as a merely occupational insertion, but as an insertion in specific social environments. For example, the living conditions prevailing in the rural estates and landed estates complexes, or in the marginal populations in the suburban belts of the large cities.

The socio-political contributions of José Medina Echavarría

In the more socio-political sphere, at the beginning of 1960, the ECLAC Secretariat published: *The Social Development of Latin America in the Post-War Period*[21].

This publication grew in importance with the passage of time and ratified its foundational and programmatic character for the work of more than a generation of Latin American sociologists. Its introduction, which we will discuss here, prefigures the main themes and problems that were addressed by Latin American sociologists - or those from the rest of the world concerned with the problems of Latin America - in the following decades.

As we also did with the first section of the 1949 Study, its main conclusions can be summarized telegraphically as follows:

The document: a) begins by recognizing that there has been economic development in Latin America but that its balance is unsatisfactory. b) Suggests that this dissatisfaction derives in part from the limitations of the restrictively economic vision. c) Also recognizes the limitations of the sociological interpretation and restricts it to a specific and apparently complementary area of the economic vision: the abnormally low productivity of the active population in agriculture. d) It proposes an explanation of the above problem based on a structural analysis of urban-rural relations and on a broad preliminary hypothesis: namely, that the "bottleneck" of agricultural productivity is an aspect of the social and cultural "bottleneck" of the modernization process (or rationalization in the Weberian sense) as a phenomenon distinct from dualism. e) Refuses to

[21] ECLAC. The Social Development of Latin America in the Postwar Period. Library Dimensión Americana, directed by Gregorio Weimberg, Solar Hachette, Buenos Aires, 1963. In spite of being -like the Study- an institutional work without explicit mention of an individual author, its core ideas and writing were basically in charge of José Medina Echavarría. It consolidates and strengthens the theses already insinuated in Medina's own 1955 proposal.

submit to an immediate empirical verification of that great starting hypothesis. It introduces the epistemological resource of Weberian ideal types. It marks the contrasts between the process of urbanization (vehicle of modernity) of industrial societies vis-à-vis that of Latin American societies. It expresses the contradiction between urban expansion and the stagnation of agricultural productivity. f) It reveals a pace of urbanization that does not correlate with the pace of industrialization either. g) Proposes to investigate the "social constitution of the agricultural enterprise" within which the old hacienda refuses to die. He suggests a causal study that transcends the agricultural-rural and includes the urban sphere. h) Rejects the dogmatic correlation between urbanization and economic development. He traces historically the origin and functions of Latin American cities and their enormous centralizing weight prior to the process of urbanization. i) He then proposes the central hypothesis of the whole work: that the traditional social structure has been relatively permeable and that this porosity has allowed it to absorb the elements of "modernity" (rationality) it needed without breaking its very structure.

He goes on to elaborate on concepts such as clientele, patronage, bossism, and other related concepts that imply the previous hypothesis. He attributes the subsequent crisis of this structure (1960s) to the wear and tear of this adaptive mechanism "due to use and demographic pressure".

He explores the ramification of that central hypothesis on the meaning of the Latin American "middle classes". It highlights the great contrasts between the economic and social attitudes of the Latin American middle classes vis-à-vis those of the great industrial societies. It suggests the "assimilation" (in a sense close to that of co-optation) of the Latin American middle classes by the traditional system. It deals with the precariousness of the Latin American trade union movement, the existence of urban "marginal masses", and its connection with the general hypothesis formulated above. He outlines the "ideological protoforms" of the situation described: nationalism, populism, and traditionalism (or "modernizing" conservativism). The same paragraph attributes the importance of these "ideologies" to three main reasons: all seek economic development, all are "steeped in irrational elements", all reflect the logic of clientelist domination and the decline of traditional society's capacity for assimilation.

Finally, and in the more propositional sphere, as a symptom of the implementation of a new (more rational) structure, he suggests replacing these "ideological protoforms" by a development policy to be assumed by the "practical programs of the (political) parties required by the new age". The "programmatic value" of the work referred to in this long introduction was a starting point (to which today we ascribe an enduring foundational value) of considerable practical repercussions in the long run.

Before concluding with this section, it should be pointed out how Medina rescues the ideal of democracy and links it to capitalist development, through the need to formulate a development policy to be assumed by the "practical programs of the political parties required by the new age". This ideal of democracy is unequivocally contained in the need to respond politically to ideologies steeped in irrational elements and reflecting the logic of so-called "clientelist domination", which genuinely belongs neither to the rationality of democracy nor to that of capitalism.

Dependency theory in the Cardoso and Faletto version

Fernando Henrique Cardoso and Enzo Faletto, both ECLAC/ILPES officials, published in the late 1960s, Dependence and Development in Latin America. In this essay, a etymologization of export economies is adapted to derive effects in the socio-political sphere, corresponding to the period under analysis: "In this sense, the hypothesis put forward in this paper is that the patterns of social integration and the types of social movements, through which the political life and profile of Latin American societies were differentiated, assumed different connotations depending on whether they were countries in which it was possible to maintain national control of the export system or, on the contrary, in those where the enclave economy prevailed in the phase of outward growth." (...). "In each of these two basic situations, in addition, the internal differentiation of the productive system and the fractioning of social groups in each Latin American country opened up different perspectives for the formation - still within the general channels of the export system - of new alliances between social groups. The success and the variable possibilities of these alliances explain the greater or lesser degree of persistence of the exporting "constituted order", or on the contrary indicate the moment or the forms of transition of the "exporting system" towards societies in which groups linked to the domestic market, such as the urban bourgeoisie and the "middle classes", began to acquire growing importance" (1969: 55-57).

Based on the previous approach, the authors dedicate the rest of the chapter to a historical exemplification of their typological criteria. On one side, among the societies with nationally controlled production, they include the agro-exporting experiences of Argentina (Buenos Aires and the rest of the humid pampas), of Brazil (the coffee complex of Sao Paulo articulated with temperate agriculture in Rio Grande do Sul), or the coffee producing societies of Colombia and Costa Rica.) On the other hand, the enclave economies at the time of transition include such divergent cases as Mexico, Peru, Venezuela, Bolivia and Chile in the extractive mining sector, or Central America, especially since the creation of the banana enclaves with U.S. capital.

Gino Germani's contributions outside ECLAC's institutional framework

It is now worth contrasting some of the reflections of dependency theorists with other social scientists from very different visions. Thus, Gino Germani, starting from a perspective more typical of what, at that time, was called "scientific sociology", highlighted from his early work the peculiar features of the democratization process in Latin America and the transition from traditional society to mass society. The fact that both approaches (the "dependentistas" on one side and Germani's "scientific sociology") started from very different epistemological perspectives was not an obstacle to the fulfillment of a constant feature of the ELADES: the discovery of the specificity and unity of Latin American historical reality, which made possible a dialogue and an implicit collaboration between different interpretative approaches. Both approaches knew, accepted and adapted in their intellectual contributions the language of the structuralist economists of ECLAC within the framework of the center-periphery vision.

Gino Germani (1964), to explain the political evolution of Latin America in general, and Argentina in particular, elaborated a system of stages to explain the historical transformations of Latin America, distinguishing between: a) traditional society, b) representative democracy with limited participation, c) representative democracy with expanded participation, d) transition to a regime with full participation, e) transition to a regime with full participation.

In a later book, Germani (1969) assimilated the vision of the ECLAC economists and reworked his scheme of stages, now applied more broadly to the modernization process, to which he explicitly incorporated the concept of dependency in relation to the formation of primary export economies, and of industrialization and "inward development" in the phase he called mass social mobilization.

The scheme of stages presented by Germani not only covers the phase of "outward growth" but also, and especially, outlines the social changes derived from the "inward" transition.

But in this section we will comment only on a few paragraphs of the "outward" phase. These paragraphs highlight not only the recognition of the economic periodization of the Latin American structuralists, but also an approach to social discontinuities which, in this author's view, can be linked to his concept of asynchrony in change as presented in his previous book. Thus, Germani says:

> The historical significance of the external impact is quite obvious, but its role in accentuating the homogeneity between nations and, in turn, the discontinuities within them was often ignored. The same oversight occurred with the role played in this double effect by the interaction between exogenous and endogenous factors. Perhaps it can be said that this effect increased over time or, at least, that it tended to become more visible in the third stage (Germani refers here to the stage he calls "dual society and outward expansion") and even more so in the fourth stage (which he characterizes as one of industrialization and "inward" development).
>
> It could also be suggested that, with the growth of international interdependence in all spheres - and especially with the growth of the global structure of power stratification - external factors may have become more powerful. This may have occurred even as the internal forces of many nations grew as a result of economic development, increasing social modernization and increased national consciousness

(or perhaps decreased alienation), features that some say characterize the "inward growth" stage.

On the other side, as time went by and the distance between the countries of the region tended to increase, the generalized effect of the external impact may have accentuated the internal discontinuities, especially in all those cases in which such impact produced the acceleration of certain component processes, while at the same time slowing down or decelerating others.

The joint effect of the exogenous and endogenous factors in the third stage is known: "economic expansion" on the basis of the primary export economy, and consequently stimulus of "limited" modernizing effects in the social and political orders.

The extent of the "modernizing effect" was a function of three main variables: 1) the type of primary export economy; 2) the degree of success it achieved in promoting "economic expansion" (as defined above); and
3) the existence of internal modernizing elites and their level of effectiveness. It is the type of primary export economy that determined, to a large extent, the variety and scope of the repercussions on the rest of the social structure. Again, however, these repercussions were limited or expanded, delayed or accelerated by the action and orientation of the elites.

Economic expansion based on a type of primary production, which required the mobilization of a small part of the population, or whose repercussions on the rest of the economy were limited, did not have a far-reaching impact on the social structure. This was the case of certain mining or plantation economies, or other economic activities, which were really "enclaves" dependent on foreigners and relatively isolated from the national economy. Here a typical dual society and economy was likely to emerge, characterized by a deep cleavage between archaic and modernized sectors. Social modernization could affect some aspects of behavior and institutions in some restricted areas and some rather social groups-usually the upper and middle strata of urban centers or, more often, of "primate" cities. Nevertheless, some basic value orientations remained unchanged even in these sectors, coexisting with other overt symptoms of modernization.

> In those countries where the primary export economy demanded, or at least indirectly induced, the participation of large sections of the population at both low and intermediate occupational levels, an expansion of the domestic market and/or some other "dispersion" effect, as well as other processes of social modernization, took place at an accelerated pace and prior to the "corresponding" or "equivalent" level in the economic order (pp. 37 and 38).

It should be pointed out that one of the leading theoreticians of the sociology of modernization applied to the Latin American case, such as Germani, derives social consequences from the outward growth model that depend on the same strategic factor that two of the leading exponents of "Latin American structuralist dependency" (if we may use this simplified term) also coincide in mentioning.

As we have seen, Fernando Henrique Cardoso and Enzo Faletto also start from the features of exporting activity to make their typological characterizations, dressed in a much more dialectical garb, but in essence, starting from similar historical aspects.

Chapter V

The 1970s - the repressive reaction

In the 1970s, together with the hardening of U.S. strategies towards Latin America, there was the repression of the social turbulence of the 1950s and 1960s and the establishment of military dictatorships, especially in South America. At the economic level, this historical juncture generated the conditions for the gradual installation of open economic models, in line with a market logic, and with the growing participation of the private sector, especially transnational corporations.

Contribution of ECLAC economists

Just as the decade of the 1960s was marked by the obstacles that inequality in the social structure imposed on development, ECLAC's reflections in the 1970s focused much more on the need to create jobs and to promote and guide capital accumulation in that direction. At the risk of being too narrow in the orientations of ECLAC's thinking, its Secretariat undoubtedly had to respond to the general orientations provided by its principals, the governments of Latin America, and this may have influenced the de-emphasis in this historical period on aspects of distributive justice and the emphasis on the study of the dynamics of Latin American growth and the factors that drove it.

At the heart of Transformation and Development, the Great Task of Latin America (1972) (prepared by ECLAC for the IDB, under Prebisch's intellectual leadership at ILPES) is the issue of the dynamic insufficiency of the economic system. This approach is totally complementary to that proposed by Prebisch in his previous book, because this dynamic insufficiency recognizes ultimate causes that also concern the social structure, but the approach focuses on the economically concrete ways of promoting capital accumulation that overcomes this inability to generate jobs with increasing productivity in order to overcome the redundancy of the labor force.

The close conceptual similarity between the concept of structural heterogeneity discussed in previous sections and the more operational and concrete concept of dynamic insufficiency can be seen. Precisely the concept of dynamic insufficiency of Latin American economies -which Prebisch had already introduced in "Towards a Dynamic"... (1963)- refers to the fact that the incorporation into the economic structure of new layers of the economy is not always possible. (1963) - refers to the fact that the incorporation into the economic structure of new, more efficient and productive technical layers, necessary to overcome the heterogeneity of the productive structure, does not occur at a sufficient pace to absorb productively the majority of the labor force, which - unlike what was happening in those years in the developed centers - continued to vegetate underemployed in the lower strata of productivity and efficiency.

In his last book, "Peripheral Capitalism, Crisis and Transformation" (1981), which exerted much less intellectual influence on ECLAC, Prebisch, now retired from his institutional positions, spoke of reproductive accumulation based on a reasoning of a dynamic nature. According to his interpretation, reproductive accumulation had a socio- political and a technical component. The socio-political component of this modality of accumulation was that the increases in labor productivity derived from technical progress - the surplus in the language used in that book - should be supported by an austere and productivism ethic, oriented towards accumulation and not consumption, and promoted by public policies endowed with such an orientation. In this sense, there would be more savings and investment and the pressure to consume would be diminished. The technical component of this strategy consisted in favoring those technologies that would imply a more rapid growth of labor productivity and therefore of new portions of surplus. The key (with obvious socio-political implications) of the process then consisted in reinvesting as much of these productivity gains as possible in order to accelerate the creation of jobs with increasing productivity and income. The opposition between average macroeconomic productivity growth and total employment growth was to be resolved by reducing the consumption ratios and increasing the investment-to-output ratios.

Main socio-political contributions of the time period under analysis originated in ECLAC

The "Cepaline" sociologists and political scientists translated these problems of exclusion or insufficient inclusion in the labor and employment spheres into the social field through the concept of marginality, which was the object of multiple meanings and interpretations[22].

The subject of social marginality is an excellent example of the conscious or unconscious appeal that the different interpreters of the concept make to the two basic institutional complexes within which it is possible to frame it: capitalism and democracy as systems historically reprocessed and theoretically reinterpreted within the framework of center-periphery relations.

---

[22] Marginality in Latin America was, above all, a "sensitizing" term in the search for theoretically founded interpretative meanings or contents. The central idea denoted by this word was that of exclusion, but it was necessary to determine the social or economic spheres in which this exclusion was predicated. As noted in one of the analyses of the subject: "It is possible to affirm that at the beginning of its use in Latin America, marginality was simply an empirical generalization of certain situations considered similar for several combined reasons: i) the rapid urbanization of the 1950s generated ecological segregations that gave rise to the emergence of marginal populations. However, it was soon recognized that not only in the suburbs but also in the urban slums of the center, the same housing shortages were also present; ii) ecological segregation was followed by the verification of other multiple forms of social exclusion, for example in the field of economic and political participation; iii) marginality was interpreted in some pioneering work of ECLAC as a form of limited citizenship, based on theoretical interpretations of T. Marshall; iv) finally, the scope of social exclusion, as well as its impact on the social and economic development of the poor, was also analyzed. Marshall; v) this linked the issue of social marginality with the cultural issue, within which different theories were formulated according to which marginality was an expression or consequence of internal colonialism (for example González Casanova), or of the cultural superimposition derived from that colonial heritage". Solari, A. Franco, R. Jutkowitz, J. 1976. Theory, Social Action and Development in Latin America. Second Part. Chapter VIII, ILPES texts, Siglo XXI Editores.

Authors such as Medina Echavarría (1963, 1973), Germani (1964, 1969), or González Casanova (1965), from different angles link marginality to a situation of exclusion that can only be understood in its historical features, specific to the Latin American reality.

In any case, it is clear that the term marginality was used in Latin America to signify collective situations of exclusion compared to certain social or economic structures. But its theoretical status depended on the epistemological conception of each author for the characterization of these structures. Within Latin American structuralism in its most multidisciplinary expression, it is possible that the most important link between political economy and the political sociology of development has been located around concepts such as structural heterogeneity (Pinto 1965, Pinto and Di Filippo 1979, Furtado 1968), dynamic insufficiency (Prebisch 1963, 1970) on the side of the economists, rural marginality and clientelism (Medina 1973), and internal colonialism (Stavenhagen 1969 and González Casanova 1965); and asynchrony of change (Germani 1964, 1969), rural marginality and clientelism (Medina 1973), and internal colonialism (Stavenhagen 1969 and González Casanova 1965).

However, there seems to be little doubt that the peripheral condition within the framework of the colonial heritage, on one side, and, on the other side, the dialectical counterpoint between the institutional complexes of democracy and capitalism, from the point of view of their Latin American historical and structural peculiarities, always reappear underpinning the examinations of these and other scholars.

External contributions to ECLAC: Dependence and modes of production

In contrast, other authors strongly influenced by Marx's thought, such as José Nun (1969), take as a starting point the class positions of capitalism, and try to understand the Latin American specificity regarding this exclusion. Other authors such as André Gunder Frank or Theotonio Dos Santos will also take explicitly Marxist positions as a starting point, to critically reformulate these ideas in order to use them to understand the so-called Latin American dependence.

This Marxist version of Latin American development, despite its undoubted theoretical quality, blurred the epistemological foundations of the ELADES, and, from this perspective, was placed in another theoretical context where the connection with democratic principles as a precondition for policy recommendations was lost.

The theory of dependency to which, in general, these sociologists and political scientists could ascribe themselves, was launched into a radical revolutionism and took as a rather "bourgeois" or formalist datum the observance of the principles, practices and institutions of representative democracy. The only categories of analysis clearly present were, within the Marxist categories assumed, those of capitalism, interpreted with visions very close to those of the ideal type that Marx had constructed for the interpretation of the European realities he had to study.

This critical commentary on the direct application of Marxist categories to a different context, clearly applicable to Nun's (1969) reflections on the industrial army and relative overpopulation, or to those of Gunder Frank (1967) on satellite-metropolis relations, cannot be extended to the same extent to Theotonio Dos Santos' view of dependency theory.

Theotonio Dos Santos: dependent or peripheral capitalism?

Dos Santos describes dependence as a conditioning situation, that is, as a situation that determines the limits and possibilities of human action and behavior. This conditioning, according to Dos Santos, is not definitive for two reasons:

a) because the concrete situations of development are formed both by these general conditions of dependence, and by the specific characteristics of the conditioned situation, which redefine and particularize the general conditioning situation;
b) the very situation of dependency can be changed, and in fact is altered, according to changes in the hegemonic structures and in the dependent structures themselves.

> These changes can occur without breaking the dependency relations but simply re-orienting them (the passage, for example, from mercantile to industrial-financial dependency); or breaking those relations and seeking to consolidate an independent economy (the case of the socialist countries of the third world, such as China, Korea, Vietnam, and Cuba, in spite of the problems they may still have due to the legacy left by the old situation and the old structures) (Marini and Dos Santos 1999: 297 and ff.).

It should be pointed out that the historical examples referred to by Dos Santos have in common the non-existence of democratic regimes of government in the Western sense of the term. That is to say, the conception of democracy that originated theoretically in the foundational reflections of Aristotle, developed conceptually in the 18th and 19th centuries during the expansion of liberalism, and became politically valid with the American and French revolutions. By rejecting the national and international institutions of capitalism Dos Santos also rejects (implicitly) the national institutions of democracy that in their different versions coexist with the current capitalist order. He leaves the door open for the determination of a legitimate political order different from the former. That political order does not seem to be, for Dos Santos, the popular democracies associated with the dictatorship of the proletariat in the vision of Marx and Engels' "Communist Manifesto". Nor does it seem to be that of the real socialisms of the Soviet Union and its Central European satellites. A question remains open regarding the political regimes that are compatible with societies that break their dependent links with the Soviet Union and its satellites in Central Europe.

These questions also arise regarding the content to be given to the word socialism. For example, given China's current economic evolution and its increasingly close links with global capitalism, questions arise as to its status as a "socialist country.".

It is interesting to note that although Dos Santos is a sociologist, he develops his fundamental categories of dependency in economic terms and within the framework of a Marxist vision.

But unlike, for example, Gunder Frank, whom he criticizes in a friendly and constructive manner, Dos Santos rejects the idea that there was a capitalist order in Latin America, in the formative phase of those economies, as suggested in the German author's satellite-metropolis view[23].

In short, taking the foundational aspect of structuralist economists, Dos Santos' historical diagnosis is also based on the formation of peripheral export economies. Thus, the basic coincidence with the Cepaline dependency theorists such as Cardoso and Faletto, and also with modernization theorists such as Gino Germani in his later works (1969), is once again apparent. They all start from the initial conceptualizations of the founding fathers of the ELADES, all of them, although in a tangential way, refer to the establishment of the center-periphery system, to the economies exporting primary products, to the constitution of internal markets, to the modalities of industrialization by import substitution, etc., as structural foundations of the Latin American economic formations.

This leads us to question ourselves conceptually with relation to two ways of denominating Latin American capitalism. First, Theotonio Dos Santos, who speaks of dependent capitalism, and,

---

[23] Thus, Dos Santos observes: "How to characterize this regime of production, as a case of capitalist regime, as a distinct mode of production or as a regime of transition from an incomplete feudalism or slavery to capitalism that assumed the colonial exporting form, just as in Europe in that period there was a stage of transition from feudalism to capitalism, characterized as a mercantile manufacturing period" (...) "It seems to us that the latter characterization is the one that comes closest to the dependent reality. The Industrial Revolution in England at the end of the eighteenth century created the conditions for the expansion of the capitalist mode of production in Europe, transforming it into the dominant regime of production in these countries, precisely because the mercantile manufacturing period had prepared the division between the ownership of the means of production and the free labor force; It had also prepared the conditions for an intense primitive accumulation of capital, based on the monopoly of international trade, on the concentration and acceleration of financial activity, on the destruction of the private peasant economy; it had, in short, advanced the international division of labor in manufacturing, which faced a steadily growing internal and external market. Another was the situation in Latin America, a producer of metals and tropical products: an important market for Europe and not for Latin America, which had the remains of this market to spare and which had to pay large sums to the Crown and the merchants. All this has led Latin America, after the limitations of the colonial period, to a dependent capitalism based on the export sector. The traces of a colonial export regime give the parameters of the 'liberated' Latin America. Not only because a large part of our surpluses was taken away from us, but fundamentally because our economic and social structures were dependent and the liberating revolutions did not succeed in changing the bases of these structures, dominated as they were by the Creole oligarchy".

secondly, that of Prebisch who speaks of peripheral capitalism. However, Prebisch's concept of peripheral capitalism is examined in a counterpoint with another socio-political process: the process of democratization, which runs with a certain independence from the economic processes and concerns the mechanisms of formation of political power in Latin America, the validity of human rights and freedoms, the formation of a civic conscience, etc. At this point, Prebisch's peripheral capitalism gives room to sociopolitical theorizations on democracy such as those developed by Medina Echavarría, or even by Gino Germani.

These reflections were not present in the theorists of dependence. This is paradoxical, since they were not, nor are they, economists but sociologists or political scientists and, therefore, they should have all the more reason to pronounce themselves on this subject. By not doing so, they seem to suggest that the theoretical instruments of the analysis of capitalist societies were sufficient for them to interpret Latin American history, without penetrating into issues such as democratic institutions, citizen rights and obligations, different cultural roots, rights and freedoms of native peoples, etc.

In the period we are analyzing, which was the 1970s, these debates on modes of production coincided with the installation of authoritarian regimes that lasted until the mid-1980s. This repressive right-wing authoritarianism put an end to the potential authoritarian expectations of the left, which were brutally repressed along with the precarious and incipient institutions and practices of democracy.

Chapter VI

The 80's - return to democracy

Historical context

The main historical facts of this decade included the gradual return to democracy and the consolidation of the economic structures of capitalism on a global scale. After the various forms of the so-called "dirty war" in which State terrorism confronted leftist revolutionism in order to crush it with blood and fire, the reestablishment of the institutions of Latin American democracy as they were registered in the constitutional charters that were suspended, but not suppressed during the period of the military dictatorships, returned with great difficulty.

In Prebisch's vision, corresponding to the last stage of his intellectual life, as information technologies facilitated the transformation and growing trans nationalization of large corporations in the developed world, the dichotomy between capitalism and democracy, in its new historical versions, took center stage in his theory. His final legacy to the ELADES was precisely an examination of the conditions of peripheral capitalism and its apparent incompatibility with the process of democratization. His last book was written under the influence of the authoritarian governments of the 1970s and, in it, the need for the structural transformation of the system was raised. However, unlike the pro-dependency advocates, he attempted a conciliation between the principles of political liberalism, expressed in the validity of democratic institutions, and the need for a socialization of the economic surplus in a version that recalled Keynes' previous recommendations included in his General Theory related to the socialization of investment[24].

The contributions of economists

Peripheral capitalism as seen by Prebisch [25]

In his last book, "Peripheral Capitalism, Crisis and Transformation" (like Germani, in his theory of stages ten years earlier), the analysis of the phases of peripheral development is made explicit by taking into consideration their impact on the democratization process. By linking the democratization process with the dynamics of peripheral capitalism, Prebisch explicitly attempts for the first time to integrate the concepts of capitalism and democracy in his analysis[26].

---

[24] Keynes said: "The implications of the theory outlined are moderately conservative in other respects, for while it indicates the vital importance of establishing certain central controls in matters which are at present left almost entirely to private initiative, there are many fields of activity which it does not affect. The state will have to exert a guiding influence on the propensity to consume, through its tax system, by setting the interest rate, and perhaps by other means. On the other hand, it seems unlikely that the influence of banking policy on the interest rate is sufficient by itself to determine another optimal investment policy. I believe, therefore, that a fairly complete socialization of investments will be the only means of approaching complete occupation; though this need not exclude any form, transaction or means by which the public authority co-operates with private initiative. But apart from this, a system of state socialism embracing the greater part of the economic life of the community is not frankly advocated" (Keynes 1943: 362).

[25] Prebisch's focus of analysis was always peripheral capitalism. However, in the institutional framework of the United Nations to which ECLAC belonged, during the Cold War and the East- West geopolitical dichotomy, the expressions capitalism, socialism and communism were preferably ignored. It should not be forgotten that ECLAC's research had as its final destination its conference documents and its technical assistance missions to Latin American governments. However, Prebisch, in the 1980s, now completely retired from his leadership positions, firmly established the term peripheral capitalism in his last works; likewise, his arguments on power were more clearly associated with an analysis of the class structure not in the Marxist sense but according to the position occupied in the strata of productive power and in the sphere of markets.

[26] It is worth noting here the important contribution of the Argentine sociologist Adolfo Gurrieri, who was Prebisch's main interlocutor during the preparation of the sociopolitical dimensions of the aforementioned book. Gurrieri, who was director of ECLAC's Social Development Division in the early 1990s, carried out an important

For Prebisch, the democratization process is not restricted to the political dimension of democracy, but also includes other dimensions of equity linked to equality of opportunities in the economic, social and cultural spheres. Greater equity in the distribution of income[27], even if only in overcoming a poverty line, is, for Prebisch, an expression of economic democratization in which people are more than mere bearers of class positions. Nor does his analysis of class, linked to the concept of power, deny or underestimate the autonomous role that individuals play in historical processes.

According to Prebisch, peripheral capitalism is specific to Latin American societies and, as such, is marked by certain processes of technological, institutional and organizational change that are historically and structurally determined. The inclusion of the term peripheral capitalism is thus predicated on a systemic framework (that of capitalism as a generic ideal type) but structurally limited in the world order (the peripheral international positioning), and historically referred to the specific Latin American societies. In turn, peripheral capitalism is conceived only as an economic dimension coexisting with other social and political dimensions. In his approach Prebisch explicitly recognizes the multidimensional, and not only economic, character of the concept of development, and examines the power structures, not only economic, but also social, trade union and political, of peripheral societies.

---

task of systematizing Prebisch's contribution to ECLAC's thinking, and published a compilation entitled Prebisch's Work in ECLAC, preceded by a study of Prebisch's thinking, which includes this last period of his reflection. Gurrieri also faced this task with the works of Medina Echavarría and must be considered as one of the sociologists who contributed most to the dissemination of the thought of these two great thinkers of the Latin American social sciences.

[27] A significant point in Prebisch's analysis that he shares with the other main economists of the ELADES -Furtado, Pinto, Sunkel, Ferrer, etc.- is the central role played by personal or family income distribution in the composition of effective demand. In fact, this approach to personal or family income distribution is the only one compatible with the study of the incidence of poverty. This is because poverty is predicated with respect to individuals or families and not with respect to abstract economic agents, mere bearers of class positions in the different markets. It is true that it is possible to say that the minimum wage of a country's workers, conceived globally as a class, condemns them all to poverty if it is very low, but the measurement of the number and percentage of the poor requires an examination at the level of individuals and families.

The issue of development styles that can be predicated on national realities can be framed in this context historically specified, which we will now consider. In his last book, Prebisch also establishes a series of historical stages through which peripheral capitalism passed in its advance towards the democratization process. The issue of styles can be located within any of these stages.

Development styles: an interdisciplinary debate in the 1980s

Considering the contributions of other Latin American structuralists, the issue of development styles can be examined in the light of the interpretations of three Cepaline thinkers: Aníbal Pinto, Fernando Enrique Cardoso and Jorge Graciarena.

The three authors emphasize that, in the concept of styles, the issue of essential needs and their satisfaction stands out. The first author observes: "In summary, when we speak of styles of development we have in mind -as a first and fundamental approximation- the degree and manner in which a given economy satisfies the basic needs of the population, expands its productive potential for that purpose and establishes a margin of national autonomy that allows it to fulfill that purpose".

Strictly speaking, it is clear that Aníbal Pinto is referring to styles of economic development, but even restricting the subject to this dimension, what is new and specific to the traditional structuralist cepalina vision is the issue of the degree to which the basic needs of the majority of the population are satisfied. Note that, without forcing the terms too much, the above can be considered as the economic dimension of democracy, both because of the emphasis on equity, which stricto sensu implies an orientation towards situations of economic equality, and because of the very concept of basic needs, the operational concreteness of which requires going down to the examination of specific individuals or families (sex, age, health, etc.).

The priority on equity oriented towards the satisfaction of basic needs is, as Pinto himself states, a way of responding to the unequal and marginalizing (excluding) growth in Latin America. In other words, the concept of equity is coming to intercept, as a policy goal, the concept of marginality. Thus, there is an increasingly explicit rescue of people understood as human beings, as opposed to classes as bearers of objective interests associated with their positions in the economic structure, and representatives of "ideologies" understood as conscious or unconscious legitimations of these objective interests.

In relation to the concept of styles, Fernando Enrique Cardoso, from a sociopolitical perspective, addresses the issue of the agents of change and the strategic recommendations that can be elaborated on the basis of this conceptual content. Thus, he emphasizes: "It does not require much theoretical subtlety to perceive that the new approach has some undefined parameters. On one side, basic needs - the very center of its analysis - ended up expressing two concerns: eradication of poverty and the belief that, under the current productive and technological conditions, this objective will only be achieved through a redefinition of lifestyles and, consequently, of development styles"[28].

Jorge Graciarena also establishes a link between the concepts of basic needs and poverty that is particularly revealing and anticipatory of the later reflections that eventually led to the current concepts of human development. Graciarena contrasts the concept of basic needs and "other development" with the more conventional strategies for combating

---

[28] It is interesting to note that Cardoso, in his analysis of styles, establishes a dichotomous counterpoint between the "developmentalist Enlightened State" (which, according to him, occupied the leading role in the developmental strategies of ECLAC economic structuralism) and contrasts it -perhaps also self-critically- with "dependency revolutionism". As an innovative element in the new controversy on styles, he recognizes the theoreticians of the new development as claiming "the valorizing category of human dignity", but oscillating in a pendulum-like attitude that, at the level of concrete recommendations, leads them to "bureaucratic-institutional reform, at the level of the United Nations". The issue of institutional bureaucratic reform to which Cardoso alludes, was also addressed by Marshall Wolfe (1976), in a pioneering way to the later approach to the issue of development styles. Marshall Wolfe, an American sociologist who was director of ECLAC's Social Development Division, was a great "ironizer" who took his skepticism to truly masochistic limits. His book of those years, entitled "El Desarrollo Esquivo (Elusive Development"), is full of caustic comments on Development and its styles. One of the most incisive chapters is the third one entitled: "Approaches to development, from whom and to what?" Although somewhat devastating, Wolfe's critique (which is also a self-criticism of his status as an international civil servant) healthily aims at demystifying the role of techno- bureaucracy as an "agent" of development, and the need to subordinate it to values that can only be expressed in the political sphere through concrete social processes and forces in each society.

poverty, and highlights the greater depth of the former as opposed to the palliative character that the latter can assume[29].

---

[29] Graciarena says: "The other development approach, which emphasizes the satisfaction of basic needs (NB), starts from a very different assumption, which is to assume the elimination of poverty as the consequence of a profound reorganization of society and human coexistence. Unlike the poverty approach, which is highly malleable and mimetic (these properties are the basis of much of its credibility and capacity to appeal to technocratic and hegemonic sectors), the basic needs approach explicitly proposes as its goal the achievement of a model of egalitarian society" (...) "As can be seen here, it is no longer possible to establish an order of more or less between poverty and BN because the differences are not aggregate and the starting assumptions and their objectives differ radically. In one case, the eradication of poverty is at the end of the road, while in the other, the satisfaction of basic needs is constituted from the beginning, in the structural principle of a model of society where the situation of poverty is, in principle, excluded as a real possibility" (Graciarena 1982: 93, included in Franco 1982).

Chapter VII

The 1990s - Neostructuralism

Historical context: capitalism and democracy in the global era

The 1980s were to profoundly change the historical scenario of Latin American societies. On one side, it was characterized as the economically "lost" decade due to the economic depression that dealt the coup de grace to the process of protected development inherited from the post-war period; on the other side, however, that same decade was "won" in the political field, reinstalling democratic regimes. Thus, at the beginning of the 1990s, a profoundly different scenario offered itself to reflections on development.

To discover why the new scenario was so different, it is necessary to return to the foundations of the center-periphery vision. Indeed, the late 1980s not only marked the end of an era in Latin America - the end of the post-war development model and the recovery of democracy - but also the end of a world era and the beginning of another based on new technological and economic conditions linked to the process of economic globalization: the installation of information technologies, the trans nationalization of business on these new technological bases, the "financialization" of international economic processes, and other well- known processes that promoted the installation of globalized capitalism, parallel to the growing diffusion of the institutional complexes of representative democracy also to centrally planned authoritarian societies.

The contribution of economists: Neostructuralism

An important methodological observation insisted upon by Celso Furtado was the degree of abstraction in which scientific problems were posed. Structuralism, as the foundational approach of the ELADES, always worked at the highest conceivable degree of abstraction, confronting directly the main categories involved in contemporary social sciences such as development, capitalism, democracy, etc.

The neo-structuralists took up the challenge of grounding these categories in the more concrete and pragmatic field of public policies, beyond the great guiding strategies of structuralism. It should be pointed out, however, that neo-structuralism is predicated as a continuation or reorientation of structuralism in the narrow field of political economy. Therefore, it must be evaluated in this sphere as a response to the new international conditions associated with the installation of global capitalism and as a reaction to the new rules of the international economy linked to consensuses or agreements reached by the central economies.

In particular, neo-structuralism can be explained for several reasons: first, ECLAC is an intergovernmental agency, a trustee of its member governments and respectful of the development strategies adopted by those governments. The fundamental values and principles of ECLAC are not set in economic terms (e.g. capitalism versus socialism) but rather in socio-political terms linked to the ideology of the United Nations, but these values are only a vague background that must be pragmatically reconciled with the political and economic processes actually in force in the historical reality; second, the historical scenario of the 1980s was transitioning towards the new styles of open, privatized/trans nationalized economies, regulated in ways that were functional to the trends of the new global capitalism. This new neoliberal philosophy had taken root in several of the most important economies of Latin America, in the heat of authoritarian governments that emerged after the repression of the revolutionary turbulence of the 1960s and 1970s.

Therefore, ECLAC had to respond to the directives of economic authorities who were embarking on the new development model; third, ECLAC had to try, for reasons of historical coherence and even institutional inertia, to reconcile the new historical facts with its more global diagnoses, and to do so from a much less transcendent position in terms of its interpretations and policy recommendations (Di Filippo 1998).

Even so, ECLAC found interpreters who managed to rescue the essential foundations of its thinking in order to apply them to a plausible interpretation of the Latin American processes of the 1980s. At the beginning of the 1990s, ECLAC, under the instigation of the Chilean economist Fernando Fajnzylber, launched its document: *Productive Transformation with Equity: Latin America's Great Task (1990).*

By that time, the development model still in force in Latin America, oriented towards economic stabilization, opening up to the outside world, deregulation of markets, and privatization (and trans nationalization) of productive processes, had already been implemented. The "magic word" of the last decade of the century had already been spread: *international competitiveness.*

Fajnzylber's ideas mark the advent of a new Eclectic vision that has come to be known as Latin American neo-structuralism. The neo-structuralism of the 1990s maintains the foundational structuralist vision regarding the importance of Latin America's international positioning and the priority of technical progress in the causal explanation of economic development processes. It also maintains the (at first somewhat rhetorical) recognition of the issues of equity and social justice.

However, the approach of the 1990s is strongly influenced both by the new historical circumstances of globalization and by the resurgence of neo-liberal ideology that impacted the economic policies of Latin American countries. The focus of analysis returns to the strictly economic perspective where the new macro-economic strategies and policies associated with the process of stabilization, liberalization, deregulation and privatization (trans nationalization) in terms of resource allocation are absorbed and institutionally digested. Neostructuralism paid much attention to the analysis of the economic policy instruments and mechanisms that Latin American countries were applying in the installation of their new development models, and reflected on the links between the "micro", "macro" and "meso" levels of economic processes. The hegemonic intellectual climate of neoliberalism in the spheres of academic reflection and public policy was not favorable to strengthening and deepening interdisciplinary links between economists and other social scientists.

Productive transformation with equity

In its approach to Productive Transformation with Equity, ECLAC accepted as a "fait accompli" the new development model generalized since the 1990s and the central role of international competitiveness in the economic viability of open economies. However, it attempted to place this concept within a broader conceptual framework that, in accordance with its intellectual traditions, would take into consideration structural elements and systemic logics. Thus, he distinguished between illegitimate or unsustainable competitiveness, as opposed to another, which he termed legitimate or sustainable competitiveness.

In this terminology, illegitimate or unsustainable competitiveness would be based, as the facts used to denounce it, on the exploitation of salaried workers, the destruction of the environment, or the not always scrupulous use, in the field of macroeconomic policies, of exchange rate devaluations. These illegitimate forms of competitiveness had been tried during the 1980s when Latin American economies were desperately struggling to increase their international reserves, decimated by high debt servicing and the low price of primary exports, in order to service their bulging foreign debt.

Note that in this approach ECLAC addresses three central issues: first, it recognizes the historical impact of disastrous macroeconomic administrations from the point of view of long-term stability (galloping inflation, depletion of reserves, etc.) that had contributed to discrediting protectionist and industrialist governments during the 1970s and 1980s; second, it recognizes the historical impact of the economic crisis in the region.

Second, it vigorously incorporates in its analysis the effects of the most decisive phenomenon in the future of humanity, the environmental imbalances induced by a narrow economistic criterion in the management of natural resources. Third, it rescues the issue of distributive justice and equity that was at the origins of the center-periphery vision, emphasizing the historical non-sustainability and the moral illegitimacy of labor exploitation as a way of facing the profound external imbalances that caused the collapse of the Latin American economy in the 1980s, the environmental imbalances induced by a narrow "economicist" criterion in the management of natural resources.

In contrast, the legitimate or sustainable competitiveness sponsored by ECLAC was proposed as that which would achieve cost reductions and quality increases not based on such illegitimate measures.The new current of economic neo-structuralism, led by Fajnzylber, proposed that these objectives could be achieved in a sustained manner only with the systematic assimilation of technical progress. In this way, ECLAC once again rescued the central role of technical progress, but redefined it in the framework of the new institutions and organizations of globalized capitalism.

The other feature of sustainable international competitiveness that ECLAC emphasized is its systemic nature. This approach linked the development of productivity and competitiveness with the new ideas (for example, those of Michael Porter) on value chains and systems. These ideas were extremely close to the Latin American neo-structuralism of the 1980s. It is interesting to understand that the new microeconomic (and mesoeconomic) visions put forward by Porter, Ohmae, Druker and other theorists of business management and managerial performance are based on the study of international competitiveness strategies with visions of markets that explicitly deny the distorting neoclassical assumptions of perfect competition, and restore all the frictions and positions of power that are typical of real markets.

However, despite the series of documents on Productive transformation with equity, in the neo-structuralist economic approach of the 1990s, the formulation of policies aimed at promoting equity remained a pending issue, partly due to the budgetary restrictions on public action resulting from the new development model.

In fact, the concept of socially sustainable international competitiveness, as formulated by Fernando Fajnzylber, at the end of the 1980s, included an improvement in participation in world markets with a parallel improvement in workers' wages. On another side, this sustainable competitiveness, according to ECLAC's approach, could only be truly and legitimately increased based on the introduction of technical progress capable of increasing factor productivity and, in particular, that of the labor force. As can be seen, the issue continued to be, as in more classic ECLAC formulations, that of the distribution of technical progress and its fruits in a way that could simultaneously satisfy the increases in international competitiveness and the growing participation of workers in these productivity gains.

Socio-political perspective: emphasis on poverty issues

The main recommendation in the social area formulated by ECLAC was the so-called integrated policy approach put forward at its 1992 session. The integrated policy approach (ECLAC 1992 b) attempts to overcome the compartmentalized visions according to which there are economic policies located at the level of resource allocation and fundamentally oriented towards growth and, on the other hand, social policies aimed at alleviating, in a targeted and a posteriori manner, the social inequalities and inequities produced by economic growth.

The integrated approach postulates that there are policies capable of simultaneously addressing economic and social problems. Such is the case, for example, with those aimed at human resource development, capable of increasing the labor skills of the population, increasing its productivity and therefore the growth potential of the system and, at the same time, improving living conditions and the skills and knowledge to improve its participation in the socio-political and cultural spheres. This approach responds to a long-standing concern of ECLAC to integrate the dimensions of its diagnosis, for example, along the lines of the efforts already mentioned to delimit styles of development.

The decade of the 90s did not bring any important new theoretical contributions to the macro-social interpretation of the issues of equity and poverty. There was a more systematic monitoring of data on the subject, together with the application of new measurement techniques that are more comparable on a Latin American scale. These advances were disseminated through annual studies such as the Social Panorama of Latin America, published by ECLAC's Social Development Division in collaboration with the Latin American Center for Economic Projections (Centro Latinoamericano de Proyecciones Económicas).

That publication was in that moment one of the most important sources of information and diagnosis on Social Development in Latin

America. In particular, it kept alive the concern and concrete follow- up of the issues of income distribution, employment and poverty. The director of the Social Development Division, Rolando Franco, included in his curriculum vitae a leading role in one of the most complete sociopolitical studies on the ELADES from its origins until the mid-1970s (Solari, Franco and Jutkovitz 1976)

Another important analytical deepening was verified in the study of the main paradigms guiding the approach to social policies, and the way in which the different changes in this field corresponded to the different phases of Latin American development that we have analyzed here. A focused policy approach compatible with a universalist vision, based on an in-depth knowledge of the basic needs of specific target groups, was advocated. This focused conception of policies was an appropriate framework for the development of methodologies for the evaluation and preparation of social projects, known as "cost-impact" (Cohen and Franco 1995), and was highly compatible with the integrated policy approach proposed by ECLAC economists (Cohen and Franco 1995).

Chapter VIII

21st century: development in a global era

As some contemporary historians have said, the 20th century was, from a historical perspective, much shorter than its chronological length. It began with the First World War and ended with a set of more or less simultaneous events: the demise of the centrally planned authoritarian systems of Central Europe, the revolution in information technologies, the consequent globalization of capitalism, and the challenges to the autonomy (and even sovereignty) of nation states that have derived from the above factors.

These far-reaching changes have also had an impact on Latin American societies. The economic opening to globalized capitalism, the growing presence of transnational corporations, the democratization (at least in terms of formal political institutions) of Latin American states, the strengthening of municipal governments, and the reduction in the maneuvering capacity of national authorities in the formulation and execution of their public policies, are all part of a new scenario characterized by rapid and important technological, organizational and institutional changes.

At the beginning of the 21st century, ECLAC addressed the complex changes that had already taken place in Latin America. The first was related to the new regional development model integrated into the global capitalist order, and the second to the generalization of the democratization process throughout Latin America.

The first issue was formulated in the work presented at the April 2000 session and the second in the report presented at the April 2002 session.

The common feature of these two studies was undoubtedly the categorical framing of the content of development within a multidimensional framework that included not only economic, but also political and sociocultural factors. This is the most notable feature of both studies: the evident multidimensionality of their approach.

To conclude this review, we will only transcribe a few summary paragraphs related to these two documents, which were prepared under the inspired guidance of José Antonio Ocampo, Executive Secretary at the time and a keen interpreter of both the history of the ELADES and the new processes and challenges of the emerging millennium.

In "Globalization and development", the first section of the synthesis of the Study refers to the feature mentioned above, entitled "The historical and multidimensional nature of globalization":

Today's world is characterized by what is known as mundialization or globalization, i.e., the growing gravitation of world economic, social and cultural processes at the national and regional levels. Although this is not a new process, since it has deep historical roots, the changes in terms of space and time brought about by the communications and information revolution have given it new dimensions that represent qualitative transformations with respect to the past.

The same introductory synthesis highlights central aspects such as the "globalization of values", the emergence of environmental problems and the contrast between the increasingly global character of capitalism vis a vis the local or national character of the institutions of democracy[30].

---

30 "There are other processes, which have a dynamic relatively independent of economic globalization. One of the most positive is what ECLAC has called the "globalization of values", which is understood as the gradual extension of common ethical principles, the most important manifestations of which are the declarations on human rights - in their dual dimension of civil and political rights and economic, social and cultural rights - and the declarations of the United Nations world summits, including, most especially, the Millennium Declaration. As in the economic sphere, this "globalization of values" has a long history rooted in the struggles of international civil society: while the civil and political rights enshrined in the United Nations Universal Declaration of Human Rights have their historical origin in the liberal movements of the late eighteenth century, the International Covenant on Economic, Social and Cultural Rights is the product of social movements of the 19th and 20th centuries, and the principles of gender equality are the result of the long struggle of international feminist movements."
"International political relations have also undergone far-reaching changes in recent decades. The end of the Cold War marked a turning point in the prevailing climate between sovereign states. The accentuation of U.S. primacy, European efforts to create a leading bloc in the world economy and politics, Japan's backwardness, the

In these new scenarios, ECLAC highlighted the promotion of economic, social and cultural rights (ESCR) as the spearhead through which it hopes to build conceptual and operational bridges of union and integration between the institutional complexes of capitalism and democracy in this globalized world.

This approach is particularly representative of the values and principles of the United Nations traditionally established since its foundation. We are therefore not in the presence of a new political or ethical value-positioning. But the contemporary human rights offensive (and its specification and deepening in the field of ESC rights) aims at promoting a new global consensus based on a growing and unrestricted respect for the dignity of each and every human being. In this endeavor, the promotion of ESC rights can play a key role[31].

These ideas fully coincide with those expressed in the ECLAC Conference Document presented at the 2002 Session. The following

---

rise of China and India, and the abrupt transition of the socialist countries were the most salient features. The profound political changes brought about by these phenomena gave representative democracy a preponderance never seen before.

"These political changes face a recognized deficit of global governance, which reflects another deep conflict: the contrast between global problems and local political processes. There are no decision-making mechanisms at the global level that make possible an adequate representation of the interests of countries and of the less powerful social sectors. This situation causes tensions, since the spaces for the exercise of citizenship and democracy continue to be national and local" (ECLAC 2000, pp. 3-7).

[31] A special study prepared jointly by ECLAC with decisive contributions from Ernesto Ottone and the Inter-American Institute of Human Rights (IIDH) states: "...the possibility of establishing a synthetic indicator of equity based on the notion of economic, social and cultural rights of individuals, which would make it possible to measure their level of realization in societies, has not so far provided an answer to the issue of the full recognition and enforceability of these rights. (...) It would be illusory to think that, through the International Covenant on ESC rights, wealth could be generated or that the non-existent could be distributed. However, this does not condemn ESC rights to ineffectiveness or make them dispensable in a social development strategy. On the contrary, their value lies in the fact that they help build the institutional legal order in which authorities and citizens operate. (...) From the above, there is a profound relationship between the fulfillment of ESCR and an adequate response to the challenges of development in Latin America, which takes into account the achievement of an equitable development that allows the exercise of a modern citizenship". ECLAC/IDHR. 2004. The equality of modern people, reflections on the realization of economic, social and cultural rights in Latin America.

paragraph is transcribed in extenso, as it reflects the last act of our study of the evolution of ELN:

> This integrated vision of development goes beyond the complementarity between social, economic and environmental policies and democratic order, between human capital, social welfare, sustainable development and citizenship: it must be interpreted as the very meaning of development. In other words, integrated development cannot sacrifice people or their natural habitat for the sake of economic growth. On the contrary, progress and growth must translate into an ever-increasing satisfaction of their needs. This means that development should not only aim to respond to people's growing desire for consumption, which, however legitimate, does not exhaust aspirations for quality of life. Development must also aim to build a social and human climate of greater security and mutual trust; to consolidate a democratic political order with greater participation of people in management and public decisions; to spread well-being to those who have less access to the benefits of modernity; to take shape in collective projects in which citizens acquire a greater sense of commitment and belonging to the society in which they live; and to seek the protection and improvement of the natural habitat for those who live there today and those who will do so in the future. This set of virtuous processes is the matter that gives integral form to development.
>
> The concept of integral development has been at the core of ECLAC's proposals throughout its history and was also the starting point for those it formulated in the early 1990s (...). We increasingly understand the relevance of this concept, which has been expressed for a long time in many visions of development similar to those proposed by our institution, such as the concept of human development (UNDP 1994) or the more recent "development as freedom" (Sen 1999) (ECLAC 2000: 51).

The concept of integral development proposed by ECLAC at the dawn of the 21st century synthesizes decades of interpretative efforts that we have attempted to summarize in these pages.

The evolution of Latin American thinking on development can be summarized by saying that it begins with an economic definition of the concept (but endowed from the outset with a historical specificity given by Latin America's peripheral position in the world order) and concludes with a multidisciplinary vision encompassing the main dimensions of Latin American societies.

The results obtained, both by ECLAC social scientists and by other participants in the debate, show that theoretical categories derived from European or American history, used in a direct and uncritical manner, tend to confuse rather than clarify the study of social class relations in Latin America, be it capitalism (as Gunther Frank claimed) or feudalism (as suggested by Puigross and other representatives of orthodox Marxism).

The Latin American reality is structurally heterogeneous within itself and only responds to the dynamics generated in its own history, as Medina Echavarría (1963) emphasized early on, as confirmed by Sergio Bagú (1949), and subsequently ratified by the studies on Latin American rural society by Gonzalez Casanova (1965), Stavenhagen (1965, 1969), etc. The issue of social inequality is raised in all its crudeness when contrasted with democracy in Latin America or with the survival of internal colonialism, especially in societies with a strong colonial heritage. The issue was originally studied and debated with respect to rural areas, but later moved to urban areas as well, linked to what came to be known as social marginality. All these processes are profoundly different from those that gave rise to the emergence of contemporary capitalism in developed Western societies.

The original economic ideas of the ELADES were action-oriented, far removed from the abstract neoclassical models of positive economics, especially in their neoclassical aspect, and much closer to the concept of political economy in the traditional conception already present in Adam Smith. The presence of the State was presupposed at all times, whether as a vehicle of exploitation or inequality, as in the most radical branch of the dependency movement, or as an instrument of development, as in the industrialist policies recommended by the founding economists of the ELADES, or as an instrument of development, as in the industrialist policies recommended by the founding economists of the ELADES.

In this journey, the encompassing concept was that of capitalism, since all contemporary theoretical currents in economics are ultimately devoted to its study. But the concept escaped the limits corresponding to purely economic logic. Around it, hypotheses on the genesis and dynamics of Latin American societies were interwoven. This explains why the debate essentially brought together two great visions of capitalism: that of Max Weber and that of Marx.

The subject of democracy was then approached in the search for Latin American specificities. Societies less linked to the colonial heritage were examined from the angle of democracy by authors such as Gino Germani (1964), who used the term to elaborate a theory of the stages of Latin American development. Societies more closely linked to the colonial heritage, in the light of the concept of democracy, were examined in the light of the conditions of internal colonialism, as González Casanova (1965) did in his studies on democracy in Mexico.

In Latin America there were elements of capitalism and democracy, but they were "peripheral", "incomplete", "distorted", "impure" versions, adjectives that implied an explicit or implicit comparison with the ideal types of these same systems in developed countries.

When Prebisch and Furtado, in the 1950s, laid the foundation stones of the so-called "Latin American structuralism", they did so implicitly or explicitly considering that the principles, practices and institutions of democracy were an indisputable fact of the permanent order of Latin American societies, and that development-oriented transformations implied moving through the rules of the democratic game or approaching them as an unrenounceable ideal. This is obvious in the case of Prebisch because many of his writings, especially those at the end of his life, make explicit this adherence to the principles of democracy. Furtado, too, not only attended ECLAC but also wrote pages that reveal an unequivocal commitment to the institutions of democracy (Furtado 1965).

However, when the contributions of political sociology sought to theorize on the basis of the economic categories of structuralism, Latin America was going through the most turbulent period of its recent history, aggravated since the early 1960s by revolutionary movements based on violent strategies and ideologies that sought to radically transform the conditions of social injustice prevailing in Latin America.

From the point of view of the "dependentist" sociologists, the concept of democracy was minimized, or at times interpreted as just another instrument in the bourgeois strategies of domination. This was an early "radically critical" strand, with predominantly Marxist roots, including its Leninist, Trotkyist, etc., versions.

It should also be emphasized that in Latin America "democracy" was directly linked to political regimes marked by various forms of populism, clientelism, authoritarian and personalist presidentialism, etc. The history of democracy was and, in part, still is, in Latin America, a chapter yet to be built and the critics of dependence were more concerned with achieving a revolutionary overcoming of existing inequalities.

The other political science vision of the ELADES (Medina Echavarría, Gino Germani, Aldo Solari, Rolando Franco, etc.) could highlight the long Western cultural tradition in the field of democracy and, above all, the significant fact that all Latin American nations, almost without exception, had begun their independent life supported by political constitutions based on democracy, which were never abrogated and were only "suspended" during the authoritarian military regimes of the 1970s. Therefore, there was a commitment in Latin America, at least formally, to this political regime of government. Also, ECLAC, the binding center of many of the ideas of the ELADES, was, according to the founding principles of the UN, an institution oriented towards the defense of the values, principles and practices of democracy.

Those who were on the sidelines of the more radical perspective (to some degree Cardoso, Faletto, but above all Dos Santos and Gunder Frank) did not explicitly repudiate the legitimacy of the representative democracies of the central countries, but their criticisms of the capitalist order, their theorizations on dependence and their allusions to imperialism, along with their ambiguous judgments regarding the government regimes that might emerge from their revolutionary positions, cast doubt adherence to the basic principles and values of Western democracy applicable to the Latin American reality[32].

There was no doubt, and on this point all the ideological strands of the ELADES agreed, that, as in the case of capitalism, the democratic model of the developed countries of the West did not hold true in the

---

[32] We are thinking here of principles such as: rule of law to which all citizens (rulers and ruled, majorities and minorities) are subordinated; separation of powers of the State, right to form political parties, to compete for power, and to participate in the Government, in accordance with the rules of democracy itself; the right to free information and to criticize the performance of those in power; the adoption of free and informed universal suffrage as a method of alternation in power; the defense of human, civil, political, economic and cultural rights and freedoms, both of minorities and majorities, etc.

peripheral societies of Latin America. To this day, 2007, the struggle for the values, principles, practices and institutions of democracy in its Latin American version continues to be an open page.

The essential feature of Latin American societies was, and to a significant degree continues to be, precisely the hybrid nature of their economic and political institutions, in which historical remnants of values originating in the European conquerors and colonizers are mixed with the pre-Hispanic and Afro-American roots of our societies.

Latin America, considered in its defining features, is Western not only in a geographic but also in a cultural sense, but its institutions combine in a complex way three different cultural strata: first, pre-Hispanic cultures, partially assimilated to Western culture in language, religion, and customs, but claiming their own values that tend to be strengthened in this 21st century; second, that of the pre-modern Western culture with a Catholic base, inherited from the Spanish and Portuguese colonial domination that included the institutions of servitude in native peoples, and of slavery, especially for immigrants from Africa; and, third, that of the culture of Western modernity with Anglo-Saxon roots, transplanted from the 19th century onwards. None of these historical stages or realities has disappeared in the 21st century, but neither has it been preserved in a pure form, giving rise to a hybridization that constitutes the cultural basis of Latin America's so-called structural heterogeneity.

Chapter IX

Development, vicissitudes of a concept

The institutional complexes derived from Western modernity, in force in the economic and political spheres, are today, respectively, the contemporary versions of capitalism and democracy. The joint consideration of both, in a different historical context such as that of Latin America, was the theoretical challenge posed to the ELADES.

The economic origin of the foundational structuralist reflections, and the strong influence of Marx and Max Weber on the theoretical currents of political sociology predominant in Latin America, implied a preferential option for the study of the categories of capitalism and the class dynamics linked to this economic system. This is not accidental, since the great hegemonic centers were not concerned with exporting their democratic institutions (except perhaps England when, tactically, it supported the political independence of Latin America at the beginning of the 19th century), but above all with capturing markets and obtaining primary products by taking advantage of the economic advantages of a peripheral capitalism founded on profound social inequalities.

Thus, the very nature of the structuralist economic approach in the field of center-periphery relations did not, in theory, easily allow for the examination of democratic regimes, a topic relevant to the political organization of States, but not fundamental to the study of international relations. The categories and values of democracy correspond to another body of theory that is different from that which corresponds to the study of capitalism, not only because they belong to the field of political science but also because they constitute a transhistorical cultural heritage, typically Western, with foundations and principles that are rooted in Judeo-Greco- Latin values, and are, therefore, well before the emergence of capitalism as an economic system that is a "child of modernity".

The concept of democracy establishes a bridge between pre-modern values and ethical conceptions - such as, for example, the Aristotelian vision of democracy in Classical Greece - and those of modernity - such as the democracies that emerged from the thinkers, ideologues and social fighters who promoted the British (1689), American (1776) and French (1789) political revolutions.

Today, not only Latin America, but also the rest of the world faces the difficult task of framing the institutions of global capitalism within the framework of the institutions of democracy whose principles, practices, and institutions summarize the most enduring values of Western culture. Putting this dilemma in Aristotelian terms, we could say that the principles of commutative justice as they are posed in the neoliberal world of global capitalism must be framed within the values of distributive justice as they have been debated in a long historical journey that goes back to Aristotle and ends up in contemporary Rawls.

If we had to summarize the contribution of the ELADES in one sentence, we would say that it highlighted the structural foundations of social inequality within Latin America and between this region and the developed centers. In addition, it explored multiple ways to achieve standards of equity without which the functioning of democratic institutions is illusory.

In the ELADES perspective, which is in line with the Universal Declaration of Human Rights, development is increasingly predicated on human beings and not only on the economic, political and cultural systems in which they live. In other words, when we discuss development today we place human beings at the center of the debate. Thus, social systems acquire meaning in reference to each and every human being who is integrally immersed in them.

The theme of human development was a new chapter that, within the UN, has been more closely linked to the contributions of the United Nations Development Program. Other strands have also emphasized the human dimension of development as essential to graduate and guide studies in this field. and orient studies in this field.

However, at that historical moment, in the mid-1950s, when the political and theoretical duel was posed in terms of power ideologies and purely systemic considerations, ECLAC and the ELADES were able, in a pioneering way, to raise the issues of the search for equity in the fruits of development. These issues remain fully relevant and urgent in today's Latin American societies.

Part Three

Latin American Structuralism and Integration

Chapter X

Latin American historical structuralism[33]

This essay attempts to synthesize the main features that characterize the current of thought we call Latin American structuralism (L.A.S). In the first section, these features are presented conceptually in a summarized manner in an attempt to highlight their validity and relevance in the 21st century. In the second section, the historical-structural perspective of this school of thought is explored in greater depth. To this end, a periodization is made within which the main factors of change of capitalism on a world scale are characterized and the connection or counterpoint between the processes occurring in the hegemonic centers and their impact on the Latin American periphery is emphasized. A synthesis of the main currents of economic thought that emerged in the western world in response to those historical changes and, according to the interests of the hegemonic powers that, in each period, led the world order, is included for each period examined. An examination is made of the influence of these currents of thought on Latin American structuralist thought.

Defining features of Latin American structuralism

Latin American structuralism (L.A.S) can be examined (i) as an economic theory, (ii) as a political economy, (iii) as a set of development strategies, or (iv) as a worldview and history. We will examine

[33] Paper published in Revista SaberEs (www.saberes.fcecon.unr.edu.ar/), School of Economic Sciences and Statistics. Universidad Nacional de Rosario, 2016.

synthetically each of these perspectives of analysis trying to emphasize for each one the value and relevance of the structuralist postulates (Di Filippo 2017).

As an economic theory with its own features

One of the most important modalities of Latin American cultural dependence has been the academic acceptance of neoclassical microeconomic theory as the official expression of the dominant economic science in our universities. This abstract, timeless and static discipline, with foundations totally compartmentalized in relation to the cultural and political dimensions of the nations where they were applied, led to the great crisis of the 1930s. The recovery from this economic disaster required Keynesian macroeconomics, which at least rescued the essential role of the democratic state in the regulation of the economic institutions of capitalism.

The dogma of the self-regulation of markets (free trade) is still supported today, mainly by the utilitarian-marginalist theories of value that morally underpin the forms of consumerist hedonism predominant in the world today. Neoclassical theory, using its own terminology, assumes, for example, that individual economic progress is manifested in the rise to "higher curves of the indifference map of each consumer in which the marginal utility of goods is always positive". To put it more simply, the more goods owned and acquired, the better off we are. There is no need to dwell on the well-known cultural and environmental consequences of this consumerist vision of the world, further promoted by the strategies of programmed obsolescence imposed by industrial companies to ensure the sustainability of demand through the replacement of old models that are still usable by new ones in the automobile and household appliance industries, etc. One of the environmental consequences of this strategy has been to turn the planet into an unlivable garbage dump that contributes to the destruction of biological diversity.

The economic goods referred to in the models of "free", "pure" or "perfect" competition are theoretically characterized in the neoclassical economics by two features: utility and scarcity. The neoclassical theoretical treatment of the notion of utility endorses and promotes consumerism as a philosophy of life. Furthermore, the relative scarcity of goods traded in the market does not derive from the "invisible hand of the market", but from the "visible hand of the TCs" (sometimes quite visible) which, through their transnational planning, control and determine those consumption options with few margins of variability and real freedom for the consumers.

Neoclassical models have recognized and incorporated, it is true, the study of oligopolistic (game theory, for example) and monopolistic forms of competition, but this recognition is the best proof of the asymmetries of power in markets and of the growing capacity of TCs to generate and manage the relative scarcity (and therefore determine the relative prices) of goods traded in markets. The real long-term causal factor affecting relative scarcity in markets is the growing inequality in the distribution of wealth and income, together with the oligopolistic character of markets increasingly controlled by T.C.s, and the growing ability of T.C.s to generate and manage the relative scarcity of goods traded in markets.

The L.A.S has dealt in depth with the issues of consumerism and the biased and concentrated mechanisms of the distribution of technical change and its fruits in Latin America (Aníbal Pinto 1965, Pinto and Di Filippo 1979, Prebisch 1981). This approach continues to be relevant and valid today in a scenario of poverty and structural heterogeneity aggravated by the growing environmental problems derived from current productive and consumerist techniques.

The other alternative theoretical trend of great academic diffusion to explain market prices is the theory of labor value, either in its classical (Smith, Ricardo, Malthus) or Marxist versions. Of course, this current has greater historical realism and provides important elements to explain the logic of capitalism, social classes and theories of exploitation. But it must be recognized that the relative prices of goods and productive factors are not, nor have they ever been, strictly proportional to the quantities of labor invested in producing them. In the present historical stage, the labor-value theory becomes less and less adequate to measure relative prices in units of human labor.

The issue of robotization is raising another set of problems linked to growing structural unemployment on the supply side, and insufficient aggregate demand on the consumption side. The current process of automation and robotization (the so-called "Fourth Industrial Revolution" or "Industry 4-0") is increasingly dispensing with the human labor force, marginalizing and impoverishing large contingents of unskilled workers, and forcing us to devise new mechanisms to make the demand for consumer goods independent of wages, as is the case with the initiatives linked to the universal minimum income whose possible application has already begun to be explored.

In opposition to the previous views, L.A.S has elaborated a heterodox theory of prices and markets, very different from those derived from utility-value or labor-value. This theory of markets, which we could call power-value, says that the "social substance" that we call "value" underlying the mechanism of prices and incomes is power. The specific form of power held and exercised through markets for goods and factors of production is general purchasing power, measured as the ratio of money flows to multiple specific price indices (consumer, retail, wholesale, commodity, manufactured, etc.).

Considered macroeconomically, the average general purchasing power of a closed economic system is a function of the general productive power attained by the system according to its rate of assimilation of technical change derived from the systems of science and technology. As is well known, the labor productivity of an economic system is inversely proportional to the amount of labor required to produce a commodity. Since the most defining feature of Latin American productive structures is the exogenous, irregular and uneven nature of the technical change incorporated from the central economies, this makes the average macroeconomic magnitudes unrepresentative and reveals the segmented and heterogeneous nature of Latin American productive structures.

As Paul Samuelson once pointed out, even a parrot can learn economics if it is taught the meaning of the interactions between "supply" and "demand". The scientific work consists in finding out the causal factors (in short, medium and long terms) underlying that interaction which end up determining the degrees of relative scarcity and therefore the prices of each specific commodity.

In order to do this, it is necessary to enter into the totality of the dimensions of the social structure (not only economic but also political, cultural and biological-environmental) and to scrutinize the factors of power that at each historical moment and place are influencing the supply and demand of specific markets. At this point, however, we transcend the watertight compartments of "pure" economic theory and inexorably enter the domains of political economy.

As a political economy

A theory of power-value cannot be formulated through the elaboration of abstract models, generally mathematized, and unable to take into consideration all the dimensions of power and translate them into magnitudes of general purchasing power.

Power, following Weber on this point, can be understood as the capacity (or potential) of certain social actors (natural or legal persons) to impose their will even against the non-institutionalized opposition of the remaining members of society. The habitual exercise of this power can be called domination (Di Filippo 2013). The positions of power of natural or legal persons (organizations, corporations, various associations, etc.) that are socially structured depend on their location in the institutions of society. Social institutions are formal or informal rules of habitual behavior, effectively internalized in social conduct. The existence of institutions is the structuring foundation of human societies by generating reciprocal expectations of behavior capable of generating social order. Please eliminate Douglass North citation.

In short, for the Latin American structuralism, political economy incorporates as part of its theoretical efforts the central role of the State, which is the source of the formal institutions that structure the social order.

We are not talking here about the authoritarian State that compulsively and centrally allocates economic resources, but instead about the democratic State that assumes the existence of decentralized forms of ownership.

But cultural subsystems (where the predominant moral values propagated through the mechanisms of information, communication and knowledge are determined) refer to informal institutions and tend to have enormous power in structuring historically concrete societies. The current process of globalization requires, today more than ever in history, an examination of economic processes that take the notion of power as a starting point. The L.A.S has attempted to advance in this line of reflection by exploring the fundamentals of the (general purchasing) power exercised in markets through the determination of the relative scarcities operating in each of the value chains that determine relative prices (see for example Rofman 1999, 2000).

As a vision of the world and of history

The L.A.S's vision of the world and of history is characterized by being systemic, historical-structural, global, institutional and multidimensional, where all these features are reciprocally compatible. We defend here the profound validity of this reading of reality to understand the new world scenario of capitalism that is taking shape in the 21st century (Ahumada and Di Filippo 2013).

The vision is systemic because in its fundamental framing or starting point it examines: on the one hand the peripheral national socio-economic systems, and on the other hand the center-periphery system of international relations. Systems are complex objects whose components are linked together by stable ties that constitute their structure. They can be abstract, such as a scientific theory, or concrete, such as the physical world we inhabit. Concrete systems are subject to a permanent process of change. Human societies can be seen as concrete systems whose parts and components are human beings or associations composed of human beings. The vision is systemic because in its fundamental framing or starting point it examines: on one side the peripheral national socioeconomic systems, and on the other side the center-periphery system of international relations. Systems are complex objects whose components are linked together by stable ties that constitute their structure. They can be abstract, such as a scientific theory, or concrete, such as the physical world we inhabit. Concrete systems are subject to a permanent process of change. Human societies can be seen as concrete systems whose parts and components are human beings or associations composed of human beings.

Systemism understood as an epistemological position (Mario Bunge 1996, 1999) attempts to synthesize and articulate the atomistic and holistic approaches in a round trip. Applied to the functioning of national socio-economic systems in the capitalist era, these two polar worldviews are represented, at one extreme (atomism) by the neo- liberal approach -

where, in the search for individual profit and through the market mechanism, economic actors allegedly succeed in promoting social welfare and prosperity; and, at the other extreme, for example, in orthodox Marxist approaches - holism is expressed in that individuals are mere expressions of the position they occupy in the class struggle driven by the development of the productive forces, in a process that necessarily leads to the social utopia of communism. Both approaches allegedly lead to inexorable outcomes that evidently contradict real historical processes.

In the 20th century, centrally planned economies by authoritarian states created societies burdened by bureaucratic rigidities and lack of technical creativity. These economic systems showed contempt for the values of democracy and human rights, which ultimately contributed to their collapse, But the emerging alternative typical of the economic neoliberalism that followed, led to the processes of corruption and profound social dissolution that are now eroding the present neoliberalism.

In contrast, the systemic approach of L.A.S is not deterministic because it conceives history as an open-ended process, without the pretension of predicting inexorable outcomes. On the contrary, it recognizes and tries to unravel the complex combinations of conflict and cooperation that are driving the dynamics of this new millennium. The international order is also addressed systemically by the L.A.S through the so-called center-periphery system of international relations. What is specifically original about the L.A.S. is to have underlined the asymmetrical character of international capitalism considered as a global system. Thus, a differentiation is established between the hegemonic centers which, through scientific-technical knowledge, hold and exercise productive power, and the peripheries subordinated to the hegemonic centers, the former, whose situation of dependence cannot be expressed with abstract and formal models and is related to specific historical processes that will be synthesized in the second part of this essay. It is enough to say for now that the notions of development and underdevelopment are considered by the L.A.S as two sides of the same coin, and not as a competition in which all advance towards the same goal and the more "advanced" point the way to the more "backward" ones.

This vision is historical-structural because its interpretations permanently take into consideration the structural transformations of the capitalist order deriving from the great technological revolutions. But at the same time it is trans-historical because it always examines them under the same lens: that of the distribution of technical change and its fruits on a world scale in the evolutionary process of capitalism. This reading of the historical process is increasingly relevant and valid as the information technology revolution deepens and accelerates.

The vision is global from its very origins because the dynamics of the center-periphery system always taken as its starting point a planetary reading of the processes of development and underdevelopment that have been simultaneously generated in the course of the historical evolution of capitalism. In this sense, perhaps because of its roots linked to the founding of the UN, the L.A.S, "discovered" and studied the process of globalization (Prebisch 1949, Ferrer 1996, 2000) long before it became a commonly used terminology in the social sciences in the 21st century. It could be objected that all the great authors who studied historical capitalism (Marx and Engels, Werner Sombart, Max Weber, etc.) captured this feature of globalization of the system, but L.A.S examined this globalization in terms of the center-periphery counterpoint, and from the point of view of the peripheral societies.

The vision is institutional and institutions are understood as formal and informal (technical and social) rules of conduct internalized in the actual behavior of social actors. The notion of institutionalized power connects individual margins of maneuver with social structures. In L.A.S thinking, the notion of social structure (e.g. Prebisch 1981) can be defined as follows:

- as the interrelated and interdependent set of institutions that in each specific situation constitute this structure. In short, institutions are the natural sphere in which social actors measure and exercise their quotas of power.

Finally, this vision is multidimensional because in its analysis of capitalism on a global scale it has been incorporating in an integrated approach the political, cultural and environmental aspects that interact with the economic aspects themselves. The new issues of capitalism in the 21st century include the environmental sphere (Prebisch 1981, Sunkel and Gligo 1981) as a determining factor for the future of humanity (global warming, loss of diversity of animal and plant species, etc.). At the same time, cultural aspects are being revalued, which, in addition to being the objective basis of technical change in the scientific sphere (Furtado 1978), profoundly affect the shaping of public opinion (transnational media power, social networks, manipulation of consciences through the creation of "post-truths", etc.). This multidimensional reading of reality is an important way of incorporating these new issues and addressing the serious economic problems affecting humanity in the 21st century.

As a set of development strategies

The L.A.S. starts with a global perspective based on the center- periphery vision of international relations. On this basis, the Latin American periphery has been building its own thinking based on its historical identity, with not only economic but also cultural and political common foundations, which go back to the very moment of conquest and colonization by the Iberian powers. This historical identity implies a "Latin Americanism" or "Latin American nationalism" based on the recognition of those common roots.

L.A.S thinkers do not deny the deep Judeo-Greco-Latin roots of the hegemonic cultural institutions already sown during the colonial period, nor those inherited from the pre-Hispanic era that form the historical memory of the originary groups. To these cultural inheritances were later added the (formal and informational) institutions of liberalism incorporated in the contemporary era, converting the former colonies into politically independent republics from the 19th century onward (Sunkel and Paz 1970).

These republics were established on constitutional foundations associated with the installation of civil rights (liberty, equality, fraternity) promulgated from the French (1789) and American (1776) Revolutions, and were also influenced by the American popular democratic ideology promulgated by Abraham Lincoln after the triumph of the Yankees in the Civil War (Government of the people, by the people and for the people).

However, pre-Hispanic and colonial cultural legacies contribute to explain why the forms of capitalist development in the centers, and in particular liberal ideas, are not fully transplantable to the Latin American periphery. Even in the strictly economic sphere, the peripheral condition is linked in the long term to the typologies of economies exporting primary products. The founding of cities and the processes of urbanization in Latin America also derive from historical circumstances very different from those that prevailed in the social evolution of the hegemonic centers where capitalism flourished from the nineteenth century onward (Di Filippo 1981)

All these economic, political and cultural impacts generated in Latin America segmentations of the social fabric and deep-seated inequalities from which the L.A.S elaborated its notion of structural heterogeneity (S.H.). In its strictly economic sense, S.H. is based on the unequal distribution of the productive techniques originated in the successive hegemonic centers (the Iberian empires, Great Britain, the United States and the emerging China), which have impacted regional productive structures from their very origins.

This S.H. has been and is socially supported by the unequal social and cultural impact of these successive technological revolutions on Latin American societies. This situation of economic, political, and cultural dependence implies to a great degree a lack of technological culture in the business world capable of granting a minimum degree of productive autonomy to our nations.

The original industrialist proposal (1950s) put forward by Prebisch from the ECLAC secretariat was the core of his development strategy. This was the basis for the structural change proposed by the L.A.S. This line of action was supplemented (since the 1960s) with recommendations for structural reforms (agrarian, tax, manufacturing exports, investment planning compatible with the rules of the capitalist order, etc.) aimed at two fundamental objectives: the first was to expand the scale and "depth" of national markets to stimulate industrial development through a better distribution of wealth and income; and the second objective (understood as an underlying ethic) was to promote values of social inclusion and equality.

In this interpretative framework, the regional integration promoted since the 1960s was a crucial strategy from two different points of view.

First, to expand and integrate national manufacturing markets, favoring the formation of economies of scale in the sense already explained. And secondly, to consolidate those historical, political and cultural features that give the region its identity, helping to overcome, on a Latin American scale, the aforementioned segregation and heterogeneity of the region.

The L.A.S supported and promoted Latin American integration initiatives since its first proposals in the sixties of the last century. Integration not only of markets but also of nations that aims, at least as an ideal, to build a "large homeland" capable of presenting itself to the world as an economically more autonomous, politically more democratic and socially more just space. Only the integration of nations united by a common history can guarantee the large scale required to materialize common ideals. These ideals are still today a pending subject in the face of the instrumental rationality of neo-liberal thinking in its different versions, always based on the presumed self-regulation of global markets.

In-depth study of the historical-structural perspective

Reference framework

The historical perspective inherent to Latin American structuralist thought is already underlined in the very title of this book. The ideas that follow are organized on the basis of a periodization founded on the technological waves that have impacted our region, originating in hegemonic centers that have successively dominated the transformations of capitalism on a global scale. The perspective proposed here also allows us to historically frame the currents of economic thought that accompanied the development of capitalism, including Latin American historical structuralism itself, which to different degrees questioned, criticized, or rejected them, but also assimilated and incorporated them when the repetition of analogous historical circumstances (but never identical because history does not repeat itself) gave rise to interpretations that were partially analogous to those of those historically previous currents of thought.

The periodization that we will analyze in the following pages includes: 1) the techniques, institutions and productive processes introduced by the European conquerors and colonizers (15th to 19th centuries); 2) the techniques, institutions and productive processes introduced by the hegemonic centers (in particular Great Britain during the 19th century); 3) the techniques, institutions and productive processes introduced after the second Industrial Revolution by the United States, the hegemonic center, still emerging during the first half of the 20th century; 4) the techniques, institutions and productive processes developed since World War II (in particular the use of nuclear energy and the expansion of consumer durables) during the heyday of the American Industrial Revolution, which changed the productive structuring of capitalism and the world power scenario during the second half of the 20th century; 5) the productive techniques, institutions and processes associated with information, communication and knowledge technologies (ICTs) that are leading to the current multicentric or multipolar scenario (with China's growing gravitation) in the process of building a new world order.

In the following pages a counterpoint between the hegemonic centers that dominated Latin American societies from their very origins and the formation of the colonized and peripheral societies in our region is presented. Also in this historical counterpoint we can discern a causal sequence of the main forms of power that have operated in the system of international relations since the origins of capitalism: scientific-technical power, productive power, military power, market power and cultural power held by successive hegemonic centers from the modern era onward.

Mercantilism and the colonial heritage in Latin America

Through Iberian colonization, Latin America received the pure and harsh impact of political absolutism and monopolistic forms of mercantilism. The conquered native peoples included high urban cultures that were economically surplus to requirements and capable of developing superior forms of knowledge. However, the European powers controlled certain forms of intangible power (Ferrer 1996, 2000) derived from technically exploitable scientific knowledge (war technology, navigational instruments, etc.).

Iberian colonization installed slave and servile regimes that involved not only the native peoples but also forced migrations of African and Asian slaves. The vernacular languages were replaced by the imperial languages (Spanish and Portuguese), the ancestral religious cults were replaced by Catholicism, the economic organization was oriented towards the exploitation of exportable wealth, and the political systems essentially reproduced the predominant forms of European absolutism.

Three basic colonial situations arose: a) the exploitation of precious metals, especially in the Andean area and the central plateau of Mexico; b) tropical agriculture, in the form of slave plantations in tropical and coastal areas (including those of the Portuguese empire); and c) temperate agriculture, especially in the southern cone of South America, which was of lesser economic importance during the colonial period.

This colonial heritage was perpetuated in the hacienda, the fundamental unit of rural society that predominated during the four hundred years between the mid-sixteenth century and the mid-twentieth century. Unlike other regions colonized by the West during the same period (such as those of the Near and Far East, which kept their languages, ancestral traditions and religious beliefs), in Latin America the conquerors imposed their own cultural institutions in a definitive and irreversible manner.

Unlike North America, where the colonial period of the United States received the British inheritance of religious pluralism, and of the economic and political institutions that were to lead to the genesis of capitalism and the republic, Latin America was historically frozen in its colonial institutions even long after its formal political independence.

Capitalist or semi-capitalist rural relations in Latin America were at the service of the construction of nascent capitalism in Europe, which required monetary instruments for the expansion and consolidation of national markets (Douglass North 1993).

The main founders of the L.A.S, although not professional historians, were nevertheless scholars and interpreters of the historical processes summarized in the preceding paragraphs, which allow us to understand many of the common features that give Latin America its historical identity.

The British Industrial Revolution and the Classical Economists

From the British Industrial Revolution (coal, iron, steel, steam engines, railroads and metal steamships, etc.), the starting points for the study of capitalism proper and, consequently, of economic development emerge.

The initial understanding of these processes was based on the work of the classical economists and, in particular, the so-called "father of political economy", Adam Smith, who associated the growth of the social product with technical progress, linked to the technical division of labor in manufacturing. On the other side, he introduced the notion of effective demand not only on a local scale but also projected to the international market in order to absorb supply surpluses and stimulate labor productivity, highlighting the absolute advantages of international trade.

The classical British economists (Adam Smith, David Ricardo, Robert Malthus) unveiled the structural features of capitalism, and the economic foundations of the class structure inherent in it. They also raised the main problems of economic value, underlying the market prices that ponder the social product. They did so through the introduction of the labor-value theory to explain the dynamics of markets for both products and factors of production.

Understanding the dynamics of markets and the determination of prices involve the enormous and complex subject of the theories of economic value. In the study of economics as a science, the expression economic value implies, on one side, ethical backgrounds that mark different worldviews and, on the other, ways of measuring or quantifying the prices and quantities of goods traded in the markets.

Regarding the ethical background, with the arrival of contemporary capitalism, after the installation of the British Industrial Revolution, the old and medieval critical views (inherited from Aristotelian Thomism) on the sinfulness of profit and interest as a mechanism to obtain income were overcome in Western Europe. (Di Filippo, 2013, chapter 1).

Adam Smith, the father of economic liberalism, repudiated the monopolistic nature of the state regulations of the mercantilist era and proposed the virtues of free trade, where in the pursuit of personal interest (through the invisible hand of the market) the behavior of the participants manages to promote general welfare and prosperity. This economic liberalism had its counterpart in political liberalism from the American (1776) and French (1789) political revolutions.

The classical school of economics interpreted the behavior of markets through different versions of the labor theory of value, where market prices have some kind of correspondence with the amount of labor contained in the goods (Ricardo), or with the amount of labor that can be commanded (Smith, Malthus), based on the possession of wealth (money, or other pecuniary goods that can be valued as merchandise).

L.A.S.'s economic interpretations were strongly influenced by economic liberalism, especially by the importance he gave to the study of the Industrial Revolution and the introduction of the notions of surplus and profit, but he always categorically rejected the liberal dogmas of the "invisible hand" and the self-regulation of markets.

With respect to political liberalism, the L.A.S has underlined the profound contrast between ideals and historical realities. Indeed, the Latin American nations were born to politically independent life as republics, quickly rejecting some imperial and monarchical pretensions of internal organization. However, the precepts of "liberty, equality and fraternity" of the French Revolution, or those of the government "of the people, by the people and for the people" (Abraham Lincoln) of the American popular-democratic ideology, clashed from the beginning of independent political life with the harsh Latin American oligarchic reality inherited from the colonial phase and consolidated during the 19th century. Through its historical-structural approach, the L.A.S highlighted these sharp social contrasts which, in practice, negated those democratic precepts.

Without prejudice to his revolutionary role as a critic of capitalism and promoter of new political movements, Marx can be studied as a classical economist who adopted a labor theory of value very close to that elaborated by Ricardo. In his philosophy of history he gives a central role (as a starting point) to the Industrial Revolution, and more broadly or generally to the development of the productive forces within the capitalist mode of production. (Di Filippo 2013, chapter 13).

Also like Marx, the L.A.S takes as the main dynamizing factor of Latin American history the technical progress coming from the developed hegemonic centers. However, in matters of international relations Marx believed that backward nations saw in the development of the mode of production of the advanced nations the mirror of their own future. By opposition, the L.A.S considered that this alignment of countries, following a line where they move from less to more developed, is not a correct interpretation of history. For the L.A.S, what has been called "development" and "underdevelopment" are two sides of the same coin evolving simultaneously in the dynamics of global capitalism (Sunkel and Paz 1970, Furtado 1964). The L.A.S looks at capitalist development from the point of view of its impact on our peripheral societies and, from this point of view, constructs a great historical interpretation of Latin American socioeconomic formation.

In addition, and unlike historical materialism, Latin American historical structuralism emphasizes and privileges to a high degree the autonomous role of cultural factors as a structuring element of Latin American societies. The impact of the different ethnic groups that populated the region was reflected in the forms of Latin American art and culture, generating situations very different from those of Europe in terms of human exploitation and social structuring.

The U.S. industrial revolution

The American industrial revolution is linked to the control of electrical energy (Tesla, Edison, Marconi) and petroleum energy associated with the internal combustion engine (Rockefeller, Ford). Throughout the 19th century it was promoted by the ideas and initiatives of the so-called American School of Economics: an industrialist movement that opposed the free trade that predominated in the world under British control with the support of the classical school of economics.

This current of economic thought was born at the dawn of the American nation with the Report on Manufactures written by Alexander Hamilton at the end of the 18th century. In the mid-19th century, this industrialist movement gained strength in the United States through the work of Henry

Carey, in favor of the protection of nascent industries. These same ideas also emerged in Germany, promoted by Friedrich List, who found inspiration and support in the processes taking place in the United States. These ideas have been the foundation of the nationalist, industrialist and protectionist currents developed in nations that were late to join the expansion of industrial capitalism in the Western world.

Carey was an economic advisor to Abraham Lincoln and a great enemy of the slave regimes established in the South of his country.

After the Civil War, his ideas helped initiate the American industrial revolution that would flourish in full force in the late nineteenth and early twentieth centuries. Once the American industrial revolution had been consummated, the American School of Economics had achieved its main objectives and the new strategic interests of the United States, a country already competitive on a global scale, moved away from protectionism and began to move towards the very ideas of free trade that it had previously fought against.

Friedrich List, in the same line of the American School, was a promoter of the union of the German nation that was consummated with the Customs Union established by Chancellor Bismarck. His nationalist, industrialist, and integrationist ideas were embodied in his main work *National System of Political Economy*.

Like Carey, List contributed to formulating the arguments that the structuralist current took up in Latin America to promote the development of our region (Prebisch 1949, Ferrer 1996 and 2000). Consequently, these currents of economic thought are the most important antecedents of the strategies promoted by ECLAC at the end of World War II.

The emergence and prevalence of neoclassicals since the late 19th century

The labor theory of value as the main basis for explaining the behavior of markets and prices predominated during a good part of the 19th century. However, once the capitalist economic system was consolidated throughout the Western world, from the last third of that century, the neoclassical school of economic thought began to emerge in Europe (the Austrian Carl Menger from Vienna; the Swiss Leon Walras from Lausanne; and the British Stanley Jevons and Alfred Marshall from

Cambridge). This school of thought, which originated in Europe, was fully adopted in the United States at the end of the Second World War and laid the foundations of the microeconomic theory that still predominates academically in that country today.

This school proposes a specific theory of value and prices (radically different from that of the classical school) which, on one side is based on a specific ethic and, on the other, seeks to quantify market transactions.

The dominant microeconomic theory taught today in Latin American universities, with rare and honorable exceptions, belongs to this current of thought, updated with nuances and ingredients of neo-liberal economics. All its premises based on the self-regulation of markets essentially contradict the worldview and epistemology of L.A.S economics.

For neoclassicals, the value of goods depends on their utility and scarcity. The utility of a good depends on the subjective and free judgment of those who consume it, and its scarcity depends on its supply and demand in the market. It presupposes the existence of a hedonistic or utilitarian behavior on the part of consumers in the elaboration of their preferences. However, in order to avoid the compromising issue of distributive (in)justice, neoclassical theory does not interpersonally compare the inequalities between the levels of utility or welfare attained by each consumer. Consumers are "monads" or micro-worlds operating within a "perfect market" and are not part of a larger social system. Therefore the purchasing power of each consumer is not compared with that of other consumers, ignoring the fact that the relative scarcity of different goods is determined to a significant degree by the personal and family distribution of purchasing power (Di Filippo 2013).

For the neoclassicals, the issue of distributive justice is excluded from their central theoretical corpus, since it corresponds to normative economics and, according to them, economic theory refers to positive economics. In other words, microeconomic instrumental rationality prevails over moral rationality, which would be proper to normative economics. Milton Friedman wrote a famous essay called "Methodology of Positive Economics", in which he justifies neopositivist epistemology-logic as clearly distinguishable from the postulates of normative economics.

Neoclassical epistemology excludes not only the ethical aspects of normative economics, but also the study of the historical frameworks in which capitalism has evolved. For this reason, capitalism being a category loaded with historicity, the notion itself has been excluded from its basic theoretical foundations. Its epistemological criteria are based on logical-mathematical formalization through the use of models, and on empirical verification through the use of statistical inference, and on the application of correlations and regressions linked to specific functional relationships.

American institutionalism and its critique of the neoclassical school of thought

Shortly after the expansion of the neoclassical school in Europe, the institutionalist school of economic thought developed in the United States. For Thorstein Veblen (Di Filippo 2013), the founding father of this school of thought, institutions are above all mental habits that guide the usual behavior of human beings in society. This habituality or reiteration is the essential feature of the notion of institutions, on which it is possible to build the notion of social relations, based on reciprocal expectations of behavior (Max Weber). An essential part of capitalist institutions is based on the development of the productive technology associated with the successive industrial revolutions.

The notion of social structure used by the L.A.S (Prebisch 1981, Furtado 1978) can be seen as a set of social relations structured by an institutional background that gives foreseeability and continuity to social processes, and a central aspect of this background is constituted by technical change in the sphere of economic processes.

There are many points of contact between North American institutionalism and L.A.S. The main difference lies in the fact that the former studied technological change as an expression of the dynamics of the American social structure itself, while L.A.S is based precisely on the study of the impact of technical change generated in the centers on the Latin American social structure. This impact is an essential explanatory factor of the segmentations and structural heterogeneity that characterizes and continues to characterize Latin American societies.

Nuclear energy and new war technologies, Keynesianism and consumerist society

At the end of the Second World War, important technological changes took place in two different fields.

In the first place, revolutionary changes took place in the war technologies whose control was indispensable for the countries vying for hegemony on a world scale. The countries that pioneered the control of these advances were only those endowed with the necessary productive power, without which they would have been neither military powers nor great hegemonic centers of capitalism.

The Second World War was a paradigmatic case of struggle, not only for war supremacy but also for the control of nuclear energy sources required for the new weapons of mass destruction. In 1939 Niels Bohr succeeded in producing the fission of uranium that releases enormous amounts of energy. In 1942 Enrico Fermi at Princeton built the first atomic pile, which gave rise to controlled nuclear energy and the possibility of producing atomic bombs. After the explosions of Hiroshima and Nagasaki decided by the United States (1945) (which abruptly ended World War II), the Soviet Union (1949), Great Britain (1952), France (1960), and China (1964) also joined the "nuclear club". In 1956, Great Britain inaugurated the first nuclear power plant as a source of energy for peaceful purposes. The United States, European countries, Japan and China soon followed. With the oil shock of the 1970s, nuclear power plants spread throughout the developed world.

At the same time during the Second War, Werner von Braun designed the V2 rockets with which Germany bombed Antwerp and London in particular, but without being able to equip them with nuclear charges. After Germany's defeat, Von Braun was left in charge of NASA's space program. Soon Russia, China and other European countries entered this astronautical competition.

Secondly, the end of World War II was a period of great economic growth, and of enormous diversification in the production of consumer goods, in fact the appellation of "mass consumer society" emerged, which underlined the consumerist orientations in the productive structures in the United States and Europe.

There was a consolidation of solid middle classes in those countries where this productive expansion was combined with the provision of public goods, both infrastructural (roads and highways) and social (education, health, housing, social welfare, etc.). In European countries, social democracies were installed, which took the political form of parliamentary democracies. The period between 1945 and 1975 has been considered in extraordinarily laudatory terms by historians and economists. It has been called "the thirty glorious years" or "the golden age of capitalism".

The Keynesianism that prevailed throughout this period legitimized the intervention of the democratic state in the economy. Intervention that was compatible with the basic rules of the game of capitalism. Since then, the flood of new consumer products (long- lasting goods, household appliances, white goods, etc.) has not ceased to flow to feed the aggregate demand, so necessary in turn to maintain the "prosperity" of the capitalist system. This consumer society, understood as a philosophy of life, has only deepened the hedonistic and utilitarian messages of neoclassical economics in versions that have become compatible with the dominant presence of Keynesian economics in the field of macroeconomics.

It is in this context that the so-called programmed obsolescence began, where products are deliberately manufactured so that their duration does not exceed a certain period of time, so that their renewal or replenishment will stimulate aggregate demand.

This set of processes associated with nuclear energy, Astro- navigation and the proliferation of durable goods (in particular electric household appliances) can be considered in part as a new energy- industrial revolution and in part as the maturation of the Second Industrial Revolution that took place during the first half of the twentieth century. This maturation could only come to fruition during the long period of relative peace that characterized the second half of the 20th century.

Development and underdevelopment: the emergence of L.A.S in the post-war era

The notions of development and underdevelopment acquired special political and academic relevance at that historical moment from the process of decolonization accompanied and promoted by the founding of the United Nations Organization (1945).

The study of the situations of poverty and deprivation of nations that were abandoning their colonial status and entering the process of political independence emerged. This historical process was accompanied by the study of development and underdevelopment as an autonomous discipline of economic science.

The international capitalist order was structured through the International Monetary Fund to safeguard the new dollar-gold standard, and the General Agreement on Tariffs and Trade to promote free and open international markets.

The promotion of the economic development of peripheral countries was left to the International Bank for Reconstruction and Development, originally created for the recovery of war-torn Europe, but which later became the World Bank to promote the development of the poor regions of the world.

From the point of view of theoretical interpretations in the economic sphere, the subject of underdevelopment and development has been approached from different epistemological and ideological perspectives by authors from the developed world such as Colin Clark, Albert Hirschman, Arthur Lewis, Gunnar Myrdal, Paul Rosenstein Rodan, Walt Whitman Rostow, Hans Singer, Jan Tinbergen, etc.

The founding of the United Nations was a decisive step in transcending the economistic character of economic development measured merely by increases in the productive power of labor and the purchasing power of the population. In the face of these strongly economistic-reductionist interpretations, the UN would open new paths for reflection on development and underdevelopment, and for action in terms of development policies for the world's poor and peripheral countries.

Two of the mechanisms through which these new fields of reflection and action were opened up were, on one side, the UN Economic and Social Council, which included the contributions of the Economic Commission for Latin America (ECLAC), and, on the other side, the sectoral agencies (UNESCO, UNICEF, FAO, WHO, ILO, etc.), which incorporated and propagated the philosophy of the Universal Declaration of Human Rights, strengthening economic, social and cultural rights, strongly associated with a broader and more profound way of conceiving development.

Development policies for Latin America proposed by ECLAC in the post-war era

It was at that time that the initial contributions of Latin American structuralism (composed of authors such as Raúl Prebisch, Celso Furtado, Osvaldo Sunkel, Aníbal Pinto, Aldo Ferrer, etc.) took place. This school of thought, established under the auspices of ECLAC-UN to study the specific features of development and underdevelopment under the conditions of peripheral capitalism, formulated an important historical perspective for the interpretation of Latin American societies from the very moment of their conquest and colonization by the Iberian powers.

A specific feature of Latin American thought in this sphere has been the incorporation of notions of power associated with situations of domination and social dependence. These notions are naturally linked to the issues of social justice understood as a projection of this thinking to the sociopolitical and cultural sphere. As the notion of development has become multidimensional, the issue of distributive justice has ceased to be confined to the economic sphere and has begun to be approached in a multidimensional manner: economic, cultural, political and even environmental.

The rise of Latin American historical structuralism took place during the post-war period (1945-1970), coinciding with the development of Keynesian macroeconomic theory in the central countries, which provided national States with important elements of monetary and fiscal policy to regulate the functioning of capitalism in democratic societies.

There were two main contributions of Latin American historical structuralism to the issues of underdevelopment. First, its vision of the center-periphery system of international economic relations originated in the personal and institutional work that Raúl Prebisch elaborated at ECLAC/UN.

Under this vision, the hegemonic powers that held scientific-technical power, productive power, market power (productivity-competitiveness) and normative power on a global scale were the centers. On the other side, the peripheries lacking these powers were subordinated to (dependent on) the hegemonic powers of the day

This foundational approach was formulated with a methodology that allowed for a historical-structural interpretation of the main phases of the formation of Latin American economies following periodization criteria quite similar to those adopted in the present essay. Osvaldo Sunkel and Pedro Paz (1970), Celso Furtado (1969), Aldo Ferrer (1996, 2000, 2012), and Aníbal Pinto (1965) contributed to this interpretation, supported by the great vision formulated by Prebisch.

Secondly, Latin American historical structuralism elaborated economic development strategies that have been schematically labeled as "Cepaline developmentalism", which implied policies and strategies that had an enormous influence on Latin American nations during the period 1950-1975, chronologically coinciding with the consolidation of Keynesianism in the Western Hegemonic countries.

The Latin American structuralist-historical approach was probably the first that from its own starting point examined the development-underdevelopment relationship in global terms within the framework of the center-periphery vision adopted by Raúl Prebisch in ECLAC and gave rise to diagnoses such as structural heterogeneity (Di Filippo 1981, Pinto 1965), and to specific strategies recommended to Latin American governments. These recommendations were widely applied in our region, and included proposals such as: i) import substitution industrialization, protected by the State (1950s); ii) structural, fiscal and agrarian reforms (1960s) aimed at redistributing wealth and income; iii) development planning compatible with the functioning of democratic societies (1960s); and iv) regional integration (from the 1960s onwards). The period covered by these policies (1945-1975) was the most dynamic in the history of Western capitalism both in the centers and in the Latin American periphery. The rates of economic expansion were only surpassed from the 1970s onwards by the Asian economies, which were the most dynamic in the history of Western capitalism, both in the centers and in the Latin American periphery.

ICT revolution and neoliberal capitalism from the 1970s onward

The importance of continuing to consider capitalism as the frame of reference for studies on economic development was once again highlighted in the mid-1970s, when new processes began to emerge that ushered in a new era in the history of humanity. Capitalism continues to be the systemic axis that lends instrumental rationality to current economic development. But this instrumental rationality has a purely microeconomic meaning in the behavior of TCs. On a macro scale, the development process includes a moral rationality that is rooted in the political action of democratic states.

Neoliberal capitalism is based fundamentally on that instrumental rationality of a microeconomic nature, eroding and denying the social advances achieved by the democratic states of the post-war period. However, understanding the future problems of development will require, first, a multidimensional view and, second, a return to the political rationality of the democratic states. The historical processes that have modified the world scenario since the 1970s are essentially the following: a) the emergence of information, communication and knowledge technologies (ICT), b) the worsening of environmental problems on a planetary scale and the awareness of their seriousness (Club of Rome 1968), c) the growing interdependence and trans nationalization of the world economy, d) the emergence of Asian countries (in particular China) as rising economic powers, e) the hegemonic position of transnational corporations in the neoliberal phase of globalized capitalism.

In the field of ideas, there was the decline of Keynesianism as the foundation of regulation and growth policies in the developed world and its growing replacement by monetarist growth policies that ended up leading to the installation of neoliberal political economy. This process included the "conservative revolution" at the beginning of the 1980s, and the growing adherence to the rules of the so-called "Washington Consensus" (1989).

At the beginning of this new millennium, new events have taken place that are leading to positions that are increasingly critical of the neoliberal model. Among other events that mark a watershed in this new millennium are the civilizational and cultural problems anticipated by Huntington in his book “The Clash of Civilizations”, which had an abrupt and violent creation in the attack on the Twin Towers in New York in a style of terrorism unheard of until that moment in history.

In the United States and Europe so far in the 21st century, protest movements have been developing against the growing social inequality and the progressive dismantling of the social state (Piketty 2014), whose institutional mechanisms protected the economic, social and cultural rights of its citizens.

In Latin America, the beginning of the 21st century witnessed a shift in the political systems in force towards forms that sought to reverse the neo-liberal (or ultra-liberal) features. In South America, the governments of Lula Da Silva in Brazil, the Kirchners in Argentina, Hugo Chávez in Venezuela, Evo Morales in Bolivia, Rafael Correa in Ecuador and José Mujica in Uruguay, initiated new strategies for understanding Latin American underdevelopment and promoting development policies, these have been baptized with ideologically charged denominations such as (favorable) "21st century socialism" or "national and popular democracies", or others (unfavorable) of "populism", "demagogy", "personalisms", "authoritarianisms", etc.

From an economic perspective, these regimes had to recognize and acknowledge their situations of acute dependence derived from the peripheral nature (exporter of primary products and importer of industrial inputs and equipment) of their productive apparatus, especially in South America. In this sense, the structuralist diagnoses applied to these countries in this period are still as valid today as when they were formulated at the end of World War II. Given these productive structures, inherited from colonial times and continued during the period of independent life, these contested models did not discover or apply anything new when they tried to use the export surpluses originated in the exploitation of natural resources (copper, tin, oil, natural gas, etc.) to promote social protection and progressive income redistribution measures. They were able to do so fully while the bonanza in commodity prices allowed them to do so, taking advantage of the vertiginous growth of the Chinese economy, which was a major demander of these products during the period. However, with the slowdown of China's economy in the second decade of this century, the segmentations and shortcomings of its peripheral productive structures reappeared, aggravated by the reciprocal isolation of its nations in terms of trade and investment ties. However, the integrationist spirit of these regimes translated into the founding of integration schemes giving rise to the formation of new organizations such as UNASUR, ALBA and CELAC. This integrationist effort revealed a perspective that we have called Latin Americanism or alternatively Latin American nationalism.

As of 2015, the social-political viability of these historical experiences began to falter, especially as a consequence of the processes of deficits and public and private indebtedness. Redistributive strategies became unsustainable for economies whose primary export base was too fragile and dependent on the industrial cycles of the hegemonic countries (pre-existing and emerging). In summary, the productive power needed to promote stable and diversified economic growth in the long term was lacking.

In addition, it is necessary to register and recognize a cultural fact: these regimes have not managed to escape the generalized era of corruption that compromises political leaders with big capital on a global scale. It is a transversal movement of global reach that compromises and splashes political personalities of all ideological tendencies (Di Filippo 2016).

One of the consequences of the wave of short-term speculation and corruption that has become more acute since the beginning of this century was the great recessionary crisis of 2008, which has continued to affect the functioning of the world economy to this day. These facts demonstrate once again that the issue of development cannot be confined within the narrow limits of capitalist instrumental rationality, and much less within the narrower short-term rationality of the financial capital that today increasingly controls the political processes of the main Western nations.

A structuralist interpretation of the global and Latin American crisis in the 21st century

The so-called financialization of Western capitalism has its structural roots in the inability of the Western powers to compete against the rapid and overwhelming expansion of Asian productivity. The process of deindustrialization of the Western powers had its beginning in a "flight of transnational American and European companies" to the free zones processing industrial exports where there is strong tax, labor, energy, etc. franchises. It is within the framework of this structural mutation that neoliberal financialism began to expand in the main economies of the West. In order to avoid the fiscal, labor, environmental, etc., regulations of the European social state, the major TCs prefer the transnational monetarist political economy, not subject to the national limits of the fiscal restrictions of the Keynesian era.

The rules of the game of neoliberalism, initially conceived, propagated and sustained by the US Central Bank (the "FED") since the end of the 1980s under the leadership of Alan Greenspan, were based on a permissiveness that was the starting point for the installation of the new transnational financial order. Ten years later, this new order led to the greatest recession suffered by capitalism since the crisis of the 1930s.

Also at the beginning of this new century, the European Central Bank (ECB's) monetary policies have implemented financialist mechanisms of transnational domination, linked to rules of the game coming from organizations not sufficiently controlled by the state authorities of the member countries, such as the Bank for International Settlements. An essential strategic goal for this new order has thus been achieved: the decoupling of central banks' monetary policies from the control of national economic authorities, and the relaxation of the regulatory rules applied to the large transnational investment banks (Di Filippo 2013)

The new transnational financial order was also supported by the emergence and/or consolidation of risk rating agencies, which evaluate the creditworthiness of the most indebted nations, of Europe (Greece, Italy, Spain, etc.) and even "grade" (give marks to) the major capitalist powers, including the United States. This new order, of course, also includes tax and financial havens, where the black money from tax evasion and tax avoidance originating in organized crime (drug trafficking, trafficking of migrants, women and child prostitutes, etc.), which today hit the three largest economies of Latin America especially hard, is laundered.

This transnational financial order is based on the ideology of self-regulation and free trade and, through the mechanism of indebtedness, subordinates and controls the fiscal policy of the most indebted countries.

From the perspective of the center-periphery vision, and beyond the evolution of their internal political, economic and cultural systems, all the nations that have achieved global hegemony in the capitalist order since the nineteenth century have ended up preaching free trade as the ideal of international economic relations. But of course they have done so after they have achieved their own productive power, understood as the foundation of their military and market power. Even China, the new emerging power (with a "sui generis" capitalist economic system and a non-democratic political system) has surprisingly become a world free market leader, especially in the face of the protectionist and nationalist tendencies that have been emerging in the United States and Europe, managers and pioneers of Western capitalism and democracy. However, before adhering to world free trade, not only China but also several of the emerging Asian countries have managed to develop their autonomous productive power by internally controlling access to their capital, goods and services markets, in order to launch themselves competitively into the conquest of the world market. These processes should be studied carefully and unprejudiced within the structuralist current of economic thought.

To use a terminology popularized by Aldo Ferrer (1996, 2000), the precondition for achieving not only "tangible" power (magnitude of territory and population) but also "intangible" power (control of science and technology at the service of a nationally controlled productive power) will increasingly require the multidimensional integration strategy of nations, which has been proposed in Latin America since the time of Simón Bolívar as the common destiny of the region. We live in the era of the mega-markets and only large political and economic blocs can confront each other with any prospect of success in the multipolar or multicentric world that is already taking shape on a planetary scale.

However, the national control of domestic technological and productive processes preached by the L.A.S should not be confused with the current extreme nationalist outbursts emerging in the Western world. These movements of deeply conservative authoritarian and xenophobic ideology have given rise to self-destructive policies such as those faced today by Great Britain with Brexit and other continental European countries seeking to break away from the European Union (EU), forgetting the enormous benefits derived from that great post- war strategic project that saved Europe from fragmentation and irrelevance.

The social dissatisfaction and the deep recessionary crises experienced today in the EU do not stem from its integration process, which has been extraordinarily successful as a paradigm of what should be understood as multidimensional integration. The crisis facing the European project today is attributable to two factors. The first is the "invasion" across the Mediterranean Sea of migratory masses from Africa and Middle Eastern countries devastated by the wars unleashed after the fall of the Twin Towers in New York. The second dissolving factor has been the consolidation of the neo-liberal economic system since the installation of the euro in the EU at the beginning of this century, before the fiscal integration of its economies had been achieved.

Of course the recent war between Russia and Ukraine is opening up another scenario of danger and conflict in the very heart of Europe whose consequences cannot yet be foreseen.

Looking to the future of capitalism in the 21st century, it is possible to imagine at least two alternative scenarios.

The first scenario evokes the apocalyptic processes that led to the catastrophic Second World War, which was a political "solution" to the recessionary conditions derived for the United States from the great crisis of the 1930s and for Germany from the burdensome debts for reparations for the First World War. The world scenario today is politically very different from that of that historical moment, but the economic scenario augurs serious risks of recession and unemployment resulting from technical progress itself (robotization, 4-0 industrialization) and of shortages in the supply of vital elements for human survival caused by the environmental crisis.

The second scenario would be a rearrangement of the capitalist order derived from the presence of new productive poles or centers (in particular China and, behind it, India) of planetary scope. In a world order governed by the principles of the UN (preservation of peace, international negotiation, respect for the self-determination of peoples, consolidation of democratic regimes, etc.), the United States and Europe would give way to the new powers, giving rise to new rules of the game that transcend those established at the end of World War II.

The world would then be reorganized on a multipolar (or, if you will, multicentric) basis in a new order regulated by the UN. From the point of view of the L.A.S's own ideology, this second scenario would give new relevance to Latin American integrationist ideals.

Regarding the risks of the world sinking into the first scenario, it is necessary to return to the issue of xenophobic nationalism, cultural conflicts with religious roots and other forms of clash of civilizations in the style anticipated by Huntington. In this world of large economic blocs, such as those being formed by Russia, India and China, the fragmentation of Europe would be truly suicidal for the values of Western culture.

However, the defeat of xenophobic nationalist movements is one thing; the continued triumph of equally extremist political movements aligned with the neo-liberal agenda is quite another. It is only stated here that nationalism is the greatest danger of political origin in the short term as long as the massive exodus of Arabs and Africans to Europe continues. Latin American integration (not the one-dimensional integration of markets only, but the multidimensional integration of nations) continues to be the pending issue and the starting point of any future development strategy (Di Filippo 2013). Progress towards higher forms of supranationalism (moving from free trade agreements, to customs unions, to common markets, and to economic unions on the road to the ideal of a political union) may be a realizable utopia at least in South America in the framework of the second scenario outlined above.

The pursuit of this ideal requires the increasing harmonization and unification of national fiscal budgets, under the control of democratically elected national governments. The monetary order cannot be subordinated to the financial dictates of central banks which do not respond to democratically constituted political power.

From the integrationist ideology developed by the L.A.S, the pursuit of the above objectives, at least for South America, would require major structural changes with respect to the primary export character of its national economies, seeking more autonomous ways of developing an industrially based productive power on a subregional scale. The attainment of these goals presupposes the development of a business sector with entrepreneurial capacity that does not flee its capital abroad or focus its profits on purely speculative and rent-seeking activities.

The ideal of Latin American integration remains more valid today than ever. This type of regional or subregional project aimed at diversifying joint productive power involves the coordination and harmonization of: (i) technical, phytosanitary, etc. standards and norms

university curricula; (iii) the granting of subregional valid diplomas and certificates in the technological sphere; (iv) migration, labor and social security regulations and other related issues. Many of these preparatory actions have already been addressed in a deeper way, at least for South America, by working groups created in Mercosur and the Andean Community (Di Filippo and Franco 1997, 2000). This integrationist ideology cannot be put into practice on a national scale, nor exclusively through bureaucratic-administrative measures. Its promotion requires the development of a social awareness resulting from the action of transversal political movements that build concerted regional platforms for the construction of a shared culture of progress toward multidimensional integration at the service of the citizenry and not of large TCs (Di Filippo and Franco 1997).

Chapter XI

Latin American Structuralism and economic theory[34]

At the heart of any economic theory of the capitalist order is the study of economic values, the market and prices. They are the central focus of this essay and its guiding thread. The broader context in which these reflections are situated is the process of structural change in capitalist societies as a consequence of the successive technological revolutions that have promoted the expansion of the productive power of human labor. Consequently, the analysis carried out here does not refer to market prices under conditions of stable equilibrium, but to the variations in the structure of markets and prices that accompany the process of development. In this essay we read some of the pioneers of Latin American structuralist economic theory, in the belief that we will discover in their fundamental writings a theory of economic value, the market and prices that is radically different from those established in the academic sphere.

In comparison with static theories, which tend to isolate and compartmentalize market activities in the formative process of the price system, Latin American structuralist economic theory takes as its starting point a systemic, multidimensional and historically dynamic vision of human societies.

To begin with, it is worth clarifying two fundamental restrictions that limit this work. First, the institutional thinking of the Economic Commission for Latin America and the Caribbean (ECLAC) is not examined here. To avoid any misunderstandings, for the purposes of this book, will distinguish

---

[34] Published in ECLAC Review No. 98, August 2009

between the notion of political economy and that of economic theory. We conceive of political economy as a discipline supporting the legislator and the statesman (Adam Smith 1999: 539), while economic theory includes, first, an underlying perspective loaded with values, and second, the theory itself. The latter is a system of hypotheses about the behavior of reality that can be verified with the help of the scientific method.

This notion of political economy formulated by Smith -different from that of the rest of the classical economists and Marx, who make it synonymous with economic science- is very appropriate to show the type of tasks that are typical of an intergovernmental organization such as ECLAC. For example, in Bielschowsky's studies (1998 and 2009) on the evolution of the institution's thinking, reference is made to the strategies for action and the ideas proposed to Latin American governments. According to Adam Smith's characterization, this would correspond to the sphere of political economy and only tacitly or tangentially to structuralist economic theory.

Secondly, and for the same reasons, this chapter does not analyze neo-structuralist thinking on economic values, markets and prices. As Bielschowsky (2009) observes in relation to the structuralist period of ECLAC's thinking, "the texts of the first three decades studied in this work are mainly those subscribed by the most prominent intellectuals of ECLAC in that period, while those used in reference to the thinking of the last three decades correspond more to official documents of the institution" (Bielschowsky 2009: 174). These documents reveal a vision strongly influenced by the political will of the member governments. The examination of the personal theoretical contribution of the neo- structuralist authors is not an impossible task, but it is beyond the possibilities of the author of this book.

Structuralist economic theory between two fires

The two great schools of twentieth century economic thought have responded to the marginalist and Marxist-Ricardian theories of economic value. In the field of both schools of thought, both of which were endowed with orthodox and influential thinkers, a heterodoxy arose that would include many scientists of the American institutionalist school and others who drew from the Keynesian revolution. In the post-war period, the processes of decolonization and European reconstruction gave rise to a preoccupation with development and underdevelopment. All these strands of thought challenged the academically established theories of economic value from different angles. Structuralist economic theory forms part of this heterodoxy.

Latin American structuralism has been questioned from two different sides regarding its theory of the market and prices. This questioning originated, on one side, from Marxist theorists and, on the other, from neoclassical marginalists based on the paradigm of perfect competition or, more broadly, on the static logic of marginal calculus applied to "free" markets. For Marxists, market prices are an expression of the social labor contained in the goods traded; for neoclassical economists a manifestation of the marginal utility and scarcity of goods. Speculations on economic value and the process of price formation in Latin American structuralism have never been able to be pigeonholed into either of these two theoretical approaches.

Marx's theory of value and its structural foundations

Marx's (1946) view of the social process is clearly historical, structural and multidimensional and includes a central analysis of the institutions of property (relations of production). However, his theory of economic value is unidimensional. Prices, under conditions of stable equilibrium, correspond to value, which for Marx is a measure of socially necessary labor time under the average conditions of technique corresponding to a given time. His theory of value is not designed to register directly the effects of important institutional changes, except when these affect the average conditions of technique. The stability of equilibrium which is assumed in it implicitly demands the immobility of all factors - environmental, political, and cultural - that underlie this equilibrium. The theory of value adopted by Marx is a Ricardian transplant foreign to the historical dialectic that characterizes his global vision of society.

When Marx introduces in volume III of "Capital", published by Engels, the notion of prices of production associated with the equalization (per equation) of rates of profit in all markets, he establishes the combination of a mechanism governed by the market - the intersectoral mobility of capital- and a process of valorization that depends on the sphere of production. However, since prices of production are also abstractions, they are in fact values which -in Marx's sense- are improperly called prices, since they are not calculated in monetary units paid in specific markets (Di Filippo 1981a and 1981b)

The prices of production conceived by Marx respond to a logic similar to the classical notion of natural prices, which implies a stable equilibrium towards which markets tend to move. For Adam Smith (1999, chapter VII), this framework of stability depends to a large extent on the general circumstances of society, while for Marx it lies, restrictively, in the average conditions of technology. Moreover, Adam Smith, like Robert Malthus, understands the value of commodities as the amount of human labor that can be purchased with them and not the labor crystallized in their production. Thus, Smith's approach directly takes into consideration the social relations of the market in the very determination of his theory of value. The notion of effective demand, introduced by Adam Smith himself, continued by Malthus and further elaborated by Keynes, assumes the intervention of the market in fixing the value of commodities. The concept of effective demand is the bridge by means of which Latin American structuralism links the functional and personal distribution of income with the determination of the price of final goods.

At the level of the philosophy of history, there is another fundamental difference between Marxism and Latin American structuralism. In the case of Marx, the starting point of his historical approach, or the ultimate cause, corresponds to the economic structure. This is the basic foundation of the labor-value theory, which is supposed to be valid only under the average conditions of technique and the relations of production (property) of a given era. In this context, the cultural and political aspects appear as super-structural epiphenomena of this central datum.

On contrast, for Latin American structuralists, like the institutionalists, the main datum corresponds to the cultural system. Technique, which today underlies capitalist societies, originated as a manifestation of cultural creativity, a theme that has been examined in some depth by Celso Furtado and which is discussed further below.

Epistemological foundations of neoclassical value and growth theories

It is worth making here the same distinction hinted at the beginning of this chapter between economic theory -with the corresponding pre-analytical cognitive vision- and political economy. The theoretical vision of the neoclassicals privileges the dogma of the self-regulation of markets, so that neoclassical economic theory is fundamentally based on microeconomic logic and assumes a long-run macroeconomy with full employment, ignoring the issue of effective demand. Finally, neoclassical political economy applied to the scene of globalized capitalism is what in this essay we call neoliberalism - for example, the criteria and principles of the Washington Consensus. Consequently, not all the excesses of neoliberalism should be attributed to the neoclassical theoretical vision.

It should be pointed out that political economy in the Smithian sense is oriented towards the statesman of a national economy, but the neoclassical political economy that we call here "neoliberalism" was a specific strategy of transnational corporations, which tried - and for a period of time succeeded - in modifying the rules of the game of the world economy (Washington Consensus) in favor of their microeconomic policies. Finally, as will be seen below, some neoclassicists use the expression "new political economy" in a way that is completely incompatible with what is meant in this essay by political economy.

Marginal analysis, elaborated by Marshall for a partial equilibrium approach and extended by Walras for a general equilibrium one, was strongly based on mathematical formalization by means of differential and integral calculus. Thus, from an epistemological point of view, and following the fathers of classical mechanics at the end of the 18th century, the first neoclassicals tried to establish the natural laws of economic science. Marginal analysis was a decisive instrument for the original neoclassical formulations of consumption and production theories, for determining the stable equilibrium points of microeconomic markets and for defending their theories of the functional distribution of income based on the equality of marginal productivity and factor remuneration. The personal distribution of income and the notion of the subsistence wage have always been excluded from the central core of neoclassical economic theory.

Unlike the classics and Marx, whose fundamental economic categories were linked to historically identifiable actors - rentier landowners, wage laborers, industrial entrepreneurs and others - neoclassical theory totally depersonalized economic categories and turned them into abstract and ahistorical variables.

Subsequently, however, and especially since the end of the Second World War, undeniable historical evidence has been uncovered in the most widely circulated neoclassical academic texts. Both game theory and pre-existing studies on imperfect markets -monopoly, oligopoly, monopolistic competition- implied a limited but explicit recognition of the power asymmetries that affect market prices. These theories and studies were incorporated into the most widely used academic manuals in the Western world.

In academic centers, a "conservative institutionalism" or "new neoclassical institutionalism" began to consolidate, always based on the defense of the market and private property as the basic microeconomic foundations of the social order (Von Hayek, Nozik and North, among others), but which abandoned, or at least relativized, the concern for preserving the premises of the theories of welfare and perfect competition. The frictions that occur in markets with imperfect information were recognized, accepting, for example, externalities and transaction costs (Ronald Coase, Kenneth Arrow, Douglass North, Oliver Williamson, Stiglitz and others).

What is now called the "new neoclassical political economy" is not political economy in the sense accepted by this book, but in fact a broadening and deepening of neoclassical economic theory in relation to the forms of micro-rationality (rational choice) and its effects on the economic, political and cultural spheres. The only difference is that some members of this school have tried to "export" it to other social disciplines. For example, Olson considered the problem of the "free rider" and included targeted regulation, based on incentives or punishments, to confer social rationality to this behavior (Olson 1965). Becker, for his part, tried to extend the principles of instrumental or strategic rationality to the sphere of interpersonal, family and love relationships, among others (Becker 1964)

The neoclassicals also recognized and incorporated the role of the State in the sphere of regulation and the role of the government in the sphere of public policies (fiscal, monetary and others) from the Keynesian revolution onwards, but the theory of effective demand was relegated to the short term and the study of economic cycles.

On a different note, by introducing a rather logical or theoretical notion of time, they defined the "long run" as the sphere of economic growth processes in which full employment and self-regulating markets operate (dynamics of the equilibrium potential product). This leads us to comment on the evolution of the neoclassical theory of economic growth.

In 1956, as a first polemical response to the neo-Keynesian views of growth theory originating in Cambridge, England, Solow elaborated an alternative theoretical proposal based on the main premises of neoclassical theory: a static view based on perfect competition, remuneration of primary factors according to their marginal productivity, the tendency of the model to achieve stable equilibrium positions, production functions based on factor substitution and others. In particular, technical progress, absent in the initial foundations of neoclassical theory, was treated by Solow as an exogenous variable affecting total productivity. For this purpose, he used a macro-economic production function of diminishing returns for each productive factor and constant returns to scale for all of them.

In this sense, he was able to preserve the distribution theory of this school, which links factor remuneration to the relevant marginal productivity under perfect competition conditions.

From the point of view of price theory, the neoclassical theory of growth in Solow's version simply ignores the problem. On receiving the Nobel Prize in Economics, he observed that "the idea is to imagine that the economy is populated by a single immortal consumer, or by a certain number of identical consumers, also immortal. Such a consumer, or his dynasty, is assumed to maximize an intertemporal utility function (...).

Any market failure is eliminated from the outset by definition. There are no strategic complementarities, no coordination failures, no prisoner's dilemmas (...). Inseparable from this way of thinking is the automatic assumption that what we observe is an equilibrium path. We are asked to adopt the construction I have just sketched as a stylized description of the functioning of the capitalist world" (Solow 1988, quoted in Katz 2000: 37).

Once again, as in the post-war period, historical evidence made this neoclassical theory of growth unsustainable, giving rise to the recognition of new theoretical premises. From the original neoclassical theoretical vision, the version of growth with endogenous technical progress, led by Romer (1986 and 1990) and Lucas (1988), began to prevail.

In the theory of growth with endogenous technical progress, the notion of constant returns to scale is abandoned and that of increasing returns to scale of all the productive factors represented in the production function is accepted. Economies of scale were well known in previous economic thought: for example, ECLAC [CEPAL] had used the concept in the 1960s to defend Latin American integration aimed at stimulating industrial development.

From this new perspective, Grossman and Helpmann (1991) argued that the non-patentable technological knowledge base, derived from the generic fruits of science, manifests itself on the one hand as a public good - standards or technical instructions are not exhausted when they are used and become available to others - and, on the other hand, as a private good through research and development (R&D).

This implies enormous fixed costs whose recovery is achieved by means of an operational scale as considerable as the participation of large transnational corporations in global markets.

This updating of neoclassical theory in relation to its original Walrasian and Marshallian premises responded to three interdependent historical reasons. First, the verification of the asymmetries of economic power that occur between firms interacting in "imperfect" markets - monopoly, oligopoly, monopolistic competition and the use of game theory- Secondly, the emergence of information and communications technologies (ICTs), which historically underlie the main cases of increasing returns to scale in the production of knowledge under conditions of technological monopoly. In this sense, it is enough to think of Microsoft and the successive versions of the Windows program. Third, the leading role played by the lobbying of transnational corporations in institutionalizing their positions of power through the design of the new rules of the game of global capitalism - World Trade Organization, International Monetary Fund - especially since the so-called Washington Consensus.

The endogenous growth theory expressed through the use of production functions has not yielded good empirical estimates. Alternative explorations, such as adding, redefining or eliminating variables to aggregate production functions, have not been successful. For example, the available data have not confirmed the specific issue of relative or absolute convergence of living standards proposed, or assumed, in the early neoclassical views. Estimates are becoming increasingly "theory-empty", while "theories" are becoming increasingly out of touch with the information at hand (Martin and Sunley 1998)[35].

A synthesis of the structuralist theoretical view of the market and prices

The theoretical vision of the market and prices of the Latin American structuralism school, sometimes implicitly and sometimes explicitly, is that at any given time the existence of the market reflects the power positions of the social actors with relation to the different spheres of each society. Consequently, market prices can be conceived as a measure of the positions of power and of the specific strategies and tactics of the

---

[35] M. Olson, "The Logic of Collective Action", Cambridge, Harvard University Press, 1965; G. Becker, "Human Capital", Nueva York, Columbia University Press, 1964; R. Solow, "Growth theory and after", American Economic Review, vol. 78, núm. 3, Nashville, Tennessee, American Economic Association, 1988; J. Katz, Reformas estructurales, productividad y conducta tecnológica en América Latina, Cepal/Fondo de Cultura Económica, 2000; P. Romer, "Endogenous technological change", Journal of Political Economy, vol. 98, núm. 5, Chicago, University of Chicago Press, 1990 e "Increasing returns and long run growth", Journal of Political Economy, vol. 94, núm. 5, Chicago University of Chicago Press, 1986; y R. Lucas, "On the mechanics of economic development", Journal of Monetary Economics, núm. 22, Amsterdam, Elsevier, 1988.

contracting parties and, in turn, the variations they experience over time reveal the changes that are taking place in this situation. This thesis does not deny that prices also measure utility and scarcity, nor that they are related to the labor crystallized in the commodities being traded, but what lies behind these measurements is that, ultimately, the determinant of prices keeps the positions of power and the strategies and tactics of the contracting parties. In the market, power is calculated using units of purchasing power in general, i.e. monetary units divided by price indexes. In this context, the broader notion of prices is adopted here, which includes the price of productive inputs, of final goods and services and, above all, of the primary factors of production, which constitute the remuneration to the owners of these. In addition, of course, the price of money is included, both from the perspective of exchange rates in the international sphere and the determination of national and international interest rates.

In the more specifically distributive sphere, structuralists consider three basic structural influences. First, they associate the functional distribution of income with the positions of productive and institutional power of the owners of the primary factors of production - here comes into play the notion of distributional surplus to which we refer below - and, on the other side, they include the personal or family distribution of income, derived from the previous one, which directly affects the composition of the aggregate demand for consumer goods and personal saving and investment behavior. Third, they emphasize the role of the State as the "maker of the official rules of the game" and of the Government -conceptually, different from the former - as a strategic economic player in advanced capitalist societies. In particular, the original distribution of income is modified in the short term through the redistributive effects of fiscal policy (both tax and expenditure). In the long term, government action affects the distribution of fundamental public goods such as health, education and justice, among others.

The most distinctive theoretical feature of Latin American structuralism in the field of values, markets and prices is its multidimensional character. The positions of power that directly or indirectly affect the market and prices refer to the place of actors (natural persons or associations) in the economic, political, biological-environmental and cultural structure of human societies. The economic structure determines the position of individuals in productive and property regimes; the political structure determines the place of actors (including the government itself) in the regimes that regulate citizens' rights, freedoms and obligations, including access to the legislative, executive and judicial powers of the State. The biological-environmental structure establishes the situation of the protagonists in the systems that regulate access to the "natural biophysical environment and its successive artificial transformations, as well as its spatial deployment" (Sunkel 1980: 13), while the cultural structure determines the place occupied by the protagonists in the systems that regulate information, communication and knowledge. But there are also informal structures that determine the type of symbols or codes used, starting with language, and of the values, both substantive - ultimate ends such as truth, good, beauty, justice and others

- and instrumental - utility, efficacy, efficiency - that legitimize social behaviors and delimit the mechanisms through which cultural stratifications are generated.

This power of natural persons and organizations is considered institutionalized or structured if it is incorporated into the reciprocal expectations of habitual behavior in social interactions, including, of course, market transactions. These structural positions, which we have schematically characterized, frame the exercise of human freedom in multiple ways and ultimately determine both the quantity of labor and the utility and scarcity of the commodities traded.

The concept of institutionalized (or structured) power makes it possible to overcome or transcend the holism-individualism dilemma that underlies many epistemological debates. According to the holistic view, human behavior depends to a large extent on social structures, whereas from an individualistic perspective it is the individual actors or agents (natural or legal persons) who determine the dynamics of historical change through their decisions and behaviors. Considered unilaterally, the first approach can lead to deterministic conclusions and the second to voluntaristic conclusions, but neither exhausts the possibilities of analysis of a social system. Therefore, in a comprehensive application of the systemic view of human societies, it is necessary to go from the actors to the power structure and then from the power structure to the actors (Bunge 1999)

This systemic incorporation of the concept of power into the explanation of market mechanisms evokes the conditions imposed by Thomas Kuhn (1969) on the structure of scientific revolutions when new emerging theories broaden the worldview of pre-existing theories and incorporate them into a new explanatory paradigm.

Philosophical foundations of the structuralist vision: creativity, development and power

The concept of creativity, understood as the use of human freedom in order to interfere in the usual order of human social processes and recreate them in an irreversible way, is at the root of the structuralist view of economics and has been developed in particular depth by Celso Furtado (1978).

Aristotle anticipated the impact of technology on the structure of human societies more than two millennia ago. It seems that information and communications technologies (ICT) have begun to turn his predictions into reality: "For if every instrument could perform its own task, on receiving an order or anticipating it, as is told of the statues of Daedalus or the tripods of Hephaestus, which, as the poet says, entered of themselves into the assembly of the gods, in the same way the shuttles would weave by themselves and the plectrums would perform the zither, and the architects would have no need of servants nor the masters of slaves" (Aristotle 2005: 63 and 64).

The meaning of technical progress and its links with social structure is quite well synthesized in this "prophetic" quote, particularly applicable to the current advent of ICTs.

The most direct connection between the epistemological vision of Aristotle and that of the Latin American structuralist current is provided by Furtado himself, diving into the depths of Aristotle's causal approach. Furtado says: "The concepts of structure (form) and process (causality) are fundamental ingredients in cognitive work. Our vision of the world has its basic points of support in them. The structural approach, because it remains at the level of morphological descriptions and excludes the notion of causality, narrows the cognitive horizon. On the other side, the analytical approach leads to a localized determinism and hides the qualitative. Aristotle sought to integrate these two concepts on the basis of the principle of finality. In the methodology of the social sciences, it is conceived to obtain this integration from the notion of creativity, admitted as the human faculty of interfering with causal determinism, enriching any social process with new elements. When it reaches a certain preponderance, or when the action of several of these elements converge, innovative acts provoke structural discontinuity. The innovative faculty (creativity), of which there is full evidence at the sociological level, would thus assume a status at the logical level" (Furtado 1978: 215 and ff.).

It is worth explaining the links between this paragraph of Furtado's and the famous four causes (or four explanations) of Aristotelian epistemology to which he implicitly alludes. For Aristotle, what Furtado calls structure is associated with the idea of form or formal cause. In turn, the notion of process, as used by contemporary science in the field of physics and nature, corresponds to the concept of efficient cause understood as the generating and transforming dynamics of structure. According to Furtado, when this process takes place in the social sphere and involves, in addition, a structural change - a "transformation" or modification of the Aristotelian form -, his origin is to be sought in human creativity. The idea of creativity linked to human freedom replaces here the notion of final cause that was fundamental in Aristotle's teleology. On another side, what Furtado calls the analytical approach, which leads to a localized determinism, refers to the components of the structure, isolated and statically considered, and is close to the analysis and decomposition of matter - material cause in Aristotelian language. However, this concept supports change understood as a transition from potency -what matter can become- to act -when actualized matter becomes what it was only in potency-, while localized determinism does not necessarily incorporate this dynamic vision (Bunge 1961: 44 and 45)

The static notion of equality of conditions ("ceteris paribus") typical of the method of neoclassical microeconomic science, which still dominates Western economic thought, is one of the most prototypical samples of the analytical approach that leads to the localized determinism to which Furtado critically refers. The foregoing reflections highlight the one-dimensional and limiting nature of this analytical perspective.

Furtado's concept of creativity coincides with the "Aristotelian prophecy" that, if the advance of technology allowed it, "shuttles would weave by themselves and plectrums would play the zither, and architects would have no need of servants or masters of slaves". Undoubtedly, technical progress, which according to Furtado constitutes one of the two forms through which human creativity takes shape, has been the great transformer of the causal process that sustains social structures and has been approaching, today more than ever with information and communication technologies, this vision formulated more than two thousand years ago by the illustrious Greek philosopher.

The relationship that Furtado establishes between the concepts of creativity and development can be summarized in the following lines:

> In its double dimension of generating force of new surplus and creative impulse of new cultural values, this liberating process of human energies constitutes the ultimate source of what we understand by development (italics added). The marvelous range of cultures that have arisen on earth bears witness to man's fabulous potential for inventiveness. If anything we know from the process of cultural creativity is exactly that man's potentialities are unfathomable (Furtado 1978: 97 and 98).

Thus, Furtado relies on Aristotle to introduce at the philosophical level his own concept of creativity, in which the Aristotelian "final cause" is no longer dictated by the nature of things, but by the (creative) use of human freedom. In other words, technical progress, as it operates in the contemporary world, is the great dynamizer of capitalist societies. It is also, for better and for worse, a phenomenon whose ultimate cultural root is the fruit of Western civilization.

The most important feature of this process of creativity is the ability to confer power to those who control it scientifically, in the contemporary sense of the word science along the lines followed by Galileo, Newton and Bacon, among others. Furtado goes on to say:

> The vow formulated by Marx in one of his theses on Feuerbach - philosophers interpreted the world, now we must transform it - has been more than fulfilled. The demarcation line of what is and is not

> science, in Popper's felicitous expression, is defined by the test to which theories are subjected. Knowledge tended more and more to be that which increases the capacity to foresee, to act. The fabulous mass of resources invested today in science and its applications finds its raison d'être in this efficacy. And the central objective of this, hélas, is military power and accumulation (Furtado 1978: 14 et seq.).

This linkage between cultural power, technological power, military power and economic power is the foundation of the center- periphery view of structuralist economic theory applied to the evolution of the capitalist system and its specific peripheral features.

Epistemological foundations of Latin American structuralist economics

The concept of system, on one side, and the notion of power, on the other, are part of the original theoretical approach of Latin American structuralism on development and underlie its theoretical vision of economic value, the market and prices. Although this systemic language that includes the notion of power is present, implicitly or explicitly, in all the formulations of this school, it is more evident in some works (Furtado 1965; Pinto 1968; Sunkel 1970; Sunkel and Paz 1970; Prebisch 1981; Di Filippo 1981a).

This systemic approach went beyond the limits of economic theory and required a multidimensional study that made it possible to articulate economic issues with those of other areas of human society, such as the sociocultural, political and environmental spheres (Bunge 1997 and 1999; Di Filippo 2007).

The Latin American structuralist theoretical vision stresses the importance of change in technical rules materialized in instruments and embodied in human qualifications. The subject of structuralism is not that of the average conditions of technology in a given epoch, but rather that of the national and international institutional effects that derive from technological change imported from the centers of the world.

In the contemporary economic sphere, the technical rules in force allow human beings and their organizations to relate to the instruments of consumption and production through specific qualifications that are part of the cultural sphere, while the social rules in force link human beings and their organizations to each other through transactions carried out from institutionalized positions of power.

The notion of structures refers rather to the stability of the technical or institutional rules internalized by the actors (whether individuals or organizations), while the notion of structural change is historically dynamic and refers to the modification of rules or their internalization.

Moreover, it should be noted that the issue of technology is more complex for structuralists than for the institutionalists of the developed world, because technological change was not self-generated in Latin America, but came from the center along with the institutions and organizations imported by virtue of it. The reformulation or rethinking of these external effects produces heterogeneities, dependencies and specific vulnerabilities that are the central theme of structuralist economic theory.

After the end of World War II, the reconstruction of Europe and the process of decolonization, along with the debate on the nature and causes of development and underdevelopment began. Important contributions in the field of the economic theory of development emerged, including the contribution of Latin American structuralism.

The center-periphery vision of structuralist theory was characterized by linking two intertwined systemic visions: that of the international economic system and that of national economic systems. By highlighting the asymmetrical nature of technical progress from the center, as well as the concentrated distribution of its fruits, a theoretical field was opened up whose analysis focused on the notions of system and asymmetrical positions of power.

The structuralist theory of development and underdevelopment is more comprehensible and empirically more fruitful using an intersectoral relations approach to which important authors such as Marx, Sraffa, Leontief, Chenery and Pasinetti, among others, have contributed from different theoretical angles.

With the rise of neoclassical growth theories, the issue of intersectoral relationships was abandoned in addition with the weakening of the influence of Keynesian economics (Los 2001)

The systemic approach in economics, clearly adopted by Latin American structuralism in its versions of the sixties and seventies, generated formalizations based on the algebra of matrices and the definition of structural input-output relationships and coefficients. These conceptual tools were essential in ECLAC's contribution to the study of national accounts and growth projections for Latin America (Balboa 1961). The first elementary manual on economics, prepared by the institution and the Latin American and Caribbean Institute for Economic and Social Planning (ILPES) to train Latin American students from a structuralist perspective, was also based on a systemic reading of the economic process that privileged qualitative and institutional analysis of intersectoral relationships (Castro and Lessa 1973). In this way, the conceptual and theoretical frameworks of systemic nature prepared the ground for the study of the structural change required to understand the processes of development and underdevelopment.

In a more abstract and broader sense, the first text produced at ECLAC and ILPES on Latin American underdevelopment and the theory of development also clearly adopted a systemic view of the subject (Sunkel and Paz 1970). The representation of a system, whether quantitative or qualitative, can be expressed in matrix language. In the matrix of a system it is possible to distinguish the actors that make it dynamic, the structures that define it, the spheres or spaces occupied by the system (with an "inside" and an "outside") and the mechanisms used by the actors to develop their strategies within the framework of these structures.

In particular, the matrix language of input-output allows us to establish a coherent and fluid relationship between the Keynesian theory of effective demand and the study of the specific structures of underdeveloped or peripheral regions, as well as the structuralist theory of the positions of economic power implicit in the study of markets. Indeed, the composition of aggregate demand, both in the short and long run, depends on the distribution of income, which in turn depends on the positions of power (productive and institutional) of the contracting parties in factor, input and output markets. In Latin America, the concentrated distribution of exogenously generated technical progress translates into a situation of structural heterogeneity. In today's global capitalism, the depositaries of this technical progress are, to a large extent, the transnational corporations.

Through the logic of input-output it is possible to highlight, in comparison with current neoclassical theory, that growth is "endogenous" to large companies, but not necessarily to the small and medium enterprises of the peripheral societies in which they operate. The process of growth and investment depends to a large extent on large corporations, which may originate in the centers or in the peripheries themselves - for example, Latin American economic groups that have trans nationalized. Consequently, the accumulation process depends too much on the microeconomic considerations inherent in the interests of private business planning.

In summary, the intersectoral analysis linked to the matrix logic of input-output makes it possible to describe and interpret the conditions of Latin America's economy. Unfortunately, the development of structural models has been almost completely discontinued in Latin America. However, some efforts have been made to re-establish this approach (Infante and Sunkel 2009).

The concept of surplus in structuralist economic theory

Anthropologists and economists have used the concept of surplus to interpret historical epochal changes. The transition from primitive societies to the first urban civilizations of the ancient world was due to the introduction of agricultural technologies that made possible the emergence of a food surplus.

Marx's concept of the development of the productive forces reflects the defining importance of the successive technological revolutions, as well as the appropriation of the surplus by the ruling social classes, that have accompanied civilization. However, his historical notion of surplus differs from his theoretical notion of surplus value.

In the theory of value, Marx freezes the historical notion of productive forces and surplus and formulates the idea of surplus value associated with the labor-value theory and its law of value, in conditions of stable equilibrium within a given era. This notion of surplus, applied to the capitalist system, could be called exploitative surplus if measured in units of abstract labor (surplus value) or, more neutrally, distributive surplus when measured in units of general purchasing power -that is, nominal income flows divided by the price index corresponding to a basket of subsistence consumption. The concept of distribution surplus coincides with the structuralist approach, but structural heterogeneity -a typical feature of Latin American underdevelopment- invalidates the notion of average technical conditions on which Marx's theory is based.

Instead of focusing their theories of value on a given structural situation, defined according to the average conditions of technique, the structuralists are concerned with structural change linked to the process of development. This notion of surplus that obeys structural change could be called innovation surplus or development surplus and constitutes a direct product of human creativity in the sense proposed in the previous section. Economists usually refer to it as "productivity gains", while Prebisch referred to the results of technical progress.

In Marx, the surplus of exploitation (surplus value) presupposes a given level of development of the productive forces and describes a mechanism of appropriation compatible with his labor-value theory. In contrast, the surplus of innovation or development formulated by the structuralists presupposes, of course, positions of power or domination which are precisely the "social substance" measured by prices, but they conceive it as the historical expression of the productive forces in action. It is a new flow, measured in units of historical time, which is added to the previously accumulated distributive surplus.

The innovation surplus arises from the distribution of productivity gains between the labor force that contributed to generating it and the other agents of the productive process. This distribution of productivity profits or benefits of technical progress is part of the distributive struggles inherent in the dynamics of capitalism, whether peripheral or central.

The innovation surplus is measured at the macroeconomic level and requires a calculation in units of (general purchasing) power of both productivity gains and their social distribution. This raises methodological and econometric challenges that have been neglected by structuralist economists, who are more prone to theoretical reflection than to detailed measurement. In this study there is no room to speculate on the mechanisms of primary appropriation of this surplus by firms, through a macroeconomic process that was studied by both Furtado (1964: 141) and Prebisch (1981: 107-124), so we have limited ourselves to describing the essential contents of the concept in its structuralist version (Di Filippo 1981, chapter 1)

The concepts of power and surplus in market dynamics

The concept of power is present throughout the structuralist thesis on development. In his thoughts on the connections between the notion of the nation state and the structuralist conception of development, Sunkel has unequivocally emphasized the following: " Furthermore, this way of conceiving development places the accent on action; on the instruments of political power and on the power structures themselves; and these are ultimately what explain the orientation, effectiveness, intensity and nature of the internal and external social manipulation of culture, productive resources, technology and socio-political groups" (Sunkel and Paz 1970: 38).

The political power of the state sets the rules of the game for all power structures and spheres. Therefore, the concept of institutionalized power is not the only object of study of political science. Indeed, the rules of the game of the political system also determine the political, economic, cultural and even biological- environmental power positions of individuals. Moreover, from a systemic point of view, the intrinsic mechanism of the exercise of power includes two other interconnected concepts: human needs and situations of dependency and dependence.

Nor are the concepts of need and dependence understood only in their economic sense, since they are conceived in a multidimensional way. Situations of need and dependence can also be verified in political, cultural or biological-environmental subsystems.

We suggest that at the core of the structuralist concept of distributive surplus, linked to a given structural situation, are the relationships between needs, situations of dependence and positions of power. The grasp of these and their distributive effects requires the study of the concrete mechanisms of historically given markets and is not exhausted by an examination of the structure of production. An illustrious philosophical antecedent of this conceptual linkage can be found in the

Aristotelian idea that the interdependence of human needs constitutes the essential link of social life and the basis of all economic transactions, which require money as a measure of the terms of exchange. At the same time, Aristotle conceives of money not in its commodity form (gold, silver and others), but directly in its institutional expression derived from the existence of the political society ("Polis" or State). Thus, the Aristotelian approach to economic science is clearly institutional.

The rate of surplus value and the Marxist concept of exploitation are not directly related to the intensity of the needs experienced by people nor to their degree of dependence on those who hold economic power (owners of productive power). Thus, in an automated enterprise with the highest level of productivity, the rate of surplus value - in Marx's sense - that is "extracted" from a highly qualified engineer could be very high. However, this "exploitation" will be compatible with an excellent standard of living for him and his family and an institutional context that allows him to terminate his contractual relationship without serious consequences. Alternatively, the rate of surplus value of an illiterate peasant living in a peripheral country may be much lower in terms of abstract labor time, but may imply a situation of extreme need and dependence in the framework of structured mechanisms of domination. In his book "Creativity and Dependence", Furtado observes the following:

> Market operations are, as a rule, transactions between agents of unequal power: Indeed, the raison d'être of trade - the expression of a system of division of labor - lies in the creation of a surplus, the assumption of which is not based on any law of nature. The "imperfect" forms of the market to which the economist refers are nothing more than a euphemism to describe the ex-post result of the imposition of the will of certain agents on this assumption. Since all markets are in some way "imperfect", exchange activities necessarily engender a process of concentration of wealth and power. Hence the structural tendency, observed since the beginnings of industrial capitalism, toward the formation of large firms. Many observers will erroneously infer from this observation that small enterprises tend to disappear, but experience shows that they are irreplaceable in the exercise of important functions: without small enterprises the capitalist system would lose considerably,

not only flexibility, but also inventiveness and initiative (Furtado 1978: 17)

The previous paragraph conveniently synthesizes, for a short book such as the present one, two very important ideas of the development-underdevelopment diagnosis implicit in the reflections of structuralism. The first is that of distributional surplus, as distinct from the notion of innovation surplus, which is not considered here, and the second is the issue of the structural heterogeneity of economic systems, which is of central importance in the peripheral forms of capitalism.

Let us examine the situation of a small company coexisting and competing with a large one. Obviously, this implies the presence of deeply asymmetric market structures that prevail in most economic sectors. It also implies a technological heterogeneity that is somewhat clouded both by the concept of average conditions of technique in a given era, assumed in Marx's theory of value, and by the notion of the marginal productivity of labor in the neoclassical theory of production and distribution.

The role played by the small company, in addition to its traits of flexibility, inventiveness and initiative, is manifested in the determination of the overall distribution surplus, macroeconomically understood. By setting an upper limit to the minimum wage, as a function of its lower average and marginal productivity, the small company favors the profit level of the large company with which it coexists, capable of paying much higher wages than those that remunerate the low-skilled labor force in small companies. Moreover, in inflationary situations, when workers demand an increase in the purchasing power of wages, small firms lack sufficient productivity and financial strength to readjust wages, so that they unwittingly keep "at bay" a majority part of the less skilled and less powerful workforce, setting a wage ceiling for them. All this favors not only the expansion of the distribution surplus with respect to the social product, but also the tendency to accumulate it in the most productive enterprises controlled by the high-income groups. This occurs both in the form of the profits of large, often transnational, companies and in the form of higher and higher salaries for skilled jobs in the technical-management fields.

With markets left to their spontaneous dynamics, the result, is an intensification of structural heterogeneity in peripheral areas (Pinto 1965; Pinto and Di Filippo 1991a and 1991b; Di Filippo 1981a and 1981b) and of income concentration both in the center and in the periphery. The average wage of small firms is, then, a subsistence line from which the remuneration of the lower-skilled labor force is calculated. It is in this way that the concept of needs is linked to the concept of surplus through the notion of institutionalized power.

Center-periphery: trans-historical vision and specific historical periods

The center-periphery vision, the characteristic framework of the historical and structural approach, has always been the starting point of Latin American structuralist political economy. The power of the hegemonic centers over the peripheral societies of the world order is ultimately based on the control of the scientific and technological processes that ensure their predominance in the cultural, economic and political-military spheres. We have already examined the abstract links between culture (in the fields of science and technology), creativity and power that have characterized the evolution of Western civilization. The point to be emphasized in this context, which is essential for understanding the identifying features of structuralist economic theory, is that Latin American societies have always been the recipients of the waves of technological change that, since the conquest and colonization, have been installed in Latin America.

The "intangible power" (Ferrer 1996: 14) of the scientific and technological knowledge of the center is the starting point for understanding the historical formation of Latin American societies. The phases on which the center-periphery vision is based are determined on the basis of the successive technological waves that have had an impact on Latin American societies. In this sense, what is of interest is the starting date of these events in Latin America rather than the date on which the technological revolutions began to take shape in the center itself.

The first event (15th century) came from the Iberian powers, which used their knowledge of navigation, their war equipment -armor, horses, firearms-, their productive processes -mining and farming techniques- and their instruments of consumption and production to transform the foundations of pre-Hispanic society. The second (19th century) took place after the British industrial revolution, when, in parallel with the beginning of Latin American political independence, the emerging international capitalism settled in the coal, iron and steel industries and the steam- powered ships and railroads.

The third event (20th century) was the second industrial revolution in the United States, which resulted in the incorporation of petroleum energy and, to a lesser degree, electricity, together with procedures for rationalizing work (Taylorism, Fordism and others) and new durable products such as: the automobile and household appliances.

The most recent development (21st century), which began at the end of the 20th century, was the introduction of information technologies and "internet of things". Their consequences have given rise to a new era of "cybernetic capitalism" (including artificial intelligence (AI) that is transforming the world.

Center-periphery, economic value and terms of trade

Structuralist theories of economic value seek the connection between structural change, both technological and institutional, and price dynamics. This feature is found in world markets and also within peripheral societies themselves.

The thesis of the deterioration of the terms of trade in Prebisch's version, formulated in the late 1940s and early 1950s, illustrates this structural dynamic. Prebisch is not interested in the equilibrium prices at a given moment in time, but is concerned with certain specific international markets - commodities versus manufactures - whose determination is the result of a careful examination of the terms of trade derived from the international division of labor between center and periphery. The conditions under which this deterioration occurs are dynamic and structural (technological and institutional).

The income elasticity of demand is only the empirical expression of an explanation whose structural background is deeper. According to Engel's laws, in the sphere of consumption, the elasticity of demand for manufactures grows at a faster rate than that for primary products. The study of these baskets of goods is, moreover, an empirical foundation for the notion of basic needs, as well as for the poverty line on the basis of which it is possible to set subsistence wages that serve as a frame of reference for calculating the needs-dependence-power link on which the concept of surplus is based.

The cyclical character of the capitalist development of the center determines the instability of prices of both manufactures and commodities. Empirical evidence immediately shows that the prices of primary products are much more variable than those of manufactures and that, in the long run, world demand for the latter (inputs or final products) grows at a faster rate than that for commodities.

Moreover, in the international supply of both commodities and manufactured products, the deterioration of the terms of trade would be due to institutionalized positions of power. Prebisch notes that in the periphery there is no significant appropriation of the expansion of productive power (productivity gains), because workers lack the cultural, trade union or political influence to ensure that their incomes rise in parallel with this increase. In contrast, wage earners in the central societies, especially since the end of World War II, hold positions of institutionalized power - unionization, political participation, welfare policies - that allow them to increase their incomes in line with their productivity growth. Also in this area, the historical terms of trade are changing as a result of the participation of the emerging Asian countries. These countries are producing manufactured goods with high productivity gains which, on the one hand, are passed on to the transnational corporations located in the export processing zones and, on the other, entail unfavorable terms of trade for Asian societies because the political and social regimes, especially in China, do not allow labor wages to rise in line with these gains.

In any case, the modification of historical conditions and of empirical trends is not a failure of theory, but a signal of the changing structural conditions of the societies that participate in the world market. The explanation of the deterioration of the terms of trade of commodities in relation to manufactures is part of a theory of economic value whereby the positions of power of the contracting parties in the productive and social structure, as well as the variations they experience, determine the oscillations of the relative prices of these commodities.

For the moment it is only possible to verify that the international order is immersed in the worst crisis since the end of the Second World War. But as in any crisis, it is necessary to explore both the dangers and the opportunities of the new emerging scenarios.

The structuralist theory of inflation

Latin American structuralism does not study the general equilibrium conditions of markets, but rather the long-term structural forces that constantly destabilize them in the dynamics of economic development.

Nor does it postulate the hypothesis that the market possesses self-regulating forces that make it return to positions of stable equilibrium. A practical application of this view took place in the formulation of the structuralist theory of inflation.

Latin America structuralism studied the phenomenon of inflation on the basis of the factors that contributed to the imbalance of sectoral or specific markets as a consequence of the structural changes that accompanied the process of economic development in the post-war period and, approximately, up to the end of the 1970s. Examination focused on the international sphere, within the framework of the center-periphery view of the cyclical oscillations of the central economies caused by variations in the quantity and price of tradable goods, giving rise to a situation of external imbalance or modification of the terms of trade (Prebisch 1963, appendix)

In the peripheral national economies, and complementary to external restrictions, inflationary processes were linked to supply constraints caused by institutional or productive rigidities. In all cases, changes in relative prices were the direct driving force behind inflationary pressures and their effects on the absolute price level.

Between the late 1950s and early 1960s, several Latin American authors proposed and developed an interpretation of inflation that contributed to founding and consolidating the "structuralist" appellation by which this theoretical current has become known (Noyola 1957; Sunkel 1958; Prebisch 1963 and 1981; Pinto 1968)

Especially regarding the inflationary issue, the distinction between structure and system was emphasized. Assuming the existence and historical continuity of the latter, what may remain immobile or could change is its structure. In this context, the vision to be considered includes not only the structure, but also the actors operating within it and, on the other hand, the mechanisms of the system understood as processes promoted by these actors, either to preserve the pre-existing functioning of the system or to attempt to modify it. Given its concern with development, structural change is of fundamental interest to Latin American structuralist political economy.

From the systemic approach in which structuralist political economy can be framed, it is possible to distinguish the structural heterogeneity of economic systems, their main actors according to the position of power they occupy in them, the operational areas of the system and the institutionalized power mechanisms through which these agents influence and are influenced by inflationary processes.

The pioneers of the structuralist approach to inflation were undoubtedly Noyola (1957) and Sunkel (1958). Noyola established a fruitful conceptual distinction between core inflationary pressures (structural data) and the diffusion mechanisms operated by structurally conditioned actors.

Sunkel distinguished between basic, circumstantial and cumulative inflationary pressures. The former includes structural rigidities that not only have an impact on factor endowment and production structure costs, but also on institutionalized positions of power -for example, agricultural property rights or the capacity to import- that clash with the new dynamic demands of development. The notion of circumstantial inflationary pressures allows us to consider specific historical situations - environmental, war and others - that are unpredictable and affect structures sporadically. Finally, the concept of cumulative inflationary pressures assumes that, since inflation is an evident structural imbalance, it is not necessarily corrected by the free play of market forces or by restricting the money supply, but can give rise to circular cumulative tendencies (Myrdal 1967) that contribute to maintaining or increasing the initial imbalances (Myrdal 1967).

In turn, the diffusion mechanisms discerned by Sunkel can be interpreted as the concrete forms assumed by the distributive struggle between the different agents affected by the inflationary process, according to their positions of institutionalized power and their specific strategies of action. This type of pressure manifests itself mainly through demand, when the different social groups try to recover their positions in the distribution of income.

Subsequently, building on the foundational contributions of Noyola and Sunkel, both Pinto (1968) and Prebisch (1981) introduced the concept of social structure in an assertive and frontal form to explain the positions of institutionalized power that underlie the modification of relative prices that translates, synthetically, into the inflationary process.

Furthermore, in his last book Prebisch (1981) made an effort to link the theory of "social" structuralist inflation with a theory of power and surplus, in which the inflationary mechanism was associated with the distributive struggle through the logic of peripheral capitalism. This mechanism conspired against the development of peripheral democracy. Beyond the intrinsic merits or demerits of Prebisch's arguments, which for reasons of space we cannot address in this book, the vision of a theory of economic value that explains the dynamics of prices and the market on the basis of the institutionalized positions of power held by the actors in the social structure was once again expressed.

Values, markets and prices in the 21st century

The Latin American structuralist approach has always given central importance to the level and distribution of real income as a determinant of the behavior of effective demand that mobilizes the economic system. The contemporary process of globalization has modified both the causes and the effects of income distribution.

Structuralism rejects the notion of functional income distribution in the neoclassical sense that the remuneration of productive factors expresses their marginal productivity calculated under the assumption of perfect competition in the relevant markets. Strictly speaking, the ownership structure of the factors of production and of the markets in which they are traded depend to a large extent on the network of institutions that regulate the power positions of the individuals and families that control the factors of production.

Behind the distribution of income has always been the structure of ownership of strategic resources, both real and financial, which are traded in the markets. In fact, the analysis of social classes carried out by the classics and Marx was based on the position of landowners, peasants, financiers, industrial entrepreneurs and workers, among other social segments, in this structure.

In today's global world, this basic verification of a trans-historical nature acquires a specific embodiment. Among the real resources whose property rights largely determine the relevant prices are the so-called natural resources - arable land, forests, springs, ecosystems, mineral wealth, non-renewable energy sources - where supply is increasingly dependent on environmental and technological factors. Moreover, the ownership of "human capital" based on education has also become part of the privatization of knowledge linked to the stratification of labor markets. This factor has increased the importance of cultural power in the functioning of markets and prices. Moreover, political power is present through new rules of the game that increasingly "transnationalized" property rights.

The protagonists of this new era are transnational corporations and their property rights, which we could perhaps call "transnational rights", due to the ease with which they are transferred through stock exchange mechanisms, the fact that they have direct access to global financial capital and that they control cutting-edge technologies developed in their own research and development departments that allow them to increase their productivity gains.

A large part of the productivity profits of transnationals is generated in the affiliates and subsidiaries installed in peripheral societies (Di Filippo 1998). The mechanism for capturing the surplus lies precisely in the fact that they reach a "central" level of productivity (and profits) on the basis of "peripheral" wages.

In the modern era, the notion of center and periphery from the point of view of the world power structure has been linked to the mechanisms of creation and control of technological power. This "intangible power" (Ferrer

1996: 14) is generated in politically unified national societies as a result of their internal cultural dynamics.

The idea that the process of globalization has made it possible for transnational corporations to operate autonomously and independently of the political and cultural power of their countries of origin is a mirage. Firstly, because the great technological revolutions are the cultural fruit of the hegemonic countries, and secondly, because these companiesvstill require institutionalized rules of the game to enable them to operate on a global scale. The investment, services, intellectual property and other codes adopted by the World Trade Organization (WTO) are an example of these institutional frameworks.

For example, events such as the failure of negotiations for the Organization for Economic Cooperation and Development (OECD) to adopt the Multilateral Agreement on Investment (MAI) in 1998 led to an institutional vacuum that may have contributed to the current (2009) disastrous collapse of investment banks in the United States and its contagion to the rest of the world's weak financial architecture.

In fact, the growth processes that have taken place in Latin America since the 1990s are essentially a transplant of market institutions developed on a global scale, which are not always compatible with the political institutions of democracy. The frequent crises experienced in the last 20 years have been due to the absence of a "financial architecture" to regulate the behavior of the major transnational players.

First, the need for "own" institutions, adapted to transnational agents and markets and transcending the political and cultural frameworks of national States, has led to the proliferation of norms that set quality standards not only in procedural, sanitary or environmental matters - for example, the rules of the International Organization for Standardization (ISO) - but also in the political and economic fields - the case of the classification established by risk rating agencies such as Moody's - and, secondly, the need to have "own" institutions, adapted to transnational agents and markets and transcending the political and cultural frameworks of national States.

The quality standards required by international investors are set by inter-governmental bodies or private organizations, but of a global nature, on all kinds of issues: competitiveness, legal security, stability of macroeconomic policies and others. Although these are reasonable guidelines in view of the need to compete in a globalized world, one-size-fits-all recipes that do not take into consideration national or regional specificities have always been questionable.

In the area of dispute settlement between global investors and governmental authorities, agreements are often both multilateral and regional agreements containing clauses that hand over relevant jurisdiction to panels of experts who rule on environmental, health and even labor issues, "over and above" national and local regulations (Di Filippo 2008).

In the technological and productive sphere, there is no doubt that the aforementioned standards are backed by the enormous efficacy of the pragmatic methods of Western science in the terms analyzed by Furtado and examined in previous sections. These form part of the "intangible power" that is propagated from the great universities of the developed world and on which the technological future of humanity instrumentally depends.

However, there is also an attempt to transfer similar "objective" standards to the economic, social and political spheres, confusing neoliberal market dogmas with the theoretical foundations of economics, politics and culture.

Education tends to become, partially or totally, a commodity. The same happens with other public goods such as security (segregated residential neighborhoods), the administration of justice (high cost of legal advice) or the privatization of parks, beaches, highways and even public safety. The rules of the game inherent to the style of growth integrated into global capitalism were introduced into all political, economic and cultural institutions, establishing new positions of institutionalized power that ended up affecting the distribution of personal or family income, the geographic location of social classes and strata in the different neighborhoods of the large metropolises and the distribution of educational opportunities in those same areas, among other things.

As a result of these changes, the structuring of markets and prices, especially the institutions that regulate the supply and cost of the raw factors of production (labor and natural resources) and money, has been profoundly modified.

The global financial crisis of the neoliberal order

In a systemic analysis of the current global economic order, it is possible to establish a distinction between actors, technical and social structures, fields or locations occupied by the system and the processes or mechanisms used by the actors that move it. We will examine here the global economic system, distinguishing three main actors: i) the hegemonic centers, basically the United States and the European Union, which since the post-war period have been the "makers" of the international technical and social structures (rules); ii) the intergovernmental negotiation and credit agencies that administer and disseminate these rules of the game; and iii) the transnational corporations, which are the main beneficiaries of the new type of global transactions that have proliferated after the installation of information and communications technologies (ICTs).

Of course, the process of globalization understood in a multidimensional way includes other important transnational actors, starting with the great monotheistic churches, the transnational networks of universities and other cultural establishments and numerous non-governmental organizations of different types and orientations. However, in order to understand the current economic crisis of the global order, even the most cursory examination requires reference to at least the three actors mentioned above.

The actors in question interact within the framework of institutional structures monitored by multilateral organizations -WTO, International Monetary Fund (IMF), World Bank- and technological structures typical of today's information and communications age. The economic sphere in which the international system operates has expanded considerably with the inclusion of China, India and the Eastern European countries that formerly made up the Council for Mutual Economic Assistance (CAME). All of them are developing strategies and tactics aimed at increasing their control of global markets. However, the protagonists of the global era are the transnational corporations (Di Filippo 1998)

Following the failure of the negotiations for the adoption of the MAI, the transnational agents of the global system, particularly the US investment banks, favored and profited from the formation of successive speculative "bubbles".

The predominant neo-liberal vision, based on an individualism that was not only methodological - the whole is the sum of its parts - but also ethical - executives whose remuneration was directly linked to the sum of the parts - was not only a methodological one, but also an ethical one - executives whose remuneration was directly linked related to short-term corporate profits, gave free rein to the creation of transnational productive and financial networks on a global scale, without sufficient coordination and oversight.

To a certain extent, this neoliberal vision is also responsible for the enormous financial crisis that the world economy is experiencing today (2009), colloquially known as the subprime crisis. This was due, at least in part, to the creation of credit by investment banks (money supply) based on private or sectoral rationality, without taking into consideration the institutionalized positions of power of the contracting parties.

Information technologies have favored the creation of "plastic money" (debit and credit cards) and the spread of consumer credit, providing individuals and families with advance liquidity from wages not yet received to purchase durable goods. This type of credit has recently been extended to all types of consumer goods, including perishable goods purchased daily in supermarkets. In this way, a gap began to emerge between the liquidity or immediate purchasing power of debtors and their solvency at different maturities.

In conditions of what could be called "consumer over- indebtedness", investment bank executives overestimated the creditworthiness of mortgage borrowers to respond to the transactions they carried out. Moreover, the ability of monetary policy (interest rates and money creation) to re-establish equilibrium in the monetary- financial markets was overestimated. It is not possible to expand on this subject, but the monetary instrument, applied with a neoclassical mentality, has undoubtedly begun to fail.

Other explanations for the collapse of global capitalism (2009) include the fact that the monetary-financial sphere is not independent of the real sphere and that the creation of currency is not neutral, i.e., depending on the structural conditions of power in which it is carried out and the mechanisms used, it will generate winners and losers, passing through the relative prices of the product and of wealth to be finally reflected in the levels of activity and the distribution of income.

Within the framework of this unprecedented financial permissiveness, the "invisible hand" of the financial market has been subjected to the model of the "financial crisis" microeconomic business model of investment banks. Hyman Minsky (1992), whose ideas with strong Keynesian roots developed in the 1970s are currently in vogue because of the global crisis, considered three types of firms (financial or otherwise) from the point of view of their behavior in the credit markets: (i) "hedge units", capable of paying not only their interest but also their debts; (ii) "speculative units", capable of paying the interest but not the principal debt; and (iii) "Ponzi units", whose profitability depends on "bubbles" or artificially expanded markets through speculative feedbacks.

Minsky says: "The first theorem of the financial instability hypothesis is that the economy has financial regimes under which it is stable, and financial regimes under which it is unstable. The second theorem of the financial instability hypothesis is that during periods of prolonged prosperity, the economy transitions from financial relationships that make possible the existence of a stable system to financial relationships that make possible (or promote) the existence of an unstable system" (Minsky 1992: 8).

This behavior of individual players in the framework of a financial system with highly permissive regimes and institutions, culturally legitimized on the basis of a neoliberal individualistic ethics, has favored financial frauds based on "Ponzi models" such as the Madoff scandal, a swindle that, according to preliminary estimates, reached an amount of 50 billion of American Dollars.

It is not possible to expand on this topic, but the systemic examination of the structuralist approach suggests that when the regulatory regimes, structures and institutions of global capitalism are relaxed, or their design depends on the microeconomic rationality of companies, transnational operators exceed their attributions and responsibilities and try to increase their profits to the "limit" of what their positions of institutionalized power allow them to do. This limit was exceeded in late 2008 and early 2009, leading to the collapse of the US financial system and a global crisis that is now spreading to the real economy with uncertain long-term consequences.

Chapter XII

Latin American Structuralism and the notion of power[36]

A meaningful way to evaluate the contributions and limitations of the structuralist current of political economy that was born in Latin America in the 1950s is, as we suggest in these notes, to frame it within a systemic approach that allows us to support the concept of power asymmetries applicable to human societies. What characterizes this current of thought is that its economic categories can be articulated around the concept of structured (asymmetries of) power, examined multidimensionally. This approach makes possible a theoretical articulation of economic issues with other dimensions of human societies, such as socio-cultural and political ones. Therefore, the concepts of system and of structured power to which we will be speaking are of a multidimensional nature.

Introduction

The ideas that are used in this chapter are based on the diagnoses and proposals of the "last Prebisch" reflected in his book *"Peripheral Capitalism. Crisis and Transformation"* (1981), in which he tries to assimilate and synthesize not only all the experiences of his long public and intellectual life, but also the work of many Latin American thinkers who were influenced by his ideas,

---

[36] Article published in "Revista Ejes de Economía y Desarrollo", Vol. 2 no. 2 (2018), Universidad Nacional de Entre Ríos, Argentina.

Also this ideas contributed to the development of the current of thought known as Latin American Structuralism. One of the features that, in addition to Prebisch himself, is clearly present in the most prominent representatives (Celso Furtado, Osvaldo Sunkel, Aníbal Pinto, and Aldo Ferrer) of this school of thought was the multidimensionality of their approaches and, in particular, the use of the notion of power (Di Filippo 2009 and 2012).

Within the framework of his conceptualizations of the economic system and of the social structure of the Latin American periphery, Prebisch observed that:

> As technology penetrates the social structure, changes occur which are reflected in the structure of power. The intermediate strata expand and, as the process of democratization advances, their trade union and political power is increasingly deployed and counterposed to the economic power of those who, especially in the upper strata, concentrate most of the means of production. Likewise, it is mainly in these strata that the labor force with social power is to be found. These power relations between the upper and intermediate strata are manifested both in the orbit of the market and in that of the State. Thus, an ever-increasing pressure to share the fruits of productivity growth unfolds. And as this sharing is achieved, the imitation of the forms of consumption of the centers tends to spread downward socially, especially in the intermediate strata. But privilege is especially concentrated in the upper strata.
>
> This double pressure [from the orbits of the market and the State] is manifested through an increase in the remuneration of the labor force, either to improve its participation in the fruit of productivity, or to compensate for the unfavorable incidence of certain factors, especially the tax burdens that fall, directly or indirectly, on it and with which the State confronts the trend towards its growth.
>
> Bureaucratic and military power have their own dynamics in the State apparatus, supported by political power, mainly of the intermediate strata. And in favor of it [i.e. in favor of that dynamic], state activities unfold beyond economic considerations, both in terms of the amount and diversification of its services and the spurious absorption of labor power

> In this means, the State, through the growth of employment and social services, tries to correct the absorptive insufficiency of the system and its distributive inequity, which is an important factor in its hypertrophy.
>
> Expressed in a few words: the distribution of the outcome of the growing productivity of the system is fundamentally the result of the changing play of power relations, without excluding, of course, individual differences in capacity and dynamism (Prebisch 1981: 42)

Contents of some basic concepts

In what follows, this article attempts to conceptually frame the notions of system, social structure, and power, drawing freely on the ideas of Latin American structuralism in general, and Prebisch in particular, with the aim of highlighting the theoretical and practical importance of these categories used in his argumentation. All the forms of power (trade union, political, economic, social, bureaucratic, military, etc.) of which Prebisch speaks in the long quotation above are intrinsically dynamic and, therefore, are either structured or in the process of structuring or destructuring, and all of them are influenced, directly or indirectly, by technical change.

All the notions of power used by Prebisch are articulated with his concerns for the distribution of the benefits of technical progress among the groups or strata that contribute to its formation. In particular, he stresses the importance of economic power based on the possession of productive means; of social power linked to human qualifications that improve market positioning; and of union power based on the association of workers for the defense of their professional, economic and labor interests.

Furthermore, Prebisch speaks of the State for its significance in the distribution of the fruits of technical progress, and within the orbit of the State he also mentions bureaucratic power and military power. The following reflections do not intend to impose a unique or dogmatic interpretation of what Prebisch and the structuralist trend he led said or wanted to say, but simply draw on some of his central arguments in order to discuss the subject freely. The aim is then to contribute to an academic debate on the current validity of Latin American structuralism regarding issues that go to the very essence of both structuralist economic theory and structuralist political economy.

With this perspective in mind, the contents of some key concepts associated with the subject are analyzed below.

Systems: Following Mario Bunge (1999), a philosopher who influenced ECLAC's thinking, a system could be understood as any complex object whose parts are linked by stable ties of some kind that constitute its structure. A concrete system (as opposed to a theoretical system) exists objectively and has a physical basis. Therefore the central feature of any concrete system is that it is in a permanent process of change. A historically determined human society can be seen as a concrete, intrinsically dynamic social system, the parts of which are persons (or associations/organizations made up of persons), and the constitutive links of its structure are technical and social rules actually in force. It is worth stressing that from an epistemological point of view structuralist thought is clearly systemic.

Institutions: Those rules internalized in habitual behavior can be called institutions, on the basis of which the social structure is built. The power held by social actors derives from the position occupied in these institutions. In the American institutionalist tradition founded by Thorstein Veblen (1904) and John Commons (1934), the habits of mind governing collective action have been emphasized as defining features of the notion of institutions.
Moreover, in the Latin American structuralist tradition, the emphasis has been placed on the central importance of technical progress in the dynamics of economic development and in the distribution of its benefits, and the features of these dynamics in peripheral economies have been examined. In both theoretical traditions, the approach is multidimensional and does not admit economistic reductionism.

Power: For Latin American structuralism, the power of social actors depends on their location in the structures. Having said this, the notions of structured power and institutionalized power that we will use in this essay are to a certain extent synonymous, given the above nuances. It is a matter of agreeing in which sense they will be used. In the sphere of production technical rules dominates, and in the sphere of markets social rules dominates. Technical rules establish a person-thing link (operation of a machine or any utensil) while social rules directly establish person-person links (for example, those governed by family law). In the Latin American structuralist theory of development, the distribution of technical change and its benefits occupies a central place and, from this point of view, in order to emphasize the aspects inherent to the structure of production, it could be considered as structured productive power or productive power in the process of structuring.

In a broad sense, the term institutions (whether formal or informal) can encompass both technical and social rules, but in a narrow sense, more commonly used by conservative neo-institutionalism (Douglass North, for example), it usually refers only to social rules. Hence the convenience of using the term structured power, which explicitly encompasses also the technical rules so essential in the structuralist discourse. In summary, for Latin American structuralism the concept of structured power can be seen as the position occupied by people in the basic social structures, including most prominently and emphatically the structures of property and production.

Social actors can be broadly defined as legal persons (all types of organizations and associations) but, strictly speaking, the concept of power can only be applied to natural persons (i.e. actual human beings)

Social structure: In Max Weber's perspective (1973, 1974) the notion of social relations (as opposed to the more diffuse idea of human interactions) presupposes the belief in reciprocal expectations of behavior, whether this belief is based on calculable probabilities or on the everyday practice of the links between human beings. Power as we have defined it for the purposes of this essay is, it should be emphasized, structured power and rests on such behavioral expectations. Some of these expectations of ancient ethical or religious roots are deeply rooted in the culture of peoples, but others, of a political or even economic nature, tend to undergo a process of change. of a political or even economic nature tend to undergo more frequent modifications, for example, in the technical sphere (person-thing relations). Even so, to the extent that they are internalized as rules of behavior, they are part of the structured forms of power. Behind scientific-technical power lie the achievements of cultural systems, as is the case with the pragmatic views of Western science. On the basis of these arguments, the social structure can be examined, as the Latin

American structuralists do, from the point of view of the power structure inherent in it.
The cultural forms of structured power are associated with the legitimized control of organizations and technologies that allow the mass provision of information, communication and knowledge. The power of science is the cultural form underlying technical progress and the distribution of its fruits. In this era of information, communication and knowledge technologies (ICT), the forms of cultural power (and its manipulation by economic power) are becoming increasingly important. The political forms of structured power are associated with the legitimized control of constitutional rules of the game on which the organization of the State is based. The legitimized control of thepublic bureaucracies and the armed forces are essential prerogatives of state power.
Finally, the economic forms of structured power are associated with the legitimized control (property rights) of the organizations and technologies of production, circulation and consumption.
The economic forms of structured power that we are interested in delving into here are those that predominate in capitalist societies. In the first place, this power is expressed, as we have already said, as productive power that expands through the incorporation of technological progress originating in the development of pragmatic science. Second, economic power is expressed through markets under the specific modality of general purchasing power exercised in markets through the use of money. General purchasing power is an economic measure of (and is fed by) all forms of social power and not only those of economic power. This is why we say that in terms of the issue of economic value governing markets, the so- called "power-value" theories here are multidimensional and are not exhausted in the specifically economic field. This is because most goods and services, both private and public, that are socially distributed, although technically they are not commodities, use the market mechanism or at least are accounted for according to market values that need to be expressed in units of purchasing power.

Economic theory: The original neoclassical economists (with their utilitarian marginalist theories of value) considered both the influence of the State and cultural institutions as factors external to positive economics. That is, they considered such influence as external data not clearly linked to pure economic theory, and explicitly isolated their theories through the methodological criterion céteris páribus. In particular, for the neoclassicals, the only ethics that penetrates economic theory is utilitarian ethics through the notions of marginal utility and welfare. Furthermore, Marx (through his Ricardian theory of value formulated in abstract terms in his work "Capital") also closed the

Theoretical field that the cultural and political subsystems could exert on the economic system in general and on the operation of markets in particular. Structuralists, on the opposite, clearly affirming a multidimensional perspective, through the notion of power, open the game to all these causal influences that end up affecting the operation of markets and the formation of prices.

Stable equilibrium: The issue of the stable equilibrium of markets is fundamental in the formulation of unidimensional theories of economic value, because the relative prices taken into consideration are obviously those of equilibrium, i.e. those that will be maintained as long as some of the conditions affecting the behavior of the different markets do not change. The point to be emphasized here is to examine whether political conditions can radically and definitively affect the conditions of stable market equilibrium. And this is obviously true in several strategic markets. It should be reiterated that the political conditions referred to are those referring to stable and legitimate rules that are part of public policies and that do not only integrate the management of economic policy. This broad consideration of the political power of the State is a very clear part of the Latin American structuralist theoretical approach.

Political economy: The links between political systems and the relative price system depend on the capacity of political power to influence a set of strategic markets which, on the supply or demand side of final goods, influence almost all other relative prices. We are not talking here about direct intervention in markets through the setting of maximum or minimum prices or quotas. Nor are we talking about protectionist measures aimed at isolating markets or authoritarian forms of centralized planning, but about the establishment of general public policy regulations which, for clearly extra-economic reasons, have an impact on the structure of these markets.

For structuralist political economy, the political power of the state and the ethical aspects of equity are inextricably linked to its theory of prices and markets.

Fictitious goods: One of the methods through which the totality of the social structure affects market valorizations has been highlighted by Karl Polanyi. From his book "The Great Transformation" (1944) it is worth mentioning here his notion of fictitious commodities referring to labor power, natural resources and money. None of these three alleged "commodities", denounced by Polanyi as fictitious, are produced to be sold in the market, and the institutions that regulate them are three of the main sources of power that affect the economic value of all other genuine commodities. In this sense, Polanyi remarks:

> The social history of the nineteenth century was thus the result of a twofold movement: the extension of market organization regarding genuine commodities was accompanied by its restriction regarding fictitious commodities. While markets spread over the face of the globe and the quantity of goods involved grew to unbelievable proportions, a network of measures and policies was embedded in powerful institutions designed to curb the action of the market in relation to labor, land and money (127).

First, labor is the fictitious commodity where political conditions can most clearly affect significantly the relative prices of all final products. Modifications in labor codes, social security, welfare, etc. can permanently change the cost of labor at different skill levels. Other public policies, such as immigration policy, can and do affect the relative abundance of workers of different skills in each differentiable segment of the labor market. Therefore, when regulatory reforms affect the labor market and change the pre- existing conditions of supply and demand, changes are generated in the cost structures of enterprises, causing an effect on the prices of the social product on the supply side. Massive migrations also produce changes in the distribution of income between wages and property remuneration, as well as between the different segments of the labor market.

Second, natural resources are also a crucial fictitious commodity, especially for understanding the social and economic formation of peripheral regions in general and Latin America in particular. The distribution of land and natural resources, as well as the production and export of primary products (intensive in the use of natural resources) is a defining factor in the peripheral positioning of Latin America. But beyond these crucial circumstances specific to Latin American history, even today, in the 21st century, the turbulent conditions of the biosphere (extinction of plant and animal species, pollution, contamination and global warming, etc.) accentuate the fictitious commodity character of natural resources. For instance, the need for environmental protection to prevent the extinction of certain plant or animal species, or the preservation of biodiversity, can lead to regulations that affect the supply of strategic natural resources. Recently, the proliferation of natural catastrophes such as droughts, floods, typhoons, tidal waves and earthquakes have also modified the long-term conditions of many markets for final goods and services, including, of course, tourism. Other political considerations associated with the control of nautical miles off the coasts of countries with maritime coasts, or with international treaties, also affect natural resource markets from the political sphere. Third, money: finally, Polanyi himself eloquently illustrates the fictitious commodity character of money. Referring to the turbulent 1930s, but interpreting facts and perturbations applicable to the present time, he observes:

> The currency had become the pivot of national policy. Under a modern monetary economy, no one could fail to experience daily the contraction or expansion of the financial rod; populations became currency conscious; the effect of inflation on real income was discounted in advance by the masses; men and women everywhere seemed to regard stable money as the supreme necessity of human society. But such an awareness was inseparable from the recognition that the fundamentals of currency might depend on political factors located outside national boundaries. Thus, the "*bouleversement*" [change, disruption, shock] that shook confidence in inherent instability also destroyed the naive concept of financial sovereignty in an interdependent economy. Henceforth, internal crises associated with currency would tend to provoke serious external controversies (Polanyi 1944: 71-72).

In the face of this type of historical events that are constantly occurring, "pure" theories of economic value of a unidimensional type that close the field to the political sphere through "ceteris paribus" assumptions or based on "purely economic" considerations are not sufficient for an adequate understanding of the valorization process that operates concretely in the markets.

Especially in this era of globalized capitalism and more generally, the entire multidimensional system (economic, political, cultural, environmental and international relations) on which the functioning of

> the social structure rests, as it evolves, is permanently modifying the situation of markets, business expectations and the conditions of productive investment. This global or planetary vision of capitalism has been present since the origins of Latin American structuralist thought through its formulation of the center-periphery system of international relations.
>
> *Dependency:* If we focus on peripheral economies, through the notion of dependency, widely understood in an abstract way (and not necessarily acceptable to some versions of Latin American dependency theories), we can now link the concept of structured power with that of human needs raised at the individual, group or macro-social level.
> Human needs are the most permanent foundation of the habitual nature of social behavior; they generate a dependence on the part of those who experience them, on those who are in a position to satisfy them. This argument can be transferred to the macro-social scale at both the national and international levels: the needs of the peripheral nations generate situations of dependence in relation to the nations that are in a position to satisfy them. These situations of dependence in center-periphery relations, especially in the economic sphere, are to some degree reciprocal (they affect both centers and peripheries) and are at the basis of the existence of markets, but they tend to be asymmetrical, operating to the benefit of the centers. This legitimizes to some extent the more generally accepted concept in Western academia of asymmetric interdependencies (Gilpin 1987: 17).

Returning to the more abstract and general notions that can be used within national societies, the conceptual sequence: i) people in need of specific satisfiers; ii) people who control the provision of those satisfiers; iii) dependence of the former on the latter; iv) position of power of the latter held with respect to the former, generates causal links useful for providing an explanation of the forms of power that structuralists have emphasized in several of their intellectual contributions. Through their concern with the issue of development styles, the ECLAC economists and the structuralists in particular were deeply involved in the subject of basic needs as an essential reference point for the study of economic value and distributive structures.

An outstanding philosophical precedent for this conceptual linkage can be traced in the Aristotelian idea that the interdependence of human needs is the essential bond of social life and the basis of all economic transactions, which require money as a measure of the terms of exchange. Money in turn is conceived by Aristotle directly as an institutional product derived from the existence of political society (Polis or state). Aristotle's (1978) approach to economic science is thus clearly institutional. This last statement is reinforced if we recall that for Aristotle virtues are habits of behavior, and human needs are presented on a daily or periodic basis through the existing institutions associated with their satisfaction.

Each of the dimensions of human needs involves specific human behaviors that leave physical traces that can be studied with the instruments and methods of science. The dimensions (biological-environmental, economic, political and cultural) of a social system, examined as subsystems, are a human abstraction of a theoretical nature and are based on one side on an introspective knowledge of what we humans know to be our own needs and on the other side on a scientific knowledge based on the external meaning of the behaviors and instruments that can be studied in the fields that are considered to be theoretically relevant.

The deterministic nature of inherited economic thinking

The deterministic character of Marx's thought has been rightly insisted upon. In the prologue to his work "Capital", Marx affirms that human beings are understood as personifications of economic categories (see page XV of the prologues to volume I of "Capital"):

> A couple of words to avoid possible misunderstandings. In this work the figures of the capitalist and the landowner are not painted, far from it, in a rosy color. But it should be noted that we are only referring here to persons as personifications of economic categories, as representatives of certain class interests. Whoever, like me, conceives the development of the economic formation of society as a natural historical process, cannot hold the individual responsible for the existence of relations of which he is socially a creature, although subjectively he considers himself to be far above them (Marx 1968: xv).

There is also determinism in the original neoclassical visions where "economic man" is an "optimizing machine" that always and blindly obeys instrumental rationality until the markets of perfect competition reach optimal positions of stable general equilibrium.

One might then ask what Prebisch says on this subject: "Is there determinism in the system? We have discussed the various forms of power and the relations between them, and we have also explained how the interplay of these relations leads, over time, to the crisis of power". Here Prebisch (1981) refers to the crisis of the social system under the dynamics of peripheral capitalism that he studied in his last book; and he continues:

> But nothing has been said so far about the actors in development, except for some considerations about social mobility. The various forms of power are expressed through different actors and among them stand out those who have the greatest capacity and dynamism in the performance of their role, both to take advantage of favorable conditions for development - both in the domestic and international arenas - and to try to overcome and counteract unfavorable changes in these conditions.

It is, in fact, a deliberate action of the actors to respond to their aspirations and interests according to the intensity of their power and aptitudes. In any case, this unfolds within the system and in correspondence with the structural mutations that take place within it.

> In the course of the development of the centers, certain principles and their corresponding rules of the game have emerged, which the periphery has tried to follow in order to achieve the regular functioning of the system. But these are not automatic; the opportunity and manner of applying them depend on the aptitude and decision of the actors. And this refers both to their regular functioning and to the rules to be followed when the system has been disturbed by violations of those principles (Prebisch 1981: 166)

If the deterministic belief in the stable equilibrium arising from market dynamics (present in the "pure" theories of Ricardo [natural prices], Marx [law of value] and the neoclassicists [perfect competition]) is abandoned. The long-run trend towards crisis proposed by Prebisch (1981) then acquires special relevance and intelligibility. However, this conclusion does not contain the inexorability of any determinism, but rather induces us to propose profound transformations of a systemic nature to peripheral capitalism, which presuppose an explicit consideration of the power structures of the periphery.

The theories of economic value and the concept of market power

Unidimensional theories of economic value: It has already been observed that there are two groups of theories of economic value that, explicitly or implicitly, have been supported by the main currents of economic thought. The first group is composed of those that, using a closed theoretical field, have defined theories of economic value based on the concept of stable market equilibrium. The fundamental scaffolding of orthodox or current (neoclassical) academic economic theory and of classical economic theory in the versions of Ricardo and Marx has been built on these theories of competitive markets. The fundamental feature of these theories is that, at the operational level of markets, there are no asymmetries of power and therefore goods are exchanged for their value. This value can be referred to the labor content of the goods (Ricardian/Marxian view) or to the utility and scarcity (marginalist view) of the goods being exchanged.

It is true that Marx, in his great vision of history and in his considerations of a political nature elaborated in other works, introduces multidimensional approaches associated with the themes of the role of the State, exploitation and class struggle. But as regards his economic theory proper in its most abstract and general formulation (volume one of "Capital") Marx also presents a one-dimensional theory of economic value, understood as the average social abstract labor time contained in each commodity.

According to his so-called "law of value" in the realm of markets there are no asymmetries of power and all products are exchanged strictly on the basis of their value. The collapse of capitalism will be, for this author, a response to the development of the productive forces, to its impact on the relations of production, and to the dynamics of the class struggle. In the meantime, however, he accepts the "law of value" as the guiding principle of the relations of exchange in the market.

Subsequently, academic economic theory, both in the neoclassical and Marxist traditions, incorporated situations of "imperfect" competition (monopoly, oligopoly, etc.). Although it must be recognized that this was a decisive step in favor of the realism of these theories, the argumentation remained economistic in the sense that it only referred to economic power, but did not link it to the role of the State and political power, especially in relation to the fictitious commodities we have considered above.

The limitations of stable general equilibrium: Let us briefly examine the theoretical justifications of stable general equilibrium. In the history of economic thought, as we have already pointed out, the two theories of value on which this concept is clearly based are, on one side, the Ricardian-Marxian one according to which the value of a commodity corresponds to its labor content and, on the other side, the neoclassical marginalist one in its Walrasian version, according to which under conditions of perfect competition the prices of productive factors correspond to their marginal productivities (marshallian version) and, additionally, in the sphere of consumption the marginal preferences between two goods are considered proportional to their possible rates of substitution in consumption. In both cases the existence of forms of commutative justice is assumed which, in different ways, ensure the equality of considerations. In this second case, the equality of considerations is verified for the marginal unit traded, and there exists, in terms of "welfare" for the rest of the units, the theoretical notion of producer and consumer surplus.

Within the framework of these theories of value, the first of the above-mentioned versions (especially Marx's) is holistic because market economic values depend unilaterally on the technological conditions of production that transversally determine the amount of social labor contained in commodities. The second version is individualistic because prices measure the utility and scarcity of the goods being traded based on the opinion of individual consumers who exercise "sovereignty" by determining their scales or maps of preferences.

The neoliberal view of the subject: The contemporary neoliberal current, for example, in the views of Hayek and Nozik, has finally abandoned the neoclassical marginalist approach to utility and welfare in order to return to the will of the contracting parties. Thus, a price corresponding to any market transaction would be a fair price (commutative justice) if it expresses the "free will" of the participants in the transaction. It is the will of the owners that determines the conditions of supply, and it is the will of the solvent demanders (owners of purchasing power) that determines the conditions of demand. But remembering that power is defined precisely as the probability of imposing one's own will on third parties, neoliberals "come clean" by ultimately laying bare the crude reality of structured power. Under these premises, the issue of asymmetries or inequalities of power, i.e. the conditions of distributive injustice or inequity, are left out of the analysis, because when a transaction is consummated it has expressed the "sovereign will" of the contracting parties.

Therefore, in the language of game theory (a view originally developed by the conservative side of the new institutional economics), the "players" try to impose their will and reach a certain score that favors them in the game, but if they fail to do so, they manifest their "will" to accept the outcome. This view, applied to markets, accepts the existence of oligopoly, so that the conditions of stable equilibrium (Nash equilibrium) assume that there is no perfect competition and that each "major player" takes into consideration the behavior of the other "major players" to define his own equilibrium situation. It is becoming increasingly clear that "power" is the real name of the game.

Transaction: The concept of transaction, common to all strands of institutional economics but little used by the Latin American structuralist current, is essentially microeconomic. The transaction is, in essence, a social market relationship, and expresses a confrontation of wills. This confrontation generates asymmetrical interdependencies in the sense already explained above, and configures a situation of power, in which the reciprocal probabilities of imposing the will of the respective contracting parties are measured.

This measure ends up being expressed in prices, quantities and conditions of the operation in question. This whole process is essentially microeconomic and, among the founding fathers of American institutionalism, was especially studied by John Commons (1995).

The "micro" concept of market transaction reaches a very relevant meaning in pre-capitalist societies, such as an Arab bazaar where bargaining is an essential part of the rules of the game. As capitalism has been consolidated, we are increasingly witnessing transactions that do not admit bargaining because they are highly regulated down to the smallest details, for example, in bourse transactions, adhesion contracts, etc. Thus, the substance of transactions depends more and more on the technical and institutional rules that regulate them. This consolidates the forms of structured power.

On the other hand, the founding fathers of Latin American structuralism did not make much theoretical use of the concept of transaction, among other things because their central concern was economic development (productivity gains, surplus per worker, accumulation of this surplus, etc.). In this macroeconomic vision, the concept of transaction is implicit in the operation of markets; however, there is a structurally founded macroeconomic theory of prices, with genuine Latin American structuralist roots, linked to the bargaining power of Latin American workers.

The structuralist view of market power and Keynesian theory

Wealth and capital: Economic power is a structured power that ultimately acquires the labor of others, whether in potential form, in the form of services, or crystallized in products. This notion was originally formulated by Adam Smith, and expressed with extreme clarity in The Wealth of Nations. Capital in Marx's interpretations embodied in his main work is also, and above all, a product of power structured under the rules of the game of capitalism, but for this author this power only manifests itself in the sphere of production (production relations) but does not operate in the sphere of markets where the law of value governs (Di Filippo 2012)

Effective demand: Adam Smith introduced the concept of effective demand, understood as the use of the necessary and sufficient purchasing power to place any commodity on the market.

In the macroeconomic sphere, the idea of effective demand, also taken up by Malthus, acquires its maximum force in Keynes, who attacks the two pillars on which the neoclassical school of thought was based: full employment and equilibrium under conditions of perfect competition. Keynes did so, in a diagnosis applicable to developed economies, by emphasizing, first, that there can be an economically inefficient and socially unjust disequilibrium (unemployment), which, however, is stable in the labor market. It will be an imbalance because not all those who want to (express their willingness to) work at a given wage will find employment. This disequilibrium can be stable if there are permanent deficiencies in aggregate demand and remain stable without reaching the position of full employment promised by Say's law. Second, the labor market, in the economies of the developed societies Keynes studied, operated under institutional conditions (e.g., union power) that modeled a special labor supply curve.

Keynes' macroeconomic perspective is fundamental for understanding the approaches of Latin American structuralist political economy. A fundamental difference between the U.S. institutional vision and the Latin American structural vision is that the latter focuses centrally on the theory of development from a peripheral perspective, which requires a macroeconomic vision. It is true that the subject of economic development can also be approached at the microeconomic level and even, recently, at what has come to be called the "mesoeconomic" level, where the economic power of transnational corporations operates. However, in terms of distributive inequalities, the issue of equity, which is central to the structuralist approach, requires macroeconomic measurements for the formulation of public policies relating to consumption, production, wealth, etc.

Therefore, unlike the U.S. institutional approach whose founding fathers predate Keynes, the main Latin American structuralists could not do without the Keynesian theoretical framework. Consider, for example, the work of Prebisch (1963), Noyola, Sunkel and Aníbal Pinto on the structural causes of Latin American inflation. Recall also Prebisch's (1947) book on Keynesian economics.

The terms of trade deterioration thesis

The formal and informal rules that regulate the organization of workers' union power are fundamental data in the thesis of the deterioration of the terms of trade elaborated by Prebisch.

The notion of transaction depends on the technological and institutional rules prevailing in each human society, precisely because the imposition of will, i.e. the exercise of power, is structurally conditioned. And the degree of structuring has been deepening in direct relation to the consolidation and development of capitalist economic systems. By transversally affecting all transactions of the same type, structures condition macroeconomic magnitudes. Hence the crucial role played in this interpretation by the concept of structured power.

These existing rules, which we call structures, are not only economic, but also derive from the other subsystems that make up the "system of systems" that we have defined as human society. The feature of any transaction is that it involves an agreement of wills, but of wills framed by the technological and institutional rules in force. This is the case, for example, with an institutional system that does not recognize labor rights, where workers try to exercise unstructured factual power, for example by initiating an unauthorized strike, but if they are outside the labor institutions, their wills only express an unstructured form of power and will surely be repressed.

Here, for example, the field opens up for acute social conflicts when certain actions, such as strikes, are internalized in workers' expectations, but formal institutions have ceased to support them, for example with the passing of new and more repressive labor laws.

In short, the concept of transaction is eminently microeconomic and expresses the confrontation of wills within a market relationship. There is in it a sphere of contractual freedom where transactions can be seen as the moves of a game whose rules are established. This is the sphere where the economic categories of conservative neo- institutional microeconomics mainly prevail.

Moreover, the notion of norm or general regulation is rather macroeconomic, it expresses the technical and social rules that underlie the moves that are expressed in each transaction. This is the sphere where economic, political and cultural categories prevail, which are the ultimate foundation of the theory of prices proper to Latin American structuralist macroeconomics.

Keynes strongly influenced Raul Prebisch's ideas regarding the center-periphery system. Strictly speaking, the deterioration of the terms of trade is a macroeconomic explanation that is strongly based on the concept of effective demand and on the technological and institutional rules that regulated trade in primary products as opposed to trade in manufactured goods.

The first part of the explanation for the deterioration of the terms of trade, especially influenced by the Keynesian view, refers to the external demand for primary products supplied by Latin America, which tended to slow down, and the peripheral demand for manufactures supplied by the central countries, which tended to accelerate.

Regarding the central (or centric) demand for primary products, two factors influenced its slowdown, first, due to the technological rules of manufacturing production in the centers, there tended to be a reduction of the primary component in the final value of manufactured goods as technical progress (miniaturization, synthetic products, recycling, etc.) was introduced into production methods. Second, the technical and institutional rules of consumption were expressed in the so-called Engel laws (German statistician) on the behavior of family baskets, so that as average income increased, the component of expenditure on food and less processed products in total consumer spending was reduced (Prebisch 1950).

Regarding asymmetries between the cost of the international supply of peripheral primary products vis-à-vis the respective cost of supply internationalization of centrally-located manufactures, the unmistakable structuralist arguments of this explanation included the low union power in wage transactions on the part of peripheral workers in primary export activities in the face of productivity gains derived from the introduction of technical progress. This low union power expressed their disadvantaged position in the institutional structure regulating labor relations, associated, among other factors, with rural social inequality in Latin America.

Structural heterogeneity and the different forms of power

Rural social inequality, which explained the low bargaining power of Latin American workers, was the starting point that opened the game to other social scientists to highlight the serious problems of structural heterogeneity, internal colonialism, etc., derived from the Latin American colonial heritage and its pragmatic exploitation by the oligarchies prevailing in rural areas, especially during the period 1950-1980.

The notion of structural heterogeneity, typical of Latin American structuralism, seeks to express this historical crystallization of aggregate social inequalities over time, which on a macroeconomic scale can be judged in the light of different principles of distributive justice. Therefore, the structuralist theory of economic value, which explains the trend of market prices (including the international terms of trade), not only alludes to the asymmetric inter-dependencies of microeconomic transactions, but also to the distributive inequities and injustices measured by the cross- cutting structures that regulate macroeconomic flows.

Of course, the notion of structural heterogeneity understood from a historical-structural perspective, and associated with the idea of asynchrony in historical change (Gino Germani), acquired richness and variety in the contributions of sociologists who also explicitly or implicitly implied the issues of structured power asymmetries (Medina Echavarría, Graciarena, Gurrieri, Stavenhagen, González Casanova, etc.)

The political and cultural diagnoses of all these Latin American authors gave social and historical support to the explanation provided by the theory of the deterioration of the terms of trade elaborated by Prebisch, when studying the deep causes of the precarious organizational and bargaining power of workers incorporated into export activities. The international counterpart of this situation was verified in the workers of the highly industrialized central societies that produced the manufactures exported to the peripheries, who were able to appropriate a substantial part of the profits of the technical progress that was being incorporated, giving rise on the side of manufacturing costs to a closed appropriation of the productivity gains, translated into an increase in real wages and maintenance of the international prices of the exported products.

This meant that, in the labor markets, the transactions through which the real wages of central and peripheral workers were determined reflected the greater union power of the former to appropriate their productivity gains in a closed manner.

Note then that Prebisch's reasoning in his center-periphery vision is systemic and multidimensional in the sense already explained at the beginning of this essay. The center-periphery system is composed of national or supranational states (such as the European Union today) linked by asymmetrical technological and institutional nexuses, giving rise to distributive injustices based on different positions in the structures that grant power on an inter-national scale. The structures involved include not only those that regulate international economic relations but also those internal to the national societies of each State. For example, trade union relations in developed countries contribute to the explanation of the deterioration of the terms of trade. They include considering the bargaining power of workers, and verifying the existence of a social pact between the main actors in developed societies (employers, workers and government). The so-called French regulationist school, which can also be included in the family of institutionalist views, called the institutional complexes on which this pact was founded "Fordism".

The concept of surplus and asymmetries of power in the ideas of Prebisch and Furtado

At the end of his life, Prebisch, in his last book, explicitly deepened a conviction that had accompanied him throughout his intellectual career: that a theory of development and underdevelopment could not be built on a purely economic basis, but must necessarily include other variables, expressible through the power structure. And so he defined, in addition to economic power and the political power of the State, other dimensions of power (trade union and social) that also operate in the determination of prices and affect the distribution of real income. Prebisch's entire argument, in its specifically economic dimension, was developed in macroeconomic terms, including the dynamic mechanism of appropriation of what he called the surplus. This specific mechanism is a complex and debatable notion that for reasons of space cannot be developed here.

Like Raúl Prebisch, within the Latin American structuralist current Celso Furtado also developed explanations of the economic process that implied the rescue of power asymmetries from which specific situations of distributive (in)justice were evidenced. The point here does not lie in the ethical positions of these authors with respect to social inequalities, but in the scientific interpretations that, from a macroeconomic perspective, end up explaining the development process as tinged by social inequalities that ultimately depend on the entire structure of the societies that develop. There are "some examples" in a book by Furtado where this reading of the process of economic development, of its systemic framework, and of its multidimensional character are summarized as follows:

> The strategic points of this process [the economic process] are the possibility of increasing productivity and the appropriation by minority groups of the benefits of this increase. These two factors are what ultimately make growth possible. In truth, if the resources incorporated into the productive process did not cause a real increase in productivity, accumulation would not determine any growth, being limited to the following to transfer in time the act of consumption. Moreover, if the occasional or permanent fruit of productivity were distributed among the population as a whole, the result would be only an occasional or permanent increase in the level of consumption, the economy passing from one stationary position to another, without giving rise to a growth process.
>
> In an economy that has reached a certain degree of development, production is structured in such a way that accumulation becomes an almost automatic process. From the outset, for the productive machinery to function normally, it is indispensable that demand should also present a certain composition. Now the composition of demand is determined by the distribution of income, that is, by the way in which the different groups appropriate the product. It can therefore be concluded that the structure of production, the part of production that goes to accumulation and to income distribution, all have the same fundamental causes. These depend on the institutional system that is articulated around the process of appropriation of the surplus (Furtado 1961: 120 and 121).

Furtado's reflections, like those of Prebisch, make a systemic distinction, on one side, between relevant social actors linked by power ties that make up the production, distribution and consumption structures of the economic subsystem. But, for both authors, these structures depend on the institutional system that is articulated around the process of appropriation of the surplus.

Furtado's concept of surplus is very simple and intuitive; it refers to the remaining social product above the survival needs of the population engaged in unskilled manual activities. This implies that Furtado defines his concept of surplus starting from the concept of subsistence needs. This idea was formalized in some detail in his "Preface to New Political Economy". This point also justifies the abstract conceptual links we have established between the concepts of need, dependence and power. These links are precisely what Furtado refers to when he highlights the institutional system that is articulated around the process of appropriation of the surplus.

But, as Furtado himself repeatedly pointed out, one of the essential epistemological problems facing social science is the level of abstraction at which the issues are raised. At the highest level of abstraction the human nature or condition is transhistorical. If it were not transhistorical, that is, if it did not cross all past, present and future civilizations, history would lack a common link because it would have lost its human sense. That sense that today allows us to read, understand and learn from Aristotle, or Plato's interpretations of ancient societies in an interhuman communication that spans millennia.

The same is true of essential human needs, which are universal as long as the human condition exists as such, but the way in which these needs are satisfied or the mechanisms through which they are instrumented to create power structures depends on specific technological and institutional conditions that do not escape Furtado. The same can be affirmed in a cross-section of contemporary human societies, which are increasingly globalized. Regarding the current process of globalization, Furtado says:

> The situation becomes more complex when production is structured transnationally, the value of labor, being a social phenomenon, is defined within each society, or more precisely within the scope of national economic systems. It is true that labor can be considered in abstract terms, independently of the context in which it is performed,

> measured in physical units, but this is a notion of reduced scope, if what we want is to understand the social relations that make up the production process. If we compare contemporary economic systems we observe that the value of labor - that is, the purchasing power of the wage measured in terms of a set of goods that satisfy the basic needs of the population - varies according to the internal structure of domination (the way in which the social surplus is appropriated and utilized) and the level of accumulation, which conditions the physical productivity of labor. If we limit ourselves to observing capitalist societies with a similar internal organization, the second factor becomes determinant" (Furtado 1978: 29-30)

Again in the previous paragraph, it is clear that, in his economic reasoning associated with the concept of surplus, Furtado starts from the concept of human needs, which, for societies specific-historical and concrete needs are only existential needs that imply different sets of goods capable of satisfying the same type of basic needs (nutrition, education, health, housing, etc.). Note that in order to access specific satisfiers, workers must have access to quotas of purchasing power that depend on their wages.

In Prebisch's case, the concept of surplus that he favors is more dynamic and is associated with productivity gains arising from the introduction of technical progress. But also in this case it is clear that the surplus is the fruit of institutional relations that express structured power within each society. Moreover, for Prebisch, too, the dynamics of surplus generation and appropriation are only intelligible from the linked concepts of purchasing power and effective demand.

The reasoning of the structuralists is, for reasons already mentioned, fundamentally macroeconomic, and is based on a systemic vision supported, on one side, by the technical and institutional rules that allow the generation and appropriation of the productivity gains mediated by the difference between the value added by the less qualified labor force and the part of the social product that it manages to capture, and on the other side, by the existence of social actors capable of exercising their privileged position in these structures to carry forward the development process.

The concept of surplus that was used in different forms by social anthropology, and by classical economists, is, as we know, a central point in the theory of capitalist exploitation that Karl Marx deepened. However, by adopting the labor theory of value originally formulated by David Ricardo, Marx closed his theoretical field, and in *Capital* he formulated a totally abstract theory of the mechanisms of power that dynamize the capitalist process. Thus, beyond the ethical validity of Marx's reasoning, from the epistemological point of view that we are interested in emphasizing here, the concrete fact is that Marx, as an economist, eliminated from his central theoretical field any asymmetry of power, other than that of the process of labor exploitation, that could operate within capitalist markets through market transactions. This is precisely the mission of his theory of value (Di Filippo 1981).

The theories of labor value and prices in Ricardo's and Marx's versions do not allow us to understand the specific conditions of structural heterogeneity prevailing in Latin America; more precisely, they are not adequate for the study of price formation within peripheral economies. In particular, starting from Marx's theory of value, there is no way to link the notion of structural heterogeneity with the process of price formation in peripheral economies.

What visibly characterizes the heterodox theories of value, which in this book we suggest to call power-value theories, is the prevalence of power asymmetries in markets derived both from the structure of the markets themselves (oligopoly, monopoly) and from the overall institutional framework articulated around the capture and use of social surplus.

Within this heterodox vision of power-value theories, the institutional or institutionalist school stands out, whose founding fathers were Thorstein Veblen and John Commons. Both studied the institutionalized power relations established in capitalist societies. They did so preferably from a micro-social or microeconomic perspective. The former wrote, in addition to his famous "Theory of the Leisure Class", a critical examination of industrial capitalism called "The Theory of Business Enterprise", in which the asymmetries of power, whose cultural roots he deepened in an extraordinary way, are translated into the monopolistic structures of markets, clearly exemplified by the conditions prevailing in the United States at the beginning of the 20th century.

John Commons wrote, among other works, his "Legal Foundations of Capitalism" [1924], which is an expression of the idea of transactions subject to institutionalized power as we have suggested it in these lines. The work in question studies the influence of judicial rulings on the evolution of the concept of property in American capitalism.

Thus, the concept of power asymmetries inherent to the very structure of markets was addressed by these economists and their school, consolidating the evident idea that capitalism in the 20th century, and even more so in the 21st century, is an oligopolistic capitalism.

The study of microeconomic issues, for example those related to the internal logic that determines market transactions, was scarcely addressed by Prebisch, but in the case of Furtado we find paragraphs of great conceptual strength and transparency, referring to the microeconomic logic in the determination of prices:

> Market transactions are, as a rule, transactions between agents of unequal power. Indeed, the raison d'être of trade - the expression of a system of division of labor - lies in the creation of a surplus, the appropriation of which is not based on any law of nature. The "imperfect" forms of the market to which the economist refers are nothing more than a euphemism to describe the ex post result of the imposition of the will of certain agents on this appropriation. Since all markets are in some way "imperfect", exchange activities necessarily engender a process of concentration of wealth and power. Hence the structural tendency, observed since the beginnings of industrial capitalism, toward the formation of large firms. Many observers will erroneously infer from this observation that small enterprises tend to disappear, but experience shows that they are irreplaceable in the exercise of important functions: without small enterprises the capitalist system would lose considerably, not only flexibility, but also inventiveness and initiative (Furtado 1978: 17).

In this paragraph by Furtado, I disregard his interesting comment on small and medium enterprises to highlight the clear and simple formulation of a vision of market transactions based on asymmetrical power relations, resulting in a conception of power- value that places him in the heterodox group distinguished in this review and brings him closer to the arguments of the American institutionalist movement.

The reciprocal feedback or cross-fertilization between the Anglo-Saxon structuralist and institutionalist currents is also observed in other arguments of Furtado where, even without explicitly mentioning this author, the influence of J. K. Galbraith and his studies on "The New Industrial State" (1969) and "American Capitalism" (1952) is noticeable. For example, Furtado observes:

> The transition from the so-called market system to contemporary organized capitalism must necessarily have repercussions on the coordinating centers of economic activities and on the general configuration of power structures. In practically all sectors of activity there are enterprises or reasonably well- structured groups of enterprises whose behavior has an overall influence on the system. The same can be said with respect to trade union organizations. In this way, the political content of economic decisions, which used to be concealed in atomized markets, becomes clear, as do the social implications of the orientation adopted by the coordinating centers. In organized capitalism, the ideology according to which the activity of the coordinating centers must be an extension of the "invisible hand" of atomized markets no longer makes sense. Political power - conceived as capable of modifying the behavior of broad social groups - is configured as a complex structure in which the institutions that make up the State interact with the groups that dominate the accumulation process and with the social organizations that can significantly interfere in the distribution of income. To the extent that it broadens and diversifies its sphere of action, the State contributes to increasing the complexity of the system of social relations over which it acts, since it itself gives rise to social strata with their own interests (Furtado 1978, 20)

Conclusions

The concept of structured power proposed in this book allows us to combine the role of individual wills as agents of social change with that of the structures (technical and social rules) that channel, encourage and limit the concrete expression of these wills.

The Latin American structuralist approach is systemic and based on a conception of history that is neither deterministic nor voluntaristic. History is conceived as an open and unpredictable process, firstly affected not only by technological and economic structures, but also by the other institutional frameworks of society and, secondly, energized by the praxis of the actors within these structures.

The scientific possibility of empirically verifying the processes examined by the structuralists finds in market prices trends (especially in "key prices" such as those of money, labor, natural resources and energy, etc.) the quantitative material required, through the way in which these prices reflect the asymmetries of power of the entire social system and not only those of the economic system.

When Latin American structuralism opens up the game of the market in this way, then the utilitarian ethics that today predominates in the world under the forms of the privileged consumer society (Prebisch), loses the force it has in the caricatures of the "economic man", and gives way to considerations of political and moral philosophy.

The type of justice that prevails in markets conceived under static conditions of stable general equilibrium is commutative justice, according to which a price is obtained which, in its theoretical justification implies equivalent considerations but, in its practical justification that includes positions of power, means that the wills of the parties have reached a point of acceptance (willingly or unwillingly) of the terms of the transaction. Commutative justice acquired significance in static pre-capitalist societies such as those of the ancient and medieval world not subject to processes of economic development. There, a "zero-sum game" operated in which the gains of some could only come from the losses of others, but capitalism is a positive-sum game and its continuous process of growth raises the problem of the appropriation and social use of the incremental surplus (Prebisch 1981)

By opening the field to ethical considerations, the notion of distributive justice emerges, which is essential for judging the rationality of political behavior and the functions of States in the management of economic policy.

In Prebisch's view, the ethical reading underlying the structuralist message is essential, and it is worth ending this essay with one of the many paragraphs in which he puts forward this message. Regarding the question: to whom does the surplus belong? Prebisch answers: "There is no scientific solution. The solution is fundamentally ethical: to accumulate the surplus in order to provide everyone with the advantages of development.

It belongs to the whole collectivity and must be used for its benefit to correct structural disparities in the distribution of the benefits of technological innovations, whether they come from economic or social power" (Prebisch 1981, 334).

Chapter XIII

Multidimensional integration in the global era[37]

Introduction

Towards a multidimensional integration

The central hypothesis of this book is that the process of economic globalization currently underway worldwide has repercussions not only in the sphere of international markets, but also in the economic, political, socio-cultural and environmental institutions of the Latin American countries involved. Therefore, a possible response to these impacts, aimed at strengthening the capacity to negotiate and take advantage of the new global scenario, could be the promotion of a multidimensional regional integration with supranational decision- making mechanisms, which, as suggested here, is feasible on a South American scale. This modality of regional integration can contribute decisively to increasing not only economic dynamism, but also the political autonomy and social equity of Latin American nations. It would therefore be an integration of nations and not only of markets.

---

[37] Published under the title "América Latina, integración regional en la era global", in "Si Somos Americanos", "Revista de Estudios Transfronterizos", 9(1), 143-170. Universidad Arturo Prat, Santiago de Chile, 2007.

The processes of globalization and integration: a conceptual theoretical framework

We start from the generic notion of system understood as any complex and delimitable object, abstract or concrete, whose parts or components are linked by conceptual or real nexuses.

In this field we are interested in concrete, historically determined, intrinsically dynamic contemporary international systems: a) whose main interacting components (actors or agents) are the national States in the political sphere and the large transnational corporations (TNCs) in the economic sphere; b) whose structures are the technical and institutional rules effectively in force that channel those interactions; c) their scope or domain is framed in "spaces" that can be political (e.g. alliances and commitments in the areas of defense, security, or the preservation of certain government regimes), economic (e.g. monetary areas), cultural (e.g. language, religion), environmental (e.g. ecosystems, river basins), etc. d) their processes and mechanisms express the strategies and tactics of the main individuals that affect the transformations of the system within the framework of its structural constraints[38].

It should be pointed out that nation-states, components of international systems, can also be examined as multidimensional systems, with their own components, structures, domains and processes. However, this book concentrates only on the international level and does not address the transformations that, at the national level, end up affecting the behavior of international players.

The language of systems corresponds to the language of games, thus: a) the actors of the international system can be seen as the players or teams playing the game; b) the structures of the international system can be seen as the technical and institutional rules of the game; c) the domains or domains (political, economic, cultural and environmental) of the international system can be conceived as the technical and institutional rules of the game as the different " rings ", " fields " or " courts " in which the game takes place; and d) the reciprocal mechanisms and processes between the main players (governments of the day,

---

[38] We are making free use of ideas inspired by Mario Bunge. See in particular Bunge 1999, chapters IV and X.

intergovernmental agencies, transnational corporations) can be " read " as the strategies and tactics of the main players according to their positions in the rules of the game[39].

De facto powers and institutionalized powers

Unlike competitive team games in sports, the "game" of international relations has the peculiarity that in its course, the players themselves negotiate new rules or, alternatively, impose them on the basis of factual modalities of power derived from the control of scientific and technological progress. The introduction and control of scientific progress is the main factual modality of international power exercised by the major hegemonic centers. This gives rise to new technical and institutional rules that regulate the exercise of institutionalized forms of power in the political, economic, cultural, environmental, etc. spheres. In the strictly political sphere, the control of scientific and technological progress translates into the control of military power, and the use of force is the main expression of the imposition of de facto powers. However, the threat, implicit or explicit, of the exercise of military power is a powerful mechanism of persuasion to impose the validity of certain rules of the game.

In the first half of the twentieth century, coercive forms of imposing international hegemonic intent predominated (the prevalence of colonialism and the outbreak of two world wars). In the second half of the same century, following the process of decolonization, the emergence of the United Nations, and the democratization and regional integration of Western Europe, the negotiation and cooperation mechanisms of intergovernmental organizations became predominant.

In this new historical framework, the modes of negotiation that have been emerging since the 1980s have been decisively influenced by the spread of information and communication technologies (ICTs), giving rise to the emergence of transnational corporations (TNCs) as powerful economic players. What characterizes the ICT revolution is that the

---

[39] We are "translating" here the language of systems into the language of games, making free and proper use of ideas inspired by Douglass North. See in particular North 1993, chapter I.

global spread of its effects has been extremely rapid and knowledge of its technical rules is accessible to a number of potential hegemonic centers that can access them directly. This is the case, among others, of emerging powers such as China and India.

Global capitalism differs from previous forms of international capitalism in that there is growing cross-border mobility of productive factors and particularly of large TNCs. In fact, these companies are defined by the fact that their productive chains are deployed in different regions and nations on a global scale. It is no longer international trade in goods that characterizes the bulk of international transactions; there is now also growing mobility of services, technology and productive investments. TNCs are major economic players in the global economy and are deploying their own strategies to conquer and share markets.

In the political sphere, the governments of the nation states continue to operate with a hegemonic preponderance of the central countries. These countries (e.g. the United States), or groups of countries (e.g. the European Union), are defined as central because they are the sources of technological power and the main makers of the rules of the game of the world economic and political order. These rules of the game are administered and monitored by intergovernmental bodies both in the economic sphere (e.g. International Monetary Fund [IMF], World Bank [WB] and World Trade Organization [WTO]) and in the political (e.g. UN Security Council) and military (e.g. NATO) spheres.

Precisely the new rules of the WTO, successor to the General Agreement on Tariffs and Trade (GATT), have reflected the protagonist role of the TNCs that lobby through their governments for the inclusion of new codes or "disciplines" in the areas of investment, technology, competition, etc.

The TNCs also "play" through pressure on the governments where their parent companies are based or, alternatively, where the production chains of their subsidiaries are located (for example, the underdeveloped countries that are home to free trade zones and, in particular, export processors or “maquiladoras”).

Information and communication technologies (ICTs) have favored the operation of these companies, which have an impact not only on the economic but also on the cultural level, through a growing economic control over the mass media. TNCs also play within the political subsystems of the Latin American countries where they are established, through the weakening of the regulatory, stabilizing and redistributive functions performed by national governments.

Two types of regional integration: unidimensional and multidimensional

The presence of TNCs has also affected the "game" of regional integration whose modalities can be seen as a subset of the global processes within the international systems we are examining. This affects the "philosophy" and typologies of regional integration. As we will suggest, two types of integration have emerged: unidimensional and multidimensional. The modalities of unidimensional integration follow the logic of the WTO, heir to the GATT, and are an accentuation of its market disciplines.

Alternatively, the modalities of multidimensional integration can best be exemplified by the logic of European integration. Let us take a closer look at both options.

The various dimensions of the integration process can be examined by taking as a starting point the language commonly accepted in the intergovernmental public sphere and incorporated into the official lexicon of international treaties. The transformations introduced by regional integration processes: a) generally begin with trade or market relations (e.g. tariff preference or free trade areas), b) are then deepened by sharing certain quotas of sovereignty (customs unions), then progress in the gradual and partial creation of communal citizenships (common labor markets), and d) culminate in the gestation of increasingly shared sovereignties and citizenships (for example, through economic and monetary communities).

Finally, it is possible to reach deeper and more binding modalities of political integration. The most significant transition in this field is from intergovernmental rules of the game and mechanisms to supranational ones. This is the historical course followed by the European Union (EU), a relevant example of a clearly multidimensional type of integration.

In contrast to the previous processes, the historical dynamics of what are now called Free Trade Agreements (FTAs) have focused only on market relations. This is the case of almost all hemispheric trade agreements signed since the 1990s in the Americas. These FTAs are sometimes called "comprehensive" (but only at the level of markets) because they include not only elements of free trade in goods, but also other disciplines inherent to the current process of capitalist globalization: transactions in technology and intellectual property, investments linked to trade and services, competition and consumer protection rules, government procurement, etc. In view of the above, a more precise technical denomination would be that of "preferential market areas".

The Latin American countries that sign these FTAs acquire institutional commitments according to which they must modify their internal investment, intellectual property, international dispute settlement, etc. regimes. The most important FTAs that have been signed are "vertical" in the sense that they link a major center of the global capitalist order (such as the United States) with Latin American nations or blocs of nations. Such is, for example, the North American Free Trade Agreement (NAFTA), or the Central American Free Trade Agreement with the Dominican Republic (CAFTA-DR).

Vertical FTAs omit in their constitutive texts any attempt by the subscribing countries to share sovereignty. The political dimension involved in the signing of deeper stages of integration, such as customs or monetary unions, involves a level of sovereignty sharing that is obviously unacceptable to the main hegemonic power of today's global capitalist order.

FTAs also omit the socio-political dimension associated with the sharing of citizenship, which is essential for the constitution of common labor markets (single passport, labor rights, community mechanisms for access to health, education, recognition of diplomas, etc.) by citizens from the signatory countries.

Finally, the "vertical" FTAs (North-South) also do not penetrate specific cultural aspects (such as the recognition and reciprocal teaching of the languages spoken by the other members, or of shared values in terms of ethics, morals, art, etc.). It is in this sense that we can typify them as one-dimensional or "market-oriented" agreements. This is the "style" of regional integration accepted and promoted by the United States in the Western Hemisphere.

In contrast, the EU has used a different logic, both in the internal creation of its own bloc and in the incorporation of the countries of its strategic environment (for example, the enlargement to include the countries of Central Europe, which are former members of the Council for Mutual Economic Assistance led by the former Soviet Union). The EU is a typical multidimensional bloc, as its rules and disciplines encompass: (a) deep macroeconomic convergence (harmonization or even unification of customs, fiscal, monetary regimes, etc.); (b) sharing of sovereignties (customs unions, common currencies, etc.); and (c) sharing of citizenships (common passport, movement and settlement of immigrant workers, recognition of diplomas, labor and social security rights, etc.).

Within the framework of this dichotomous typology (unidimensional versus multidimensional), we could say that the Latin American economic groups (Mercosur, CAN, CACM, and Caricom) are incipiently multidimensional, because their agreements explicitly include political commitments (community parliaments, courts of justice, democratic clauses, commitments in the field of defense, etc.), social commitments (recognition of multiple rights of immigrants from other member countries, etc.), and even cultural commitments (e.g., the teaching of Portuguese in Spanish-speaking member countries of the Mercosur and vice versa). But progress in each of these fields is still hesitant and uncertain. It should not be denied that these blocs are experiencing acute obstacles to their consolidation and deepening. Precisely the South American strategy recommended in this chapter aims to overcome these limitations

The process of economic globalization and its impact in Latin America

The process of economic globalization is based on the spread of ICTs, which took place with great force in the late 1970s and early 1980s, a period that coincided with other dramatic changes in international relations. Politically, there was the definitive collapse of the authoritarian communist regimes in Eastern and Central Europe. On the economic front, the so-called Conservative Revolution associated with the governments of Margaret Thatcher in Great Britain and Ronald Reagan in the United States began to take place.

Another aspect of great importance in this historical stage was the emergence of the so-called "emerging" economies of Asia: first Japan in the early 1970s, and then China in the mid-1980s. India, although less spectacularly than China, is another powerful player in the new rules of the world economy.

In Latin America, the 1980s witnessed the disastrous consequences of the excessive indebtedness process that had been building up during the 1970s. This process was associated with the abundance of the so-called "petrodollars" administered by transnational private banks. The 1980s included the worst regional recession since the crisis of the 1930s. It was a "lost decade" in economic terms, but "won" in political terms with the return to democratic regimes in Latin American countries.

Finally, by the early 1990s, most Latin American countries had made their economic models compatible with the rules of global capitalism and had embarked on strategies of growth models based on open economies, oriented by private- transnational criteria in the allocation of resources.

Since the 1990s, Latin American regional integration, especially in the area of markets, has also seen the introduction of new rules of the game associated with the proliferation of FTAs. These treaties are based on trade liberalization and opening mechanisms of general and automatic application that were considered compatible with the WTO philosophy.

This reorientation of regional integration treaties in the sphere of markets was called "open regionalism". Open regionalism is a legal commitment to reconcile the "openness" philosophy of incorporation into the rules of the game of the global economy with the integrationist philosophy based on the conception of reciprocal preferences, only for the partners to the agreement, in the areas of trade and investment.

Thus, the two integration strategies conceptually examined in the previous section were put forward in Latin America. On one side, multidimensional integration emerged, expressed in pre-existing Latin American agreements or those created since the 1990s. Among the former are the Andean Community of Nations (CAN), the Caribbean

Community (Caricom) and the Central American Common Market (CACM). Among those created since the 1990s is the Southern Common Market (Mercosur)

Furthermore, one-dimensional integration emerged, the most important and earliest reference in the Western hemisphere being the North American Free Trade Agreement (NAFTA) signed by the United States, Canada and Mexico in 1994. NAFTA is based on an acceptance and deepening of the philosophy and rules of the game of global multilateralism. In particular, it relies on the disciplines of the World Trade Organization (WTO) in the area of trade relations. Since then, the strategic interactions between these two types of agreements have shaped much of the history of integration in Latin America.

The process of economic globalization and Latin American integration

Over the past 25 years or so, the information and communication technologies (ICT) revolution has increasingly transformed the structure of world trade in goods and services. Intra industry trade and intrafirm trade (trade carried out between subsidiariaries of the same transnational company, especially in durable manufactured goods as a result of the proliferation of production chains of subsidiaries of certain parent companies) have expanded. This has led to the emergence of so-called global products whose parts and components are manufactured in multiple countries and finally assembled in a given country. In the North-South sphere of the American continent, these types of global products are usually manufactured in export processing zones such as those on the northern border of Mexico, and in several Central American and Caribbean countries.

The technological background of globalized production

These new forms of globalized production are increasingly possible and frequent because of the enormous technological opportunities for reducing the coordination costs of companies and firms operating transnationally on a global, continental or subcontinental scale. The result of these technological transformations and of the convergence of the technical norms that regulate them has been a great international mobility of direct investment flows, of technology, and of new types of services.

The institutional background to economic globalization

The international mobility of technology and productive investments depends not only on technical feasibility, but also on the economic efficiency of these movements, which is largely based on the institutions that regulate transaction costs. These transaction costs can be broken down into information costs, negotiation costs, contractual formalization costs, monitoring and follow-up costs, and litigation costs.

One consequence of these processes is that international transactions on a global scale directly affect the internal economic institutions of the countries involved, beyond the traditional border impacts that were verified at customs and translated into tariff and non-tariff restrictions. The WTO disciplines related to intellectual property, investment and trade in services directly involve the functioning of codes, internal laws, or judicial and administrative procedures that take place within member countries.

Regional integration in the Americas, processes, types and trends

We could say that the Latin American economic blocks (Mercosur, CAN, CACM, and Caricom) are incipiently multidimensional, because their agreements make explicit incursions into political commitments (community parliaments, courts of justice, democratic clauses, defense commitments, etc.), social commitments (recognition of multiple rights of immigrants from other member countries) and even cultural commitments (for example, teaching Portuguese in the Spanish-speaking member countries of Mercosur and vice versa). But progress in each of these areas is still hesitant and uncertain. It should not be denied that these groups are experiencing acute obstacles to their consolidation and deepening. The South American strategy recommended in this book is aimed precisely at overcoming these limitations.

The concrete dynamics of integration agreements

Until the end of the 20th century, the existing perspective was that regional integration processes in the Americas would be reduced to five major agreements. On one side, the Free Trade Agreement of the Americas (FTAA), which would legally absorb all the other FTAs previously signed on a hemispheric (North-South) or Latin American (South-South) scale. On the other side, the four sub-regional groups that currently include almost all Latin American countries (Di Filippo and Franco, 2000).

However, the FTAA negotiations seem to have collapsed definitively in 2005, following the Presidential Summit held in Argentina. The four potentially multidimensional agreements (Mercosur, CAN, CACM and Caricom) face very different perspectives and options that are strongly influenced by political considerations. It seems appropriate to begin by analyzing the hemispheric agreements and to place within this more global framework the evolution of the agreements that are exclusively Latin American in nature.

Hemispheric integration and its one-dimensional strategy

The FTAA Free Trade Agreement of the Americas is an expression of a style of hemispheric relations that the United States has been promoting in the Americas since the end of the Cold War. Therefore, it is not exclusively the FTAA that we are interested in exploring here, but rather the philosophy of what we are calling the one-dimensional and vertical hemispheric agreements promoted by the United States in the Americas.

In June 1990, the President of the United States, George Bush (Sr.), unveiled the Initiative for the Americas, which proposed: a) the long-term creation of a hemispheric free trade zone and, in the short and medium term, the gradual trade liberalization of Latin American economies through the bilateral signing of trade and investment agreements with the United States; b) the promotion of reforms to Latin American investment regimes to favor market-friendly privatization and regulation processes, through technical and financial assistance supported with US$ 1.5 billion; and, c) the negotiated reduction of the official or governmental debt of Latin American countries that adhere to the "spirit" of the Initiative[40].

This initiative was the institutional consolidation of the new economic strategy, integrated into the emerging global economy, which had been introduced in Latin America since the late 1970s and throughout the 1980s. The strategy, during that previous period, was stimulated by the lending support of the WB and the IDB in development issues, and also by the role of financial guarantor and technical advisor played by the IMF in the pro-market reforms that were taking place. This was the first far- reaching action taken by the United States with respect to Latin America after the collapse of the communist bloc and the end of the Cold War. Until then, U.S. proposals had been rather reactive in relation to the East- West struggle. Such was the case of the Alliance for Progress in the 1960s after the triumph of the Cuban Revolution, or the Caribbean Basin Initiative in the 1980s, following the aborted revolutions in Nicaragua and Grenada.

In 1994, as part of the new U.S. strategy, the North American Free Trade Agreement (NAFTA) came into force, linking the United States with its immediate environment, consisting of Canada on its northern border and Mexico on its southern border. In terms of relations with Mexico, it is necessary to mention two significant precedents. In 1965, the United States suspended the Mexican Bracero Program, which accepted temporary labor migration from Mexico, and replaced it with the Maquiladora Program (export processing zones). This change is very important to understand the meaning of NAFTA and its exclusively "market-driven" bent. In effect, with the Maquiladora Program, the

[40] At the end of 1991, the United States had signed the following trade and investment agreements in Latin America (some of them prior to the launching of the Initiative: Mexico (1987), Bolivia (July 1990), Ecuador (July 1990), Chile (October 1990), Honduras (November 1990), Costa Rica (November 1990), Venezuela (May 1991), El Salvador (May 1991), Peru (May 1991), Panama (June 1991), Nicaragua (June 1991), Mercosur of "the four": Argentina, Brazil, Paraguay and Uruguay (June 1991). See Lucrecia Lozano (1993), La Iniciativa para las Américas: el comercio hecho estrategia, "Journal Nueva Sociedad", number 125, May-June, pages 121-134.

United States was trying to curb the alarming growth of the migration of "Hispanics" (Latin Americans) who, under the protection of the Bracero Program, were entering the United States with the intention of staying illegally. The “maquiladoras”, in the strategic intention of the United States, would "kill two birds with one stone": they would retain potential immigrants, especially from Mexico, and would allow them to take advantage of lower labor, environmental, social costs or Energy costs by the U.S. companies that will set up in the free trade zones[41].

The path of continuing to incorporate countries into NAFTA experienced setbacks during 1995 when the U.S. Congress denied the Executive Branch approval of the so-called "fast track" for the negotiation of new trade agreements, which frustrated (or at least postponed) the incorporation of Chile into NAFTA.

In the same year that NAFTA was signed, the United States promoted and installed the First Summit of the Americas (Miami, 1994), which included the official announcement of the launching of the FTAA.

The FTAA negotiations gave rise to disagreements arising from the U.S. effort to abstract the logic of international markets from the socio-political context in which these markets operate, both at the hemispheric level and, above all, at the national level of the Latin American countries subscribing to the FTAA.

The first of these disagreements was related to the issue of agriculture and the negative impact it could have on employment, production and food consumption in Latin American countries. The second was related to asymmetries in the ability to compete internationally on a "level playing field", since even the larger economies of Latin America, taken in isolation, are small and underdeveloped compared to the United States. The third was linked to the regulations negotiated in the FTAA and their compatibility with the economic, political and cultural institutions of Latin American democracies.

---

[41] “Maquiladoras” are companies that import, duty-free, industrial inputs to produce manufactured goods, which are subsequently marketed outside the maquiladora's host country. According to the Dictionary of the Spanish Language (1970), the word “maquila” means "to charge the miller for the maquila". It originated in the Spanish Middle Ages to designate milling of other people's wheat, whose owners (of the wheat) paid the miller with part of the flour obtained. Something similar operated in the sugar mills of the Antilles during the 19th century.

In 2001, with the turn of the century and the millennium, some momentous events took place. First, on a global scale, the attack on the Twin Towers in New York opened the door for the US government to initiate a punitive anti-terrorist strategy in countries such as Afghanistan and Iraq that were suspected of promoting terrorist attacks and producing weapons of mass destruction. The United States thus embarked on a costly and protracted war in which it has not succeeded, nor has it been able to disengage itself in a way that is honorable for its international image.

Second, at the Latin American level, there has been a shift towards more autonomous positions that are less complacent with the neoliberal economic strategy. This process has continued during the last five years with a radicalization of positions opposed to the rules of the game of neoliberal capitalism. The process began with the collapse of the Argentine economy at the end of 2001 and the takeover of power by Eduardo Duhalde, first, and then Néstor Kirchner; it continued with the assumption of power by Juan Ignacio Lula in Brazil, and has continued throughout the last five years with the election of Tabaré Vazquez in Uruguay, the consolidation of Hugo Chávez in Venezuela, the election of Rafael Correa in Ecuador, etc. These are governments which, up to now, have not broken the rules of the democratic process nor have they closed themselves to the global economy, but have clearly departed from the rules of the game of neo-liberal democracy. It is necessary not to lose sight of these processes in order to understand the political context that precipitated the failure of the FTAA negotiations.

As is now very clear, the original intention that led to the creation of the FTAA was modified after the eighth multilateral meeting held in Miami in November 2003. The modification was related to the negotiation procedures and the results that would be expected from the signing of the agreements. At the previous ministerial meeting in Quito (2002), the idea of a single comprehensive and complete agreement was still alive. However, in the Miami Declaration, a new "à la carte" version of the agreements emerged, derived fundamentally from the lack of understanding between Mercosur and the United States regarding agriculture and services.

The opening of the draft text of the negotiations to the public and the emergence of the issue of asymmetries in the development of the negotiators generated two potential areas of friction that would become apparent in the subsequent course of the negotiations. However, the main problems were to arise after Quebec, when the market access negotiations began (May 2002) and the need to define the negotiation modalities arose. These modalities included offers in the areas of agricultural and non- agricultural goods, as well as services, investment and government procurement.

In agricultural goods, the main area of friction was that of subsidies and other disciplines on practices that distort trade in these goods, practiced by the developed countries as components of their traditional protectionism in this sector.

Moreover, in the field of services, the developed countries were the suppliers wishing to establish themselves in the developing countries' markets, and the most heated issue was related to the so-called "commercial presence", a term that attempted to bring into the "Chinese shoe of trade" many of the defining features of the process of corporate trans nationalization inherent in contemporary economic globalization.

The issue of "commercial presence" was also at the thematic core of the investment negotiating group. So clear was this thematic intertwining that the Agreement on Methods and Modalities of Negotiation (October 2002) states: "The negotiating groups on services and investment shall, as a general rule, continue to meet separately. However, if deemed necessary, such groups may meet to deliberate jointly on common issues, particularly trade-related issues. As we shall see, one of the main areas of disagreement between the TNCs, the main economic players in globalization, and the governments of the Latin American countries, is the rules of the game that should govern the behavior of the TNCs in the region, and the procedures for settling any disputes that may arise.

The publication of the first negotiating draft gave wide access to all members of civil society (beyond the business chambers, the only ones initiated, up to that moment, in the course of the negotiations through the parallel business forums). Although the explicit contributions from civil society were rather scarce and unbalanced, the general public finally had access to information resources just when the Latin American political landscape was beginning to change its ideological shape.

It soon became clear that some large and medium-sized countries (particularly Argentina and Brazil), with temperate agricultural production and exports that competed especially with those of the United States, were unwilling to continue to negotiate the access to their investment and services markets if the central issues of agricultural protectionism were not addressed and the demands for legal and judicial reforms favorable to transnational investors were not moderated. The "Pandora's box" of small and relatively less developed countries also continued to increase complexities and tensions of a magnitude that had not been foreseen. All this ended up having categorical repercussions in the Miami Ministerial Declaration (November 2003), where the principle of "single undertaking" (a single commitment subscribed to by all participants regarding all matters under negotiation) was abandoned

Alternatively, the option emerged of a wide of alternative menu to which countries could flexibly adhere without accepting any set of rules en bloc. An "a la carte" or "light" agreement, an expression of the existence of irreconcilable disagreements that threatened the future of the entire negotiating process.

The process of erosion of the FTAA negotiations culminated in an open rupture made explicit in the Presidential Declaration of the Mar del Plata Summit (2005). On one side, the Mercosur member countries, including Venezuela, prepared a text that implied the abandonment of the negotiations because "the necessary conditions to achieve a balanced and equitable free trade agreement" were not in place. On the other side, the remaining economies of Latin America and the Caribbean signed a declaration similar to that of the Presidential Declaration of the previous Summit, insisting on the need to continue with the negotiations.

The Latin American economic groups versus hemispheric FTAs

Mexico, CACM and Caricom interests and strategies

The economic size of the United States compared to that of the MCCI countries (Mexico, Central America and the insular Caribbean) is ten times greater in terms of gross domestic product. The only country that manages to weigh significantly in U.S.-MICC relations is Mexico, but even in this case, the asymmetries are in the sphere of economic, social and political asymmetries. Since the recompositing of the Mexican political system (end of the PRI's hegemony) and its incorporation into NAFTA, political asymmetries have been reduced, but economic and cultural asymmetries continue to increase.

Mexico appears as a "small" country in economic terms compared to the United States and as a "giant" compared to the CACM and Caricom. On one side, the United States is economically almost 12 times larger than Mexico. On the other side, Mexico is economically almost four times bigger than the 17 countries of the CACM + Caricom.

In the United States-CACM comparison, the United States is 70 times larger in economic terms than the Central American countries. The countries that make up the CACM (Costa Rica, El Salvador, Guatemala, Honduras, and Nicaragua) had a population of 35 million people, a GDP of 157 billion current dollars, and a per capita product measured in purchasing power parity (PPP) prices of 4,500 USD of the same monetary unit in 2004. The member countries have liberalized their reciprocal trade, are consolidating a common external tariff and aspire to multidimensional and deep integration. Between 1997 and 2003, their reciprocal exports measured as a percentage of total exports rose from 16.8% to 26.9%. If we add Panama and the Dominican Republic, the U.S. economy is 46 times larger than the U.S. economy as a whole.

Needless to say, in the U.S.-Caricom comparison, these asymmetries reach a maximum degree, since the United States is 263 times larger in economic terms than all Caricom member countries combined. Caricom is made up of more than a dozen Caribbean island "micro-states" which, in 2004, together had a population of six million people, a GDP of $41 billion USD and a per capita product of 7,600 USD (PPP) in 1990 USD. They have liberalized their reciprocal trade and have a common external tariff. In the 1990s, their reciprocal exports, measured as a percentage of total exports, rose from 16.7% in 1997 to 18.8% in 2003.

Incidentally, this issue of economic asymmetries between the United States and the MCCI group of countries has a counterpart demographic: the masses of immigrants who, coming from these areas, try to settle in the great country of the North. This generates other types of asymmetries in the political and social spheres that affect hemispheric relations. At the present, after the failure of the immigration law aimed at providing a legal space for undocumented immigrants, there is a probable tightening of immigration laws that will particularly affect the citizens of the group of countries mentioned above. The popular reaction on the part of the tens of millions of so-called "Hispanics" who, legally or illegally, live in that country, is very significant and has the support of multiple organizations defending civil and political rights, guarantees and liberties in that country. These groups of Latin American immigrants, supported by other smaller contingents from other latitudes, are a non-negligible electoral force capable of tipping the balance in the U.S. congressional or presidential elections.

The positions of these countries with respect to the FTAA were obviously different. Mexico was relatively reluctant to move forward with the agreement because its ties with the United States are established in NAFTA and its interests would not have been better served by signing on to the FTAA. The Central American and Caribbean member countries compete with Mexico for the investments of TNCs ultimately oriented to the large U.S. market. However, so far in the 21st century it is clear that the main competitor of Mexico and the other members of the MCCI is China, both in attracting such investments and in conquering the U.S. market.

The recent signing of the FTA between the United States and Central America, which also includes the Dominican Republic (CAFTA-DR), will mean the de facto obsolescence of many pre-existing rules in force in the CACM. CAFTA-DR will imply the installation of new and updated rules in the areas of services, intellectual property, trade-related investments (commercial presence), public procurement, dispute settlement, etc. CAFTA-DR will create a new institutional framework within the philosophy of the WTO, but going further (what has been called WTO- plus). The issue is a contentious one and has given rise to mixed feelings among governments and their political tendencies in the subscribing countries.

This is demonstrated, for example, by the debate in Costa Rica that culminated in a popular consultation, which was overwhelmingly favorable to the approval of the FTAA.

This means that, despite the freezing of the FTAA, the United States has continued with its strategy of one-dimensional agreements focused exclusively on market relations, and aimed not only at promoting trade but also at installing a new institutionalism functional to the dynamics of the globalization process and its economic presence in Central America.

The main points of interest for the United States are to take advantage of low labor and environmental costs in the export processing zones, better access to tropical product exports, and to take advantage of local service markets.

Mercosur and CAN interests

In South America, Mercosur and Andean Community of Nations (CAN) not only have conflicting interests with the USA and the EU in temperate agricultural activities, but also (including Chile, which is not a full member of these agreements) are too far away from the United States to take advantage of free trade zones for exporting goods or services to the large US market. In these South American blocs, foreign direct investment in manufacturing and services is primarily interested in supplying South American markets. In addition, the traditional interest of the TNCs in exploiting the different types of natural resources in great demand in the developed countries continues. This interest has multiplied with the irruption of continental China in world markets, expanding the demand for raw materials and foodstuffs (oil, copper, soybeans, etc.). China's growing presence in international transactions in the global era is significantly transforming the dynamics of world markets.

South American countries depend to a decisive degree on the exploitation of their natural resources in the traditional style of primary exports to the developed world, and the desired expansion of their production and manufacturing exports conflicts with the powerful competition from mainland China. The large domestic markets of South American countries with high growth prospects make it profitable and attractive for developed countries to invest, not only in the typical and traditional exploitation or commercialization of primary products, but also in the installation of activities related to the provision of services oriented to the South American domestic market. The Andean Community of Nations, due to the peculiar "longitudinal" geographical disposition of its members, lacks some of the economic advantages of the natural areas of integration, and this fact is reflected in the relatively low proportion of reciprocal trade among its members. At the Trujillo Presidential Meeting (1996), a new institutional framework was created that converted the Andean Group into the Andean Community of

Nations, with a Council constituted at the presidential level and charged with providing the political orientation of the Agreement.

The countries that make up Mercosur (Argentina, Brazil, Paraguay and Uruguay) have deregulated most of their reciprocal trade and, established a common external tariff.

Note that both CAN and Mercosur have suffered significant reductions in their reciprocal trade percentages after the boom experienced in the first part of the 1990s in the frame of the neoliberal expannsion. The root of this deterioration may be found, first, in the negative impact of the global economy expressed in the contagion of some financial crises originated in other latitudes, second, in the insufficient political will of its members to seek deeper mechanisms of macroeconomic integration and, third, in the incomplete institutional evolution of the agreements themselves towards multidimensional modalities associated with the validity of democratic regimes. These types of difficulties in reciprocal trade can also be addressed in the light of the general strategy suggested in this book. The underlying idea is that market relations among Latin American countries are embedded in institutional structures that set their limits and give them their stimuli.

Union of South American Nations (UNASUR)

What has been lacking in promoting the integration of South America's internal market has been the provision of an infrastructural and institutional base to make it viable.

The foundation of Unasur was an attempt to become a political and economic community among the twelve South American countries. Created in 2004 in Cusco, Peru, during the III South American Summit, its General Secretariat was located in the city of Quito. The constitution of Unasur aimed to increase the systemic competitiveness of the South American region in world markets, and to unify and take advantage of South America's internal market.

In addition, Unasur intended to perform the functions of political and diplomatic coordination both within South American intergovernmental relationships and in the negotiations that the region could undertake with the rest of the world.

Unasur promoted the convergence between Mercosur, CAN and Chile in a free trade zone, whose negotiations were very advanced and began prior to the creation of this Union. Unasur had also become the organization in charge of promoting the pre-existing South American Regional Integration Initiative (IIRSA) aimed at advancing the physical, energy and communications integration of South America. These include the Interoceanic Highway that would link Peru with Brazil, passing through Bolivia; the South American Energy Ring to supply the Mercosur countries and Chile with Peruvian gas from Camisea; the Binational Gas Pipeline that would connect Colombia with Venezuela; the Binational Polyduct that would make it possible to export oil to the east through the Colombian coast on the Pacific Ocean; and the Interoceanic Highway that would connect Peru with Brazil, passing through Bolivia.

Considered as a whole, around 2010 Unasur covered a geographical area of almost 18 million square kilometers with a population of 370 million people, and a product that in orders of magnitude made it the fifth largest "virtual or potential" economy in the world behind other "real" groups or nations such as the European Union, the United States, China and India. [42]

The rise (2008), subsequent fall (2018) and apparent rebirth (2023) of UNASUR is another proof of the absolute dependence and fragility of South American integration with respect to the changing ideological fluctuations of the national Latin American governments in power. This is the best example of the unfinished odyssey of the development and integration process that is summarized in this book.

---

[42] From a political-social perspective, it is also worth mentioning the Bolivarian Alternative for Latin America and the Caribbean (ALBA). It was born in Havana (2004) as a result of an agreement between Venezuela and Cuba. Subsequently, Nicaragua, Antigua and Barbuda, Dominica and St. Vincent and the Grenadines have joined. It focuses its attention on the fight against poverty, social exclusion and high illiteracy rates. It attaches crucial importance to about the social problems of peasants and small farmers. It proclaims the creation of mechanisms that take advantage of the creation of what it calls "cooperative advantages" among member countries. It expresses political intentions and theoretical foundations that still need to mature and be made much more.

An institutional reading of integration processes in America

It may be useful to consider the role that multidimensional regional integration agreements could play in creating institutional convergence to facilitate economic development under conditions of increasing integration into the world economy.

The relevance of a discussion on this topic derives from the fact that most Latin American countries are members (full or associated) of one of the multidimensional agreements currently operating in Latin America: Mercosur, CAN, CACM and Caricom. For example, all CAN member countries plus Chile are currently Mercosur associates. In summary, the aim is to examine the role of regional integration agreements in the creation of common institutional frameworks to facilitate Latin America's development in the current global era.

Sub-regional convergence of institutional frameworks

This way of approaching the subject implies privileging the importance of the internal institutional frameworks (at the national, South American and Latin American levels) of Latin American countries in the success of their development models. It also implies re-examining the meaning and scope of the strategies that in the 1980s and 1990s were called liberalization, privatization and deregulation, applied to modify the development model that had previously been in force between 1945 and 1980.

In the economic sphere, the main raison d'être of the need fo institutionally deep regional agreements lies in the creation of a South American market capable of fulfilling two functions. The first is that the producers located in that market acquire the benefits of global systemic competitiveness in their exports to the rest of the world as a result of the reduction of average transportation, energy, transaction and coordination costs. This would occur as the domestic market becomes more unified and its average productive efficiency increases (economies of scale and other factors tending to reduce average costs). The second economic function that this type of agreement could fulfill is that localized producers in this integrated space, including transnational companies, will benefit from the developing domestic market as a result of the integration process. Both aspects are increasingly visible today in emerging integrated markets of maximum scale, such as China and, to a lesser extent, India.

In the area of public goods in general and public services in particular, the interconnection of infrastructures and the convergence of standards and operating procedures generate a clear reduction not only in monetary costs but also in the time and quality of economic activities.

As regards production chains and intra-firm coordination of TCs, the consolidation of information technologies helps to develop procedures such as electronic data interchange, the application of "just-in-time" procedures for stock management, etc.

For transactions between reciprocally independent firms (not linked by capital ties), the convergence of legal and juridical procedures reduces the costs of information (search for contractual counterparts), negotiation (contractual power positions), formalization (legal certainty, convergence of requirements), follow-up and monitoring of what has been agreed (various telematic procedures) and dispute resolution in case of litigation.

Migrations, community citizenship and multidimensional integration

In addition to this broad economic perspective, the creation of a South American market for goods, services and non-human factors of production facilitates the establishment of common labor markets among the member countries. In turn, these integrated labor markets necessarily imply the parallel construction of a community citizenship based on the common validity of human, citizenship, economic, social and cultural rights and obligations. We will suggest that the spatial mobility of the Latin American population is much more viable than in the North-South sphere, if it is practiced under agreements and regulations capable of safeguarding the political and social stability involved in the processes. This leads us to highlight the advantages of multidimensional integration, at least on a South American scale.

Although the socio-cultural and political difficulties of integrating labor markets should not be minimized, there are important migratory circuits that are operational (e.g. in the southern cone between Argentina, Peru,

Chile, Paraguay, Bolivia, and to a lesser extent Ecuador) and can result in a better use of the skills and availability of the South American labor force.

Democratic clauses and their impact on the agreements

Returning to our systemic perspective and the language of games, we could say that all regional integration agreements involve economic players (basically the TNCs). The economic rules of the game encompass the institutions that regulate the ownership of resources within the framework of the dynamics of global markets, and are therefore expressed through global intergovernmental organizations such as the WTO, the IMF and the World Bank.

All regional integration agreements involve the political players, which are the governments of the nation-states subscribing to these commitments. These governments have the legitimacy that emanates from the political systems on which they are based, but in any case they represent the sovereignty of the respective States. A common feature of all types of democratic systems is that, in the final analysis, sovereignty lies with the citizens who grant legitimacy to the respective governments. However, the central issue that concerns us is the link between the institutions of democracy and the regulations and commitments that emanate from the signing of integration agreements. In relation to the agreements signed between nations of the Western Hemisphere, the democratic clause is a condition that is increasingly present. In the case of the EU this was particularly evident in its founding members and in the successive enlargements of the bloc. It was only after other Western European nations (Spain, Portugal, Greece, etc.) took over democratic regimes of government that they joined the EU. The same is happening today with the enlargement of the EU to include some ten Central European nations. The four Latin American blocs also require their full or associated members to comply with the democratic clause. In South America, both Mercosur and the Andean Community of Nations (CAN) have included since 1998, democratic clauses as a condition for membership in the agreements, doing so with the Ushuaia Protocols and the Protocol on the "Andean Commitment to Democracy", respectively".

Belatedly, the FTAA negotiations included the requirement that the countries entitled to sit at the negotiating table should have democratic political regimes, and the Inter-American Democratic Charter of the OAS (OAS-IDC) was quickly approved in September 2001. Therefore, it would seem that all agreements, both one-dimensional and multidimensional, show equal respect for the institutions of democracy. However, the impact of these institutions on the functioning of these agreements is not the same in all cases.

The only way to understand the different impact of these democratic conditions or clauses on regional integration agreements is to examine the unidimensional or multidimensional character of these agreements and the supranational or intergovernmental nature of their decision-making processes.

In one-dimensional agreements (FTAA, NAFTA, etc.) the rules of the game of global capitalism attempt to predominate over those of national democracies. These one-dimensional agreements create organisms or mechanisms that ignore or even violate the independence of the democratic powers of these countries.

In this context, it is worth considering the mechanisms for the settlement of disputes that may arise between the national governments of the signatory countries and the TNCs. These mechanisms, based on panels of experts, are not subject to the jurisdiction of the sovereign powers of the governments involved. Therefore, the principles of sovereignty and autonomy of the branches of government may be violated. Furthermore, as these FTAs are one-dimensional, they do not include social, cultural or political commitments, nor do they require bodies such as parliamentary bodies, courts of justice, or executive powers of a supranational nature.

In contrast, in multidimensional agreements, whether highly developed (EU) or incipient (Mercosur, CAN, CACM and Caricom), commitments include social clauses (multilateral social security, health and welfare agreements) and cultural clauses (reciprocal recognition of diplomas or educational certificates). These and other clauses are conditions required for the effective enforcement of minimum community citizenship, without which the rights of immigrants from other Member States would be illusory.

It should also be noted that in the case of the EU, supra-national bodies such as the Court of Justice, the European Parliament, or the Commission operate. Think also of the European Central Bank and the validity of the euro.

Let us examine an example: if the EU had signed an FTA with the United States with the clauses contained in NAFTA or those that were unsuccessfully negotiated in the FTAA, the EU Court of Justice would not have been able to apply its unlimited jurisdictional powers that allow it to impose fines of millions of euros on large TNCs that violate competition and consumer protection rules. The EU Court for example imposed a fine of almost 500 million of Euros on Microsoft for anti- competitive practices. It also imposed another fine of almost one billion euros on four major elevator manufacturers (Otis, Kone, Schindler, and ThyssenKrupp) for price fixing. No one doubts that the EU Court of Justice is an autonomous power capable of defending the interests of EU companies and citizens. But its existence is a consequence of the supranational and multidimensional nature of the EU.

Conclusions[43]

Like all the rest, this chapter is incorporated as it was originally published in 2007. Only the outdated statistical data have been eliminated, and a few connective paragraphs have been added. The author considers that, despite the time that has elapsed and its outdatedness, it nevertheless preserves an even more valuable Latin American message in light of the Russian- Ukrainian war, and the sharpening of the Sino-American confrontation.

The role that regional integration can play in the development of Latin American societies is not limited to market considerations, or even to institutional frameworks of an economic nature. It also includes regional convergence at the cultural, social, environmental and, above all, political levels. A multidimensional integration strategy with supranational norms and mechanisms is a way of counterbalancing and more adequately assimilating the impact of the globalization process. The transnational economic players are sufficiently powerful to require South American political counterparts with greater bargaining power.

The convergence of South American countries at the political level is based on the principles, practices and institutions of democracy. On these

[43] Explanatory note: It should be remembered that this chapter was originally published in 2007 and that it has been reproduced without any update. The author and the editors considered that it retains a historical and testimonial value and a Latin Americanist message (multidimensional integration) especially valuable, today (perhaps more than ever), given the war in Europe, and the sharpening of the Sino-American confrontation.

bases, and recalling the example of the EU, there is no reason to disregard, at least in the case of South America, the legitimacy of institutions, mechanisms and decision-making bodies of a multidimensional and supranational nature, capable of operating in the different dimensions of regional integration agreements.

Part Four

Power, democracy and social responsibility[44]

[44] The following chapters XIV, XV and XVI, were extracted from: Armando Di Filippo (2013), "Poder capitalismo y democracia", RIL Publishers, Santiago de Chile.

Chapter XIV

An "Aristotelian" theory of power and domination[45]

Proposal of the subject[46]

The starting point of the analysis of domination is the notion of power. The notion of power is a specification of the Aristotelian notion of potency. The powerful is the one who is in a position of power. In human social life, positions of power refer to the place occupied by people in the institutions of society. These positions of power are those that allow the powerful to exercise their power. The structured and stable exercise of power in a given sphere of society is a form of domination.

The position of power consists in the control of some incentive that orients the behavior of human beings in society. The dominator is the one who, in a relationship of domination, possesses and exercises the incentive that allows him to dominate. The incentive is the mechanism through which the dominator induces the dominated to act in a certain way.

In relation to human beings we can define three main incentives or, in other words, three specific mechanisms of domination. An economic mechanism, which consists in managing the scarcity of some satisfaction

---

[45] The quotation mark for the word "Aristotelian" is a reminder that Aristotle did not formulate such a theory, nor did he claim to do so. In this chapter his basic philosophical categories are freely used to propose it.

[46] This chapter originally published in 2013 by Editorial RIL in the book "Poder, capitalismo y democracia", includes, in the present version, some minor modifications oriented to give greater clarity to some fundamental concepts.

necessary for life in society (in the capitalist era, which began approximately two and a half centuries ago, that mechanism has been industrial and financial capital); a political mechanism, whose function is to administer legalized coercion or the threat of its use (generally controlled and centralized by the normative power of the State); a cultural mechanism, (generally managed by those who exercise normative power) established to administer information, communication and knowledge.

This cultural mechanism traces its roots to the origins of the great civilizations and crystallizes in the language that treasures ancestral wisdoms. In the cultural history of the West, these roots are based on important Greco-Latin sources. Going precisely to the origin of these sources, we will try to express this approach through Aristotle's four causes applied to elucidate the meaning of the notions of power and domination. The four Aristotelian causes apply to all rational action and, also, to the forms of rational domination.

By "rational" we understand here that action that seeks congruence between means and ends, but this rationality is purely instrumental, to the extent that the instruments of action themselves become ends. For example, when the ends of the powerful are those of acquiring more power. Moral rationality is that which addresses head-on the ethical significance of the ends that may eventually be pursued. Instrumental rationality seeks effectiveness and efficiency in the application of means. More precisely, it administers means with the final objective of obtaining more means. This is the case, for example, of the profit motive pursued by capital in market activities.

Every rational action that we can conceive of, be it the creation of the universe by God (if we are believers), be it the production carried out by an artisan, or the domination of a rational being over another equally rational being, can be examined from four explanatory angles.

These explanatory angles were called "causes" by Aristotle, and we wish to adapt this complex explanatory approach to the main systems of domination operating in contemporary Western societies. The four causes addressed by Aristotle are: a) the final, b) the efficient, c) the material and d) the formal. In the case of individual-rational action, the final cause responds to the conscious ends that the actor proposes, the material cause expresses that on which the actor exercises his action, the efficient cause is the action itself (or the chain of partial acts that constitute it) and the formal cause is the previously conceived or planned structure of said action (relatively lasting if it has modified a pre-existing reality).

The more the concrete result obtained is farther away from the preconceived or planned form, the less rationality can be attributed to such action. Theoretically or ideally, if the action were completely rational, then the preconceived form should coincide with the concrete result. Of course, in the practical action exercised in the framework of human societies, this coincidence may not be clearly verified, first, because in the social structure there are eco-nomic, political, cultural and biological- environmental dimensions where multiple actors and differentiated situations act and intertwine, and second, because rational action is institutionalized as well as the wills expressed through them.

Thus the formal cause, i.e. the preconceived or planned form, is not usually the fruit of an individual mind (as Joseph Schumpeter thought, for example, with the idealized figure of the innovative entrepreneur), but is expressing a social or collective result. This clarification or caveat is especially applicable in the case of rational domination.

At a purely theoretical level, the efficient cause is the action itself (with its techniques) executed or coordinated by the dominant subject, the material cause is the behavior of the potentially dominatable object (which can also be a rational subject: for example, the workers in a factory), the formal cause is the successful outcome (if it responds to the plans formulated by the dominant subject) of the structured relationship between the dominant subject and the potentially dominatable object, and the final cause is the motives for which the dominant subject wishes to subordinate the behavior of the dominated object.

Aristotle did not explicitly use his four causes to examine a process of domination, but he did approach the notion of power from his conceptual power-act duo. In this free use of Aristotle's ideas, we begin by conceiving the notion of power held by human beings in any social relation, as a conceptual variant of the notion of power, and the notion of domination is the actualization of power. Thus, domination is the actualization of positions of power, and, reciprocally, these positions are potential situations of domination.

This Aristotelian contextualization of the notion of domination is relatively adaptable to the contemporary languages of systems and games.

In the language of systems (e.g. Mario Bunge's version), the dominator and the dominated could be considered the components of the system of social domination; the efficient cause of the relation of domination would refer to the dynamic mechanisms used by the dominator to make the process of domination effective; the material cause would allude to the behavior of the potentially dominated actor (the dominatable "matter"); the formal cause would be the relationship itself (dominator-dominated) originally conceived as the structure of the domination system; and the final cause would express the motives (values, ends, interests, etc.) for which the dominator wishes to dominate the dominated.

In the language of games, for example (North, 1993), rather than speaking of effective or consolidated domination, the notion of power struggle emerges. It is a confrontation whose outcome is not defined; therefore, definitive domination can only be determined at the end of the process. The potential dominators and dominated are the players; the efficient causes that shape the process of domination are the individual or team plays with their respective weighting (for example, goals scored in a soccer match); the formal causes are the technical and social rules of the game; and the final causes are precisely to dominate the adversary by winning the game.

The Aristotelian language of causes has been originally presented and exemplified through a productive action, in a way in which it is very clear from the beginning who is the subject that dominates and places the efficient cause (for example, the artisan producer, the artist creator or nature understood as an intelligent force), and which is the dominated object that is the material cause (moving from dominated in potency to dominated in act). The condition of the dominator (artisan, producer, creator) is furthermore identified because this (etymologically from the Latin “Dominus”) sets the ends or final cause, i.e. the reasons for which he performs the act of production or creation. Finally, the result of the process of domination (also production or creation) assumes a preconceived structure that is the formal cause of the process.

It is very important to distinguish between power on the one hand and domination on the other hand, where, as we said, power is domination in potency, or domination is actualized and exercised power. In this respect we have three moments: the first is that of the positions of power, the second is that of the struggle for power, and the third is that of the actualization of domination.

The moments of domination according to Aristotelian language

Let us return to the Aristotelian language of causes and to the example of production. The craftsman producing a marble statue has before him the marble, which is the material because of his art, and the tools he will use to model it. We are at the moment of positions of power. But we can ask ourselves: is it a question of a habitual process and of a skilled craftsman, can we say that the craftsman is in potency (active) to turn the marble into a work of art, and that the marble is in potency (passive) to be turned into a work of art?

Is necessary to navigate from potency to act, and, in that journey, it is possible that we as external observers discover that the artisan does not know his trade well or has inadequate tools, or that, being skilled, he was given an imperfect material (marble). Thus, there are direct conditions of the productive process that determine the positions of power of the interacting parties, such as: the artisan's capacity for action on the material and the material's capacity for reaction or resistance. There are also indirect or remote conditions, such as: the room where the artisan works, its comfortable or uncomfortable temperature, its lighting, its isolation from external interferences, etc.

These direct or indirect conditions are, analogically speaking, the positions of power of the interacting parties. In this example we speak (strictly speaking) of production and not of domination, but production is a special case of the notion of domination. Every process of production is a process of domination of the producer over the matter he transforms in order to submit it to his ends, but not every process of domination is a process of production. The concept of production is a simpler form of the concept of domination.

In this first example referring to the craftsman's statue, the second moment is that of the power struggle in which the craftsman, with his tools (efficient cause), acts on the marble (material cause) to transform it into a statue (formal cause), in order to create a beautiful object (final cause). There is a power struggle because the marble offers resistance to the action of the craftsman, and the process of production of the statue expresses precisely this struggle, which leads to the domination of the craftsman over the marble he uses.

The third moment is that of realized domination (consummated, made effective), when the already structured result of domination emerges, which is the statue. This is the moment of values and ends. If the statue reaches the desired levels of perfection and beauty, then the success of the process of domination (production) of the craftsman over the marble he has transformed will have been consummated. All this is, of course, a theoretical and highly idealized conjecture within the framework of the vision of the illustrious Greek sage, which serves as a starting point and a source of inspiration.

The moments of domination according to the language of games

Let us now examine the language of games in the simple version presented by Douglass North (1993). Let us assume that the game under examination is soccer. The potential dominators and dominated are the opposing teams. Each of them considers itself as an efficient cause, capable of producing plays that lead to the final cause, which is victory. For each team, the opponent is part of the material cause, upon which the process of domination must fall. Most team sports are played with a ball, which is the "conductive thread" of the process and the apparent material cause of the game; however, the real object on which the action of each team falls, is in reality the opposing team. In other words, each team considers itself as the efficient cause of a process aimed at transforming the opposing team into the loser. There are technical and playful (social) rules that must be respected by the teams and that give the game its identity and specificity (which is why, let us say, it is soccer and not basketball).

At the beginning, the game is a power struggle, but as the contest progresses, a process of domination emerges (i.e., the team that scores goals provisionally dominate the match). The final result will only be known when the rules that determine the conclusion of the game are fulfilled.

Let us examine in this situation what the three moments are. The moment of the positions of power is the moment of the direct and indirect preconditions that affect the ability or probability of each team to succeed in the contest. Among the direct conditions are, for example, the state of physical preparation and skill of each player and each team. Also psychological states such as depression, euphoria or extreme nervousness. Among the indirect conditions are the physical infrastructures such as the playing field and the elements that make up its design and suitability. But there may be particular indirect conditions to be taken into account; for example, a match held at a high altitude, in very hot or cold weather, or humidity, etc., where one team is accustomed to such physical conditions, but the other team suffers from them because it is not used to those physical conditions.

The moment of the power struggle takes place during the match itself, and it is there that this dynamic, very complex picture is verified, where each team carries out its action aimed at dominating the other. These are two parallel, reciprocal and antagonistic processes. In them, the two teams assume each other, but they also oppose each other. They also need each other, because there can be no contest without contenders.

The third moment is that of realized domination. This moment takes shape throughout the game. Thus, if a team is ahead with a high score and there is little time left in the game, the matter is factually defined before the official conclusion, but the rules of the game (which configure its form) express a formal or official moment of declaration of the conclusion of the game. In any case, from a dynamic perspective, the game (contest, encounter, etc.) is the effective transition from a potential or hypothetical domination to an effective or final domination, which only takes place when the parties accept, according to the rules, that they won or lost.

In the case of a game, the moment of domination marks the end of the contest, but in the case of a war or the domination of one nation over another, it marks the historical beginning of a structured relationship that transforms the pre-existing reality and is prolonged in time.

The moments of domination according to the language of social systems

The third example is finally the most complex and refers to human societies, understood as social systems. This is the example we are interested in examining in depth in this paper. Here again, it is vital to distinguish the three moments of the processes of domination.

Unlike games (sports, games of chance, etc.), where the technical and ludic rules are prior and external to the game, in the social systems historically existing in civilized societies, the rules are modified by the social actors themselves and there is a permanent struggle to impose them. These technical and social rules are the conditions that are being modified; we call these variations structural change.

A social system is intrinsically dynamic and is composed of actors who are linked through technical and social rules, which constitute the structure or form of the system. The social process is driven by the individual and collective behavior of the actors, who are the efficient cause of its dynamics, and is oriented by the ends and values they sustain.

When we examine a process of domination between human beings, we can only know what is the efficient cause and what is the material cause of the process if this process is historically structured and reproduced over time. In that case, it is clear that, for example, in a slave regime, the master, with his behavior (with the mechanisms and incentives he uses) is the efficient cause of the process; the slave with his subordinate action is the material cause; the rules imposed by the master on the slave are the form or formal cause of domination;

and the ends or final cause of domination, whatever they may be, are imposed by the master.

It sounds strange to consider human beings as "material causes", but they are not considered as such (as human beings) when their particular ends are not consulted. Unlike what Kant asks, they are not always considered as ends, but only as means, that is, as dominatable matter, or, what is the same thing, as material causes of domination.

The historical structuring of the processes of domination in the sphere of human societies does not obey any inexorable or unmodifiable determinism, but once established, neither can it be easily transformed. This point is essential to distinguish between deterministic and non-deterministic analyses. This difference is therefore very important for understanding the mechanisms that explain the development of capitalism and democracy in Western societies.

A historical example presented schematically can be that of the process of domination installed in Latin America during the colonial era. We would have three moments of this process. First, the positions of power of colonizers and colonized, second, the struggle for power during the process of conquest, and third, the consolidation of a stable and structured process of domination that lasted at least three centuries (Di Filippo, 1981; Sunkel and Paz, 1970).

The timing of the positions of power was uncertain for the potential dominators, but in hindsight, the conquered had more powerful direct conditions of action than those of the conquered. The most obvious element was the mastery of productive and war technologies of greater efficiency and scale than those of the aborigines. In addition to these conditions (which had a direct influence), there were also other important motivations, such as the objective need for gold and silver that the European nations in the mercantilist phase had for the organization of their internal economies (Di Filippo 1981).

The moment of power struggles corresponds to the very process of the wars of conquest (late 15th and early 16th centuries), facilitated not only by the conquerors' greater productive and technological power and their strong motivation to acquire precious metals, but also by the pre-existing social structures of the native peoples, with their willingness to subordinate work, learned and practiced in the despotic societies in which they lived.

The moment of domination itself, which involves the definitive installation of colonial society, includes efficient causes, which are the incentives of a coercive nature (slavery, servitude), used by the dominators to achieve the subordination of the dominated; material causes (the dominated matter), which are the slaves and serfs who can be potentially modeled to fulfill their subordinate work; formal causes, which are the set of social and productive institutions (internalized rules of behavior) that gave structural stability to the process of colonial domination. These rules were used to administer subordinate labor in the mines, in the orders, in the mites, in the repartimientos or on the plantations). Finally, the final causes, understood as political, economic and cultural ends, were determined by the dominators.

In Latin America, the process of colonization turned ends into means, and the aim of the dominators was to maintain and, as far as possible, increase their positions of power in the spheres of political and economic domination. Thus, for example, when the missions of the Jesuit orders succeeded in organizing the Guaraní aborigines into self-sufficient and peaceful productive communities, teaching them productive techniques, fine arts and Catholic values, these communities began to acquire an influence that was considered exaggerated for the political interests of the crown and the colonial economic interests. Consequently, the success of these missions led to their expulsion, as they were not in line with those objectives of power.

The specificity of power and domination relations in human societies

Human societies can be seen as a type of social system, the basic components of which are human beings endowed with certain forms of moral and instrumental rationality; endowed therefore with freedom and framed within consciously internalized rules of habitual behavior (institutions), which together constitute the structure of human societies.

The notion of process applied to a human society refers to structured interactive human behaviors, which we denote as social relations and which, as a whole, constitute, dynamize and transform human societies.

The point to highlight here refers to the notions of freedom and power of human beings, which are derived from their capacity for rational behavior. This does not happen in other animal societies, where behaviors are much more genetically conditioned. We know, for example, that in higher primate societies there are also power struggles, but they are linked to the primary and basic needs for survival, reproduction, etc.

Aristotle defined humans as rational animals. What is specifically human in the relations of domination in civilized societies is precisely rationality (both instrumental and moral). Among other features, human rationality is characterized by the capacity for abstract thought and by the complexity, depth and subtlety of linguistic communication. Consequently, the regularities that structure human societies are not only dictated by genetic and environmental influences, but above all by institutions, which, like language, are created by humans themselves in the history of concrete societies.

These institutions are internalized (whether by genuine internal conviction or by external coercion suffered by those who submit to them) in everyday behavior and can be modified through complex power struggles which, in societies that we call civilized, are finally translated into the political sphere, giving rise to certain types of States ("polis, civitas").

The notion of power, when applied to the sphere of human beings, refers to an active power of a rational character. Reciprocally, one can speak of a passive power that is also of a rational character. Aristotle himself distinguishes between irrational and rational potencies.

Introducing the idea of rational power, Aristotle (1999) states that, being rational in nature, this power can produce opposite effects, while irrational powers produce the same effect:

> Contraries are not produced in the same being; but science is a power inasmuch as it contains the reason of things, and there is in the soul the principle of motion. And so that which is healthy produces nothing but health, that which is hot heat, that which is cold coldness, **while he who knows produces the two opposites.** Science knows the one and the other, but in a different way. For the notion of the two opposites is found, but not in the same way, in the soul which has in itself the principle of motion; and from the same principle, from the soul, applying itself to one and the same object, it will bring forth both opposites. The rationally potent beings are in a case contrary to that in

> which are found those who have only an irrational potency; there is in the notion of the latter only a single principle.
>
> It is clear that the power of good carries with it the idea of active or passive power; but it does not always accompany it. Whoever does good necessarily does something; while he who only does something does not necessarily do good (232).

The rational human condition means, in short, that human beings are capable of proposing specific ends and then trying to adapt the means required for the achievement of these ends. If there were unanimity about what are "good" ends and what are "bad" ends, the notion of the "common good" would be the general goal of human behavior. In the absence of such unanimity, power struggles arise, associated with the search for alternative ends. Consequently, there is an inversion between ends and means. Since the ends are not unanimous, the ends supported by those who have the appropriate means will prevail. These are the powerful.

The Aristotelian distinction between rational and irrational powers can be associated with the power of modern Western science, transmuted into applied science, and then into technology (Mario Bunge 1997). Basic or pure science, because it is a rational power (personified in those who hold such knowledge), can use the truth it unveils, either to produce "good" (for example, to cure the sick) or "evil" (to administer the poison that will kill them). It is good to remember this ambivalence of the effects of rational power, as opposed to the factual forms of irrational power (the burning of a forest caused by lightning, the impact of an aerolite, etc.). Consequently, in rational forms of power there are margins of freedom and, consequently, the ethical problem of the legitimacy of ends arises.

It is convenient to distinguish between the philosophical, generic notion of power and the different applied notions of power, exercised over natural entities or over social subjects. In this context, Aristotle observes (1999):

> The transition from power (or potency) to act for thought can be defined: the will realizing itself without encountering any external obstacle; here, on the contrary, for the being that is the object of healing, there will be power if there is no obstacle in it. In the same way the house will also exist in potency if there is nothing in it and if there is nothing in matter that opposes a house being built. If there is

> nothing to add, nor to take away, nor to change, matter will be the cause in potency. The same will happen with all beings that have outside themselves the principle of their production; and the same with those that, having this principle in themselves, will exist by themselves, if nothing external opposes it... Thus, the earth is not yet the statue in potency; it must become bronze in order to have this character[47] (238-239).

From this remarkable paragraph, it is worth highlighting the sentence: "The transit from power to act for thought can be defined: the will realizing itself without encountering any external obstacle". This definition of Aristotle is in itself a broad definition of the exercise of power, since power can be defined - to paraphrase Weber - as the capacity or probability of imposing one's will within a social relation, even against the opposition of the other members. When thought, that is, the thinking being imposes his will without encountering any external obstacle, he is exercising his power. In social relations, however, as Max Weber points out, it is necessary to foresee the emergence of obstacles that the dominator must overcome in order to impose his will.

Following Mario Bunge (1997), we can analyze in greater detail the more complex forms of power, as is the case of rational power: " Power can be analyzed as a binary relation: agent "a", exerts power over agent "b", or “Pab”, for short (The formal properties of P are obvious: it is unreflective, asymmetrical and transitive)[48]. If one thinks twice power turns out to be at least a quaternary relation because it is always exercised by some means "c" to obtain some end "d", or "Pabcd", for short. However, for any pair (means, end), the quaternary relation can be treated as if it were binary."

---

[47] For the Greek thinkers of antiquity there were original material principles. Some authors mention four elements: earth, water, fire and air. Earth was then, for these thinkers, an original element that, combined with some other element and after successive transformations, can end up becoming, for example, bronze, which is the material cause of sculpture.

[48] In set theory, a binary relation is called irreflexive if the elements are related to themselves; it is called asymmetric when: if one element is related to another by means of R, then the other is not related to the first; and transitive when: whenever one element is related to another, and the latter to a third, then the first is related to the third.

It should be emphasized that here Bunge speaks of the power that is exercised, and this conscious and rational exercise of power, if it acquires habituality, is what can be called domination. The quaternary relation of domination to which Bunge alludes can be analyzed (may I suggest) also in the light of the four causes proposed by Aristotle. It is clear that this is a special use of the notion of four causes:

- *Final cause of domination (corresponds to d in Bunge's previous symbology):* Aristotle's four causes become fully intelligible if we start from the final cause, that is, from the objective or motivation of an actor or of a determined set of dominant actors. Starting from the final cause confers moral (or immoral, depending on the ethical perspective) rationality, i.e., it confers full meaning to the actions under analysis. In the sphere of power relations, the final cause refers to the motivation or purpose pursued by the dominator in the exercise of his power.
- *Material cause (corresponds to b in Bunge's symbology*): In the sphere of social relations of power, the entity on which domination falls is the behavior of a human being. Its essential feature is that this behavior must have the potential to be subordinated (used or transformed according to the purposes of the rational action of the dominator)
- *Efficient cause (Corresponds to a in Bunge's symbology):* In this case it refers to the active dominant subject who subordinates the passive dominated. Note that, if the domination is exercised between human beings, the efficient cause is affected through the application of the incentive of power by the dominant agent.
- *Formal cause (Corresponds to P in Bunge's symbology):* It is the dominator-dominated relationship already established. It is the actualization of the active power of the dominating agent over the dominated patient. It is the behavior of the dominated, shaped or determined by the dominator in accordance with the final cause, responding to the action of the dominant agent. The formal cause establishes a structure of action that can be prolonged in time, where the efficient cause (represented by the dominator and his means) acts on the potentiality of the material cause (the dominated and his possible behavior) to transform it

and give it a new form in accordance with the ends of the dominant agent

It was observed above that, when the material cause is an inanimate entity, instead of being in the sphere of domination, we are rather in the sphere of production. Such is the case, for example, of a sculptor who designs a work of art (final cause) and, with his skill and his instruments (efficient cause), acts on the matter at his disposal (material cause), to leave a structure (formal cause) that is an expression of what he has acted and of the rules that guided his action.

In the realm of domination itself, but exercised over an irrational being, we can think of a tamer or horse tamer, who with his knowledge, tools and qualifications (efficient cause) acts on the animals (material cause), to achieve a stable structure of domination (formal cause expressed in a rider who habitually controls his hard-riding), destined to achieve transportation together with his personal load (final cause pursued).

The exercise of domination over animate and irrational beings, when institutionalized in a habitual manner, can become a production process. For example, a poultry farm implies: a) a final cause (producing food), b) a material cause (birds that are the basic raw material of the process), c) an efficient cause which are the productive processes executed or controlled by the dominating agent (owner or manager of the farm), and d) a formal cause which is the total structure of the process that leads to the final product sought and gives it habituality.

The specific and complex aspect of the power relationship, when applied to human beings in the societies in which they act, is that it is a matter of substituting the personal or spontaneous ends of the dominated for other subordinate ends. The same procedure of domestication of the foal, applied to the human being, can be translated, keeping the distances and deep differences, into a process of socialization and education that predispose him to accept social ends fixed by the one who controls the community.

Obviously, there is a multitude of processes and situations where structured and habitual relations of domination are manifested. What characterizes all authoritarian or coercive relations of domination is that human beings are considered as means for a finality that may be external to their intentions, as Marx expresses it in his notion of alienation. This is what Kant critically referred to when, in his moral precepts, he preached that human beings should be treated as ends in themselves and not as means for further action.

The relationship of domination will be coercive or authoritarian if the ends pursued by the dominant agent are not shared by the dominated, thus producing a dissociation between the dominator and the dominated, with respect to the ends pursued by each in the relationship of domination. The commander of troops (efficient cause) who indoctrinates and trains (formal cause) his soldiers (who are the material cause of the the power relationship) to lead them to war and perhaps to death, in order to win battles (the final cause of the domination process), is probably alienating his troops, imposing ends on them based on different types of incentives that alienate their will. Soldiers, in effect, may obey the commander and go into battle for multiple reasons: profit, love of country, loyalty and respect for their commander, or fear of facing a court-martial. The specificity of a "hard and pure" domination process is that the ends of the dominated do not necessarily coincide with those of the dominator, but the latter is forced to adopt them as if they were his own ends.

When relations of domination are structured, they are the main foundation (the form) of social systems and the basis for the existence of social classes. We could say with Mario Bunge (1999), a social class is a social group ...

> ...whose members are related to persons of other groups by some relation of domination. Let us begin by clarifying that the expression "class domination" should not be taken literally, because only individuals can dominate or be dominated, directly or by proxy. In other words, the terms or relata of a relation of domination are individuals and, more precisely, animals, in particular human beings.
>
> We will say that one animal dominates another in a certain respect if and only if the former makes the latter behave regularly in a certain way in the same circumstances. Subhuman animals can only dominate by force or sex. In contrast, one human being can dominate another in many respects: by force, by persuasion or suggestion, economically, culturally, politically, and so on. In other words, there are several kinds of human domination, and each of these kinds has several members. So much so that one individual can dominate another in one respect, while

> being dominated by the second in another respect. For example, the minister dominates his subordinates politically, but the latter may dominate the former bureaucratically (pp. 53-54).

This intertwining of dominant actions is very important, because it generates an interaction that, if it reaches stability, can give rise to complex structures of power and domination that go beyond the particular goals that the actors set themselves.

What are the four causes predicated on?

A couple of fundamental distinctions should be made at the outset. The first is related to the dynamic character of social reality, and the second to the role of human beings in social processes.

First, the four causes, when applied to the social sphere, refer to concrete systems that are intrinsically dynamic. Thus, there is a certain tension between the notions of structure (form) and process. Indeed, a structure refers to the more or less stable reproduction of a set of social institutions and organizations, endowed with specific material and intellectual instruments.

The dominant notion is that of process, since the entire universe is in permanent change, and concrete human societies, as components of that universe, are also in permanent change. Thus, when we speak of structures, we refer to the relatively stable reproduction of a set of institutions, organizations and habitual social relations. In short, a social structure is in reality a social process that reproduces itself without major changes.

Therefore, it would be wrong to consider that the process is "dynamic" and the structure is "static". If by "static" we mean "immobility," no social structure is static because all its components are intrinsically dynamic.

What may be static is the vision or model with which we represent the structure to ourselves. But then we refer to an abstract, theoretical system that we have constructed in our mind. This intellectual construction is justified, since a process can reproduce itself within its structural frameworks without major changes for long periods of time. In that case, the structure, which is always dynamic, undergoes a kind of "stabilized dynamics" through which it reproduces itself. It is in the interest of social scientists to know, using a static view, the patterns that regulate such stable change.

In a long-term perspective such as the one adopted in this chapter; the historically significant issue is that of structural change. In this case, the process does not reproduce itself in essentially the same way. The inertia of the past is broken because new forces or powers are at work that need to be unveiled.

Therefore, the four Aristotelian causes ask slightly different questions; on the one hand, when they refer to a dynamic system whose structure is stable, and reproduces itself without change, and, on the other hand, when they refer to a dynamic system whose structure changes.

Secondly, the role of human beings is not clear as to whether they participate in the social game as efficient cause or as material cause. And the immediate answer would be that in social regimes that open the possibility of governing to all citizens, all have the opportunity to participate as efficient causes. But if there are strata that are definitively excluded, they are instrumentalized as material causes on which the process of domination falls. Aristotle said that, in an ideal regime, citizens must come together to rule and be ruled.

In a human society (concrete social system) the components (material cause) of which it is "made" are ultimately the human beings or persons who obey an established system of domination; the structure of this system (formal cause) are the rules and artifacts in force that determine the social relations and the corresponding reciprocal expectations; the dynamics (efficient cause) that reproduce the structure are the established and habitual incentives of domination; and the ends that guide the dynamics of the system (final cause) are those imposed by the dominant classes.

In a human society (concrete social system) the components (material cause) of which it is "made" are ultimately the human beings or persons who obey an established system of domination; the structure of this system (formal cause) are the rules and artifacts in force that determine the social relations and the corresponding reciprocal expectations; the dynamics (efficient cause) that reproduce the structure are the established and habitual incentives of domination; and the ends that guide the dynamics of the system (final cause) are those imposed by the dominant classes that guide the process of domination. This system of ends and values is cultural in nature and more precisely presupposes an ethics.

Consequently, it is not that ethics is in itself a factor of social change, but only ethics incarnated in those endowed with power has social effects.

Today, in the 21st century, in the era of artificial intelligence, those who control the algorithms that give rise to this new form of intelligence acquire a responsibility unprecedented in the history of mankind. Hence the importance of corporate social responsibility (see chapter XVII).

Thus the behaviors of human beings subordinated to specific forms of domination are the material cause of the social process, and the behaviors of the human beings who exercise this domination are the efficient cause of that same process.

Every human society is a structurally asymmetrical social system, founded on positions of power and relations of domination, on the basis of which the system reproduces itself. The structural change of a human social system is a change in the structures of domination (of its rules and its material instruments), and is accompanied by a change in the systems of goals and values that guide the social behavior of the dominators.

Consequently, the use of the four causes or the four questions that organize our scientific investigation of human societies must refer, first, to the human beings who make them up; second, to the structure that is taken as a starting point, which is assumed to be stable; third, it must refer to the structural change of that same social system (change in the rules and instruments of social life) that corresponds to a change in the relations of domination prevailing in a society; and fourth, this change implies a modification in the system of ends imposed by the dominators.

In the contemporary era, the system of legally binding ends that guides the process of domination is found fundamentally in the political constitution of States and in the fundamental legal codes. Ever since Aristotle studied the constitutions of the Greek states of his time, it is there that we find the link between a system of goals and a system of rules that regulate the different dimensions of social life (biological-environmental, cultural, economic and political). We are talking, therefore, of civilized human societies. The etymological roots of politics ("Polis") refer us in its Latin translation to "civitas", and from there to civilization.

A fundamental and transhistorical mechanism of social change

A different question is to know what is the ultimate efficient cause that produces a change in the systems of domination and social ends of human societies. Not just any change in the domination system is possible, only that which can reach a certain structural stability. Otherwise, the change in the domination system may lead to the collapse of the human societies under analysis. The system of ends and values pursued by the ruling classes must be reproducible, i.e., it must achieve structural stability. The transition from one system of ends to another depends to a high degree on the technical, economic, cultural and political capacity to reproduce the system under new structural guidelines.

Aristotle, without referring to the four causes, distinguishes, in the “Polis”, between the material cause (the "parts" of the city, corresponding to the definable social actors), the formal cause or social structure (the asymmetries of economic, productive and cultural power) and the efficient cause or motor that energizes the city (the relations of domination that arise from these asymmetrical positions):

> The reason for the existence of many political regimes is that every city has several parts. We observe, in the first place, that all cities are made up of houses (families); then we see that, of this multitude, some must necessarily be rich, others poor and others of average position, and that the rich will have heavy weapons, while the poor will lack them. We also see that, of the people, one part is that of the farmers, another that of the merchants, and a third that of the artisans. There are also differences among the notable people, according to their wealth and the size of their patrimony, as, for example, in the breeding of horses (it is not easy, by the way, to dedicate oneself to it if one is not rich; that is why in ancient times in those cities whose power depended on their horses there was an oligarchy; they used their horses in the war against neighboring towns...). To these differences of wealth are also added others due some to lineage, others to virtue or to some similar trait that we describe as part of the city when we speak about the aristocracy. We then determine, in effect, how many are the necessary constituent parts

> of every city. These parts sometimes all participate in the political regime, sometimes few and sometimes many.
>
> It is therefore clear that there must be various forms of political regime, which differ from each other specifically, because the parts that constitute them also differ from each other specifically. A political regime is the system of powers ("Magistratures"), which are all distributed, either according to the power of those who participate in the government, or according to some other equality common to all: I mean, for example, the power of the poor or of the rich or some common to both. It is necessary then that there be political regimes as orders based on the predominancies and on the differences between the parties (Aristotle 2005: 234-236)

Thus, within the human societies of ancient Greece, Aristotle leaves open a certain variable combinatorics, considering the defining features of the social actors (the parts of the city) and the structures that link them (the relative positions of power). The political regime reflects these differences, which essentially seem to depend in all cases on the control of resources (rich classes, middle classes and poor classes).

These structural variations are verified within the social systems of the ancient world that Aristotle observes. His knowledge of history is profound, but he refers to the civilization in which he lived: a slave society where citizenship was reserved for a very small fraction of the "parts" of the city.

However, his almost prophetic intuition allows him to outline a hypothesis which, put simply and in a single paragraph, constitutes a true philosophy of history; one according to which technical change in the instruments of action and production is the foundation of profound historical change in the relations of domination:

> Just as for the arts which have a definite sphere, if they are to fulfill their task completely, it would be necessary for the appropriate instruments to exist, so also the domestic administrator must have appropriate instruments at his disposal. Some of the instruments are inanimate, while others are animate (for example, for the pilot, the rudder is inanimate but the lookout is animate, for in the arts he who renders services belongs to the class of instruments; so also, a possession is an instrument for life and property is a set of instruments,

> and the slave is an animate possession, and so anyone who renders a service is like an instrument prior to the other instruments. For if each instrument could perform its own task, by receiving an order or by anticipating it, as is told of the statues of Daedalus or the Tripods of Hephaestus, which, as the poet says, entered by themselves into the assembly of the gods, in the same way the shuttles would weave by themselves, and the plectrums would play the zither, and the architects would have no need of servants nor the masters of slaves (Aristotle 2005: 63-64).

Aristotle expresses here a philosophy of history that formulates a hypothesis of social change in the very long term (it is being fulfilled more than two thousand years after having been set forth). In short, it refers to what Marx would call the development of productive forces, Schumpeter business innovation, Prebisch technical progress, etc. In short, we are talking about a fundamental and transhistorical mechanism of social change that was strengthened at the beginning of the contemporary era with the advent of capitalism. This process was analyzed in the chapter X of this book when we observed: the periodization that we will analyze in the following pages includes: 1) the techniques, institutions and productive processes introduced by the European conquerors and colonizers (15th to 19th centuries); 2) the techniques, institutions and productive processes introduced by the hegemonic centers (in particular Great Britain with its steam engine during the 19th century); 3) the techniques, institutions and productive processes (the internal combustion engine, for example) introduced after the second Industrial Revolution by the United States, the hegemonic center, still emerging during the first half of the 20th century; 4) the techniques, institutions and productive processes developed since the Second World War (in particular the use of nuclear energy and the expansion of the nuclear industry)

The first two phases of this periodization are: (1) the new technologies (e.g., consumer durables) during the heyday of the American Industrial Revolution, which changed the productive structuring of capitalism and the world power scenario during the second half of the 20th century; (2) the techniques, institutions and productive processes associated with information, communication and knowledge technologies (ICT) that are leading to the current multicentric or multipolar scenario (with the growing gravitation of China) in the process of constructing a new world order.

Undoubtedly, the paragraph referring to Aristotle's "prophecy" that we have quoted in previous pages coincides with phase 5 of the above periodization, which has led to the algorithms of artificial intelligence, giving rise to a new social order, fraught with dangers for human freedom, which we have tried to describe in the anticipated conclusions to this book.

Are the notions of power and domination scientifically verifiable?

The fact that the essential unity of the material world and the systemic nature of the objects of scientific study are accepted does not mean that the profound differences between the nature of social processes and the nature of processes more proper to the physical-natural sciences should be ignored. In the study of the physical and natural sciences, humans examine their object of study from the outside, whereas in the historical-natural sciences they participate in a certain sense (since they are human beings) in the object under investigation. This determines that the researcher cannot avoid ascribing a final cause or a specific moral rationality to the behaviors of the people in the societies under investigation.

In the case of the social sciences, the ethical and teleological aspect of human behavior cannot be ignored. It is therefore necessary to distinguish between three notions with different meanings (Mario Bunge 1999), which vary according to the type of social system being studied: a) scientific laws, i.e. hypotheses or theories that can be verified by the methods of science applicable to all situations of the type studied; b) values supported by people in situations of the type studied; and c) formal and informal institutions, understood as internalized norms of habitual behavior in social life.

The relations of domination between rational beings presuppose the control of the motivations that drive the behavior of the dominated beings. I refer to the incentives used by the dominator, which are transmuted into values pursued (willingly or unwillingly) by the dominated; in our previous example of the battle they would be love of country, loyalty or admiration for the boss, obtaining money, fear of punishment, etc.

The question then arises as to whether it is possible to analyze in a scientific way social relations involving human ends or values. This means an important difference that Mario Bunge (1999) examines in the following way:

> Let us return to the question of social laws (in the sense of scientific generalizations). Let us suppose, for the sake of discussion, that we know some reliable social generalizations, and let us ask ourselves whether they are sufficient (together with the relevant data concerning the circumstances) to explain and predict any possible social fact. Our answer is negative, because people are inventive and value sustaining, and social systems satisfy man- made rules of various kinds-including legal and moral norms-as well as laws. Hence, the explanation or prediction of a social fact may require four sets of premises and not two: a) statements of laws, b) valuation, c) rules, and d) empirical data. Thus, explaining or predicting the observable fact that an individual or group of class C engages in actions of type A may require the following premises:
>
> Law: In social systems of the same class C, the fact (state or event) B follows the state or event A, always or with a certain frequency (constant or mutable according to laws with the passage of time).
>
> Valuation: Individuals of social systems of class C perceive fact B as optimally valuable (or just satisfactory).
>
> Rule: Try to obtain what appears to be optimally valuable (or only satisfactory).
>
> Fact: The individual, or group in question, belonging to a social system of class C, tries to make fact A occur.

Bunge's argumentation on the scientific status of the explanation of social facts comfortably accommodates the notions of power and domination, although this connection is proposed in the present work and does not compromise his opinion.

Let us exemplify the logic of the previous paragraph in the field of economic reflections. For example, let us try to explain or predict the fact that workers lacking property (apart from their own labor capacity) in capitalism (class C group) are offered in the labor market (type A actions) In order to do so, we must start from the following assumptions:

Law: In capitalist (sub)social systems (of the same class C), obtaining a personal or family wage income (state or event B) follows obtaining a job in the labor market (state or event A). In terms of power, this means a situation of dependence on the part of workers who require an income to live, which in turn depends on obtaining a paid job. But this situation of dependence requires prior knowledge of the needs and, more generally, the values of the workers involved.

Valuation: Workers lacking property in capitalist social subsystems (class group C) perceive the attainment of an income (state or event B) as valuable. Here the notion of incentive is expressed, i.e., the idea of income operating simultaneously as a "stick" (if denied) or a "carrot" (if given).

Existing institutions or internalized social rules: Power structures and reciprocal behavioral expectations induce workers to try to obtain a wage income (event B) as a valuable or socially necessary goal for survival. This internalized norm of habitual behavior derives from the position of power (or powerlessness) occupied by the actors in the economic structure of society.

Data: It is a matter of achieving a verifiable perception by different means (surveys, regular statistical records, etc.), that salaried workers respond to a certain degree and measure to the structure of domination established by capital.

The great transformation: artificial intelligence

In this brief paragraph we develop some suggestive hypotheses on the current evolution and future of capitalism. To put them forward, let us return to the paragraph quoted on the "Aristotelian prophecy". Aristotle says:

> For if each instrument could perform its own task, either by receiving an order or by anticipating it, as is told of the statues of Daedalus or the Tripods of Hephaestus, which, as the poet says, entered the assembly of the gods by themselves, so would the shuttles weave by themselves, and the plectrums play the zither, and the architects would have no need of servants, nor the masters of slaves.

This hypothetical statement posed by Aristotle as a distant utopia, today has become technically possible, and in fact has begun to become effective, as robots begin to replace humans in all kinds of tasks and disciplines from the techniques of scientific research, to human professions with various types of qualifications, such as medicine or gastronomy, for example.

Looking at the systematization cited in previous pages on the scientific method formulated by Mario Bunge and adapted in this work to the examination of the capitalist system, we have just said that: "The structures of power and the reciprocal expectations of behavior induce workers to try to obtain a wage income (event B) as a valuable or socially necessary objective for survival. This internalized norm of habitual behavior derives from the position of power (or powerlessness) occupied by the actors in the economic structure of society.

Now, the massive introduction of robotization based on artificial intelligence (AI) algorithms will definitely change the power structure in capitalist societies. In the previous capital-labor dialectic of the dynamics of capitalism both the dominator and the dominated were opposed in their interests, but they also knew and needed each other. In particular, exploited human labor was an essential component, not only of capitalism but of all class societies in human history.

But this capitalist dialectic, which implied a certain power relation, is being replaced by another system in which capital will gradually dispense with human labor, which will no longer be an indispensable component of the productive processes. Therefore, in the long run, the labor force that will be dispensed with will lack new sources of income and will be expelled from the essential logic of the capitalist markets.

Enormous transformations in the structures of human societies are foreseeable as a result of the economic systems that will emerge. On one side, there will be an acceleration of the processes of concentration of capital and monopolization of markets as large capitalist corporations invade the field of activities previously the preserve of small and medium- sized enterprises. On the other side, a labor force unnecessary for the functioning of markets on the scale of individual enterprises will be increasingly dispensed with. This will not happen overnight, but its effects will probably already be felt in the course of this century. This crucial connection in the logic of the scientific method along the lines proposed by Bunge will then have been broken. Workers will still need to perform a paid task in order to earn an income in the labor market. But companies, left to the presumably self-regulating mechanisms of the market, will be increasingly concentrated and robotized. Human workers will be replaced by "intelligent" algorithms, not only in simple and routine tasks but also in others associated with scientific and technological innovation. In this context, Aristotle said in *Nicomachean ethics*:

> The need we have for each other is, in reality, the common bond of society. If men had no needs, or if they did not have similar needs, there would be no exchange between them, or at least the exchange would not be the same. But as the effect of a completely voluntary convention, money has thus become the instrument and the sign of this necessity. Aristotle, Nicomachean ethics (1998).

Wages and salaries received in currency by the very high percentage of people who live from their work will decrease their relative weight in the income generated. Only the owners of some form of wealth, will continue to have purchasing power measured in monetary units. This will definitely change the systemic rationality of capitalism.

Human behaviors and values

Obviously, in this scientific interpretation of a social process, what generates uncertainty in relation to the scientific explanation is the field of values and rules. Thus, in the example of the commander and the soldiers, cited in the previous section, the explanation of the battle will be different depending on the values that induce the soldiers to fight for victory: defense of an ideal, patriotism, profit, fear, trust and loyalty to the commander, etc. However, it is likely that some of them are not clear about the value that legitimizes their decision to fight, but they are clear about a coercive rule that is institutionalized: "every soldier must be willing to risk his life in battle (or to lose it before a court-martial)".

In conclusion, returning to the epistemological implications, the validation of a scientific law in the social sciences requires not only empirical verification from the data, but also an examination of the values and norms that guide human behavior.

However, the values that can be analyzed scientifically are the expression of what people are or do. Regarding what people are, it is necessary to study human nature. The biological-environmental conditions of human life tell us that for our species pure air and water are good because they help us to live, and so we could cite other obvious examples associated with our biological dimension. But it is also possible to deduce other scientifically verifiable rules regarding the conditions of our rational life. The "being" of humans refers not only to their transhistorical defining features, but also to their existential ones, since each concrete human being exists in an equally concrete way, and on the basis of that concrete existence, defines what are the ends or values that allow them to exist and, therefore, are good for him.

This does not mean legitimizing any form of behavior, but it does mean understanding what is the mechanism through which human beings find certain ends to be good and not others. It means, in short, to put oneself in the place of the other and try to understand from that position what are their goals and motivations.

On a social and not an individual scale, the interpretation of the causal relationship goes from concrete human beings and their behaviors to values, and not the other way around. As we have seen, the prevailing values in a society are not understood if there is no clarity about the main systems of domination prevailing in it. This does not mean that there are no transhistorical human values that are present in every human civilization. They result from a knowledge of the essential features of every human being. That is, they result from what every person is.

In this transhistorical sense, devoid of any essentialism or transcendentalism, it is possible to speak of human nature or the human condition. But human values are historically situated and, therefore, are not discovered from an abstract notion, but from the concrete notion of human existence, that is, from concrete human beings acting in concrete circumstances. Mario Bunge (1997) summarizes this notion by saying:

> Values are relations between objects, on one side, and evaluating subjects on the other. More precisely, values are complex dispositional properties: they are not inherent qualities of valuable things, events or acts or conceptual entities, but potential relations that are actualized in the circumstances that cause certain things, events, acts or conceptual entities to be judged as valuable, in some sense, by some social unit (person or group). Indeed, a preliminary analysis of the simplest value judgments yields the following form: x is valuable in respect R for the

> social unit U in the circumstances C and in the light of the body of knowledge K (142-143).

The analysis of value judgments to which Bunge alludes in the previous quote, that explanations in the social sciences should include explicit mention of values and norms, can be made explicit by using the same example of the previous section and saying that earning a family income is a valuable behavior, in capitalist economies for workers who depend on their labor for survival, a fact widely known from the usual position occupied by these workers in the economic system.

The most widespread and unanimously accepted values in a given society are usually linked to the satisfaction of the most elementary needs on which the survival of the poorest depends. This notion of what is necessary for survival is thus linked to what is valuable, giving rise to the fact-value sequence.

As Aristotle points out, the interdependence of social needs is the basic unifying bond of social life. From this point of view, the habituality and interdependence of human interactions derives from the habituality and interdependence of human needs. If we distinguish between essential human needs and existential human needs, the former derives from human nature or essence (rational and political animal), which is universal, objective and transhistorical given; and the latter (existential needs) are particular, also objective, but historically situated. Existential needs derive from essential needs and give them a historically situated existence in concrete societies and are experienced by concrete human beings.

Seen from the individual angle of the needy, these needs are conditions for transiting from potency to act, that is, for transiting from a moment of deprivation to a moment of satisfaction. This transit is also a leap from a moment of relative impotence (lack of freedom) to a relative increase of freedom, in a dynamic process that is framed in the structures that define the system. They are, as Bunge observes in the above quotation, "potential relations that are actualized in the circumstances that cause certain things, events, acts or conceptual entities to be judged as valuable, in some sense, by some social unit (person or group)". Therefore, the needs that arise from social life demand goods, i.e., valuable instruments. The provoked and/or controlled scarcity of such goods, implies in practical terms the control of human freedoms. In other words, it is a mechanism of power and domination.

Power, domination and scarcity in the market environment

The notion of scarcity is at the heart of economic categories and market mechanisms. However, scarcity, as it occurs in capitalist markets, is not a natural given but a relationship between quantities demanded and supplied. Therefore, scarcity is a result not only of the natural environment, but also of power structures.

When viewed from the individual angle of the agent in a position of power who controls the satisfaction, human needs are conditions for the transition from a situation of unexercised power to another effective situation of domination. The possessor, and therefore potential provider of the individual in need to achieve the transition from deprivation to satisfaction, is in a position (situation) of power. When this position of power is institutionalized and is thus exercised in a habitual and interdependent manner, a structure of domination may emerge.

The subject who, within the framework of capitalist market institutions, acts as a "potential dominated" depends on the "potential dominator" because the latter controls, in a socially structured manner, some satisfying factor whose deprivation converts the potential dominated into a person who lacks the freedom (personal autonomy) to actualize the vital potentialities that allow him or her self-realization in some field or dimension of reality (be it economic, biological- environmental, cultural or political). From this angle, economic goods defined by their utility and scarcity can be instruments of market domination through mechanisms that generate scarcity.

However, any structured relationship of domination in the sphere of markets creates an interdependence that manifests itself in different degrees. The difference lies in the severity of the consequences experienced by the dominator and the dominated if the domination relationship breaks down.

This is a general principle that transcends the sphere of capitalist market relations. A rebellious slave can be deprived of his life, a deserting soldier can be executed, a striking wage-worker can be deprived of his means of subsistence, and so on. By contrast, on the side of the rulers, when it breaks down the relation of domination, the severity and intensity of deprivation is usually less.

In capitalist economies, under the instrumental rationality of capital, the objective of the productive process is not the satisfaction of human needs, but the generation of profit, and, therefore, production depends on the rate of profit capable of being achieved with a given effective demand to be satisfied. Consequently, relative scarcity, measured by the coincidence in time between quantities demanded and quantities supplied, is determined by the magnitude of this effective demand and the average rate of profit pursued by the suppliers.

Since the administration of goods required to meet human needs has a technical component, the sphere of goods-producing techniques is a necessary component of these relations of domination, and generalized technical change in the sphere of production (as clearly perceived, among others, by Marx, Schumpeter, and Prebisch) determines different types of historical periods and human societies.

Each historical epoch determines, therefore, different potential situations of domination. Aristotle anticipated that the advent of robots (instruments that replace human servants and workers, even anticipating the desires of their masters) would have powerful effects on the structures of social domination. However, the scarcity of a product in capitalist societies is not measured by the quantity of it that society can supply in relation to the quantity that people need, but in relation to the quantity demanded by those who can pay its price. That is why, even in the contemporary era, famines that generates mortality do not necessarily imply a physical or material shortage of products, but only restrictive market mechanisms.

Chapter XV

Democracy: procedural and substantive dimensions[49]

The historical roots of the concept of democracy

Democracy as a political system was originally characterized by Aristotle in his work "Politics", but he did so only for the Greek citizen, fit to rule and to obey the government of his peers. He accepted, simultaneously, slavery as a social regime compatible with Greek-style democracy. Aristotle not only characterized democracy as a regime that defends the freedom of Greek citizens, but, according to some interpreters of his thought, considered it as the best of political regimes, simultaneously supporting majority rule and the rule of law.

Since the modern era, democracy has been emerging as a social process that sought to place limits on the power of the state. It emerged as a struggle against the totalitarian, absolutist and dictatorial forms of the monarchical governments of the modern era, on the basis of which the European nation-states were organized.

Liberal democracy was developed by the industrial bourgeoisie as an emerging class, whose common interest was the defense of capital, the dominant force in the development of industrial societies. The private ownership of capital was defended as the foundation of the power and freedom of the bourgeoisie. That is why the foundations of political liberalism cannot be understood without taking into consideration the foundations of economic liberalism.

---

[49] Chapter 3, from "Poder, capitalismo y democracia", Editorial RIL, Santiago, Chile.

The advocates of political liberalism are divided between those who, like Locke, make self-ownership and individual property the foundations of political order, and those who, like Rousseau, emphasize the role of free and equal citizens in the formulation of a social contract that assures the popular will.

When political systems are studied in conceptual isolation from economic systems, this interdependent connection between the foundations of capitalism and democracy is lost. According to contemporary formulations of liberalism, in the properly political sphere, democracy has certain minimal features that are procedurally defined as a method for making collective decisions, independently of the substantive content of those decisions. Minimal political democracy is thus conceived as a set of rules that determine which bodies or individuals are authorized to make government decisions and under what procedures they can make such decisions.

The idea is of a procedural democracy, empty of shared ethical contents, with the exception of those resulting from the search for a "negative" freedom, a private sphere of action not interfered with by laws or other individuals.

The concept of "negative" freedom in the liberal sense popularized by Isaiah Berlin refers to that sphere of human action in which it is not interfered with or obstructed by external circumstances or laws. On the other hand, the idea of "negative" freedom in the republican sense that we privilege here means liberation from the conditions of dependence with respect to situations of domination.

Within the contemporary liberal conceptions of political democracy, Robert Dahl (1992) stands out, who uses the term polyarchy (government of many), a more correct term for this merely procedural version of democracy, which includes the following basic features: the constitutional basis for government decisions, the peaceful and regular election of government officials, universal suffrage as the method for such election, universally guaranteed freedom of expression, freedom of information through alternative sources other than those originated in the government, the right to form political associations (parties, interest groups, etc.) in order to form political opinion, and the right to form political associations (parties, interest groups, etc.) in order to form political opinion.), for the purpose of forming public opinion or competing for positions in the Government.

This eminently liberal concept, of political groups competing for power, is also present in the concept of democracy proposed by Joseph Schumpeter (1971):

> To simplify the matter, we have not retained, as a kind of competition that serves to define democracy, more than the case of free competition for the free vote. The justification for this is that democracy seems to imply the application of a recognized method to the conduct of competition, and the electoral method is practically the only one available to communities of any size for this purpose. But, although this restriction excludes many procedures for achieving chieftainship which must be excluded, such as competition by military insurrection, it does not exclude certain cases which are strikingly analogous to the economic phenomena to which we attach the label of unfair or fraudulent competition or restriction of competition. And we cannot exclude them, because, if we did, we would be reduced to an ideal democracy completely alien to reality (p. 346).

However, the political revolutions that opened the door to the emergence of liberal democracy were founded on substantive precepts loaded with moral values. The French Revolution stated a dictum that has remained until the contemporary era, pointing out three fundamental values of a multidimensional vision of democracy: liberty, equality and fraternity. This dictum refers us to a citizenship that is not only political, but also economic and cultural.

Although the dictum was coined by the French revolutionaries, the ideal of equality was more present in the American Revolution, which gained independence from British tutelage. Even so, the political systems of the nineteenth century, led by the industrial bourgeoisie, expressed a situation of negative freedom (in the sense already explained), without equality or solidarity. This negative freedom in the liberal vision, understood as the rejection of any interference with citizens' rights, acquires special intelligibility if we remember the central importance that, in the bourgeois revolution, the right to private ownership of capital acquired.

In Europe, particularly in Great Britain, the notion of freedom for the industrial bourgeoisie was directly linked to the right of capital property, understood as a purchasing power aimed at profit and accumulation through the markets.

The injustices of the new capitalist order in the process of being installed were soon felt by the working class of Western Europe. After the political struggles of the second half of the 19th century, socialist ideologies emerged in their "utopian" and "scientific" versions, giving rise to intense social struggles that led to the communist experiment of the Soviet Union at the beginning of the 20th century. There, an authoritarian social project of equality was practiced, but without freedom or fraternity.

Shortly after the end of World War I, the fascist and national-socialist movements in Europe and Japan, of an internationally aggressive nature, implied a form of government based on sectarian, chauvinistic and racist fraternity modalities, without equality or freedom.

A certain notion, similar to the idea of fraternity, was legitimized in the twentieth century, at the end of the Second World War, with the social democracies that built the European welfare states. The main stimulus for this idea came from Catholic political movements which, inspired by successive encyclicals (beginning with "Rerum Novarum"), insisted on the theme of universal fraternity as a fundamental ingredient of democracy.

The Catholic Church, as it lost its temporal power, gradually made the idea of democracy its own and moved away from its support for absolute monarchies in which the Pope officiated as "king of kings." However, the Church never accepted liberal principles and redefined them by postulating new relationships between the notions of equality and fraternity, associated with the Gospel message and founded on the fact that, being all children of the same God, we must behave fraternally.

The papacy of John XXIII and the Second Vatican Council introduced the idea of democracy based on concepts proper to Christian philosophy. The influence of the Catholic philosopher Jacques Maritain was felt, not only on the thinking of the Church, but also on the Universal Declaration of Human Rights, promulgated by the UN in 1948, whose drafting team was heavily influenced by him.

Article 1 of the Declaration states: "All human beings are born free and equal in dignity and rights and, endowed as they are with reason and conscience, should behave towards one another in a fraternal manner". As can be seen, this article of the Declaration includes the three elements of the dictum of the French Revolution: liberty, equality and fraternity; however, the first two principles are postulated as premises inherent to human nature, while its propositional part refers to the duty to behave fraternally.

On a national scale, the quarter century that followed the end of World War II created macroeconomic instruments that reconciled the existence of capitalism with a form of social democracy, where the notions of owner, required by the institutions of capitalism, and citizen, required by the institutions of democracy, coexisted.

The basic values of democracy are viewed differently, depending on whether they are seen through the eyes of owners or through those of citizens. The former can be defined as holders of rights and obligations of a patrimonial nature; the latter as holders of rights and obligations of a civil (political or cultural) nature. Let us now look again at the three supreme values of democracy with the two alternative views, that of the owner and that of the citizen.

The concept of freedom is not the same for the citizen who is the owner of a great wealth as for the citizen who is only the owner of his personal life. In general, the feature of political democracy that owners emphasize most is freedom. They conceive that freedom as directly linked to ownership and control over one's own life and property.

Therefore, liberty is defined for libertarians (such as Nozick) in terms of property and not the other way around. In this perspective freedom can only exist if it guarantees ownership of oneself and the property that one person legitimately controls. The issue includes, then, the ownership legitimacy of the assets that people control. In practice, the issue of the status of owner is imposed and displaces the status of citizen. This displacement implies a displacement of the human and citizenship rights of those without property.

The relationship between freedom and property is therefore also a relationship between the political concept of citizen and the economic concept of owner. For example, conservative neo-institutionalist authors such as Douglas North (1993), attach so much importance to the issue of property that the very genesis of the state is conceived in terms of a contract between property owners and those who control military power. The former finance the existence of the latter, and the latter undertake to protect the former from external dangers. This connection between the concepts of freedom and private property is essential to the development of private enterprise and, therefore, to the functioning of the capitalist order.

The notions of equality clash head-on with the combined notions of freedom-property. Those of equality, always transformative or revolutionary, are expressed in the form of ideals and utopias that drive social struggles; while those of liberty-property, rather conservative, are expressed in all the economic practices of everyday life. The combined notion of freedom-property refers us to a person-thing relationship, where it is possession that objectifies the existence of human beings and places them in the social order, while the notion of equality refers us to a person- person relationship, where it is living together that objectifies the existence of human beings and places them socially.

The theme of equality is at the basis of the Aristotelian concept of justice. Aristotle defines justice in terms of equality. He distinguishes between commutative justice - defined as equality of an arithmetical or direct nature, applicable to transactions, contracts and any type of voluntary agreement - and distributive justice, conceived as equality in terms proportional to the merits of persons who may be entitled to different types of goods (wealth, honor, education, etc.).

The first type of justice (legal or commutative) refers to a given person-thing relationship, founded on the freedom-property duality, on the basis of which the person-person relationship is constructed through the contract. Market transactions are relations between persons previously mediated by the person-thing relation, that is, by the position occupied by each one in the structure of property. Thus, the notion of freedom- ownership is the foundation of market relations. The type of equality applied to exchanges is the one most emphasized by the owners, since it assures them the conservation of their property through mercantile transactions that preserve the equality of the considerations

Neoliberal authors in the economic field and libertarians in the political field, such as Hayek, emphasize that for the proper functioning of a free market, the only type of equality compatible with the freedom of owners is that of commutative justice.

But citizens who are not (or are scarcely) owners of wealth, but only possessors of their personal capacities, belong to another type of equality associated with the concept of distributive justice, according to which the criteria for the distribution of all the values cherished by citizens are fixed: freedom, dignity, honor, life, education, virtue. Distributive justice is concerned with persons and not with goods. The criteria for the distribution of goods (civil, political, cultural and economic) are made according to the merits of persons. It is clear that these merits are evaluated differently in different political regimes. Let us remember that, according to Aristotle, the merits that define the criteria of distribution, in oligarchy can be associated to the wealth of each one, in aristocracy to the virtue of each one, and in democracy to the freedom of each one.

The theme of fraternity is the most difficult to reconcile with the condition of owners in general and of capitalist owners in particular. It expresses different legal norms that regulate forms and degrees of sharing the possession of wealth and, therefore, cannot be separated from the principles that guide distributive justice.

If fraternity is practiced in more or less hermetic "brotherhoods", it can be sectarian, mafia-like, racist or express other forms of exclusion. If it is based on universalist criteria, it is close to the contemporary concept of solidarity, associated with the criteria of the common good, promoted by the most recent encyclicals of the social teaching of the Church. Solidarity thus understood is compatible with the precepts of freedom and equality.

The issue of solidarity can be linked to the issue of democracy from the historical development of social democracies, after the second half of the last century, in which welfare states were created based on an active expansion of public budgets with spending and taxation criteria.

The Catholic conception of the common good, associated with the universal destination of goods and the consequent social function of the ownership of resources, is compatible with a conception of fraternity applicable to the functioning of social democracies.

In short, the above precepts acquire different connotations according to those who practice them, whether they are private owners or not. Only the owners of some merchandise (including money) can participate in their own right in the markets, and in that participation, the game of the market demands a defense of private interests when defining the prices and quantities that are traded. The tensions generated between economic and political liberalism are heightened when the ownership of wealth accumulates in a few hands and gives rise to an economic power that ends up imposing a specific political form of government: the oligarchy.

A multidimensional economic theory of power-value, such as the one upheld in this work, affirms that, in stable and organized markets, the monetary market value (price) of a commodity is directly based on the position of the contracting parties in the structure of ownership. This is nothing new, since everyone knows that the first condition for participating in markets is to be the owner of some commodity or legal tender. What may be a more original claim is that the process of allocating resources and setting prices and quantities in markets depends entirely on organizations (institutions, associations, etc.) and technologies in place that make up the basic structure of society. In such a case, it can be said that price is based on a theory capable of relying on, and eventually legitimizing, the concept of distributive justice. Otherwise, if we adopt a restrictive contractualist view of the market, as is the case with those who are dogmatic believers in the "invisible hand", only the commutative justice of each contract is evaluated.

It is interesting to suggest that the notion of distributive justice is systemic in nature because it can only be defined by linking the whole with each and every one of the parties that participate in the game of distribution, whereas the notion of commutative justice is atomized and takes as its starting point only the negotiating parties without considering their respective positions in the structures of distribution.

Private ownership of resources is a decentralized form of power exercised through markets and consists in the possession of wealth. The more general power behind the power conferred by the ownership of wealth is always the political power of the state, which sets the rules of the game for all social subsystems and thus determines a stable social order, capable of reproducing itself on the basis of coexisting institutions. Abstractly, we can say that economic institutions are de facto subordinate to political institutions, because the State, however unjust and authoritarian it may be, must ensure, at the risk of being destroyed, the stable reproduction of social institutions as a whole. Such reproduction cannot avoid issues related to distributive justice, at the risk of producing social crises capable of destroying pre-existing social orders. This idea can be historically applied to the type of basic structure of society in which our contemporary existence takes place. In this sense, we will say that the instrumental rationality of capitalism, in order to respect the criteria of distributive justice, should be subordinated to the moral rationality of democracy.

However, this "must be" has only been considered historically when these global crises affect the very existence of a civilization. This is precisely what happened at the end of World War II, creating exceptional psychological conditions in the ethical sphere that explain events such as the Universal Declaration of Human Rights promulgated by the UN, the processes of decolonization on a global scale, the definitive democratization of Europe and the growing institutionalization of economic, social and cultural rights.

Understood as ideal types, democracy and capitalism can be defined as institutional complexes that interact within basic social structures. Democracy, conceived as a political system defining a certain power structure, cannot evade the issue of distributive justice inherent in a given property structure, and capitalism, understood as a system defining a certain economic power structure, requires only clear rules of commutative justice.

In sum, a central referent of the present argument is the Aristotelian notions of justice. Although, for obvious historical reasons, Aristotle could not have known about capitalism, he did have a clear idea of the political implications that flow from the possession to the general power of purchasing goods. He understood, as far as the circumstances of his time permitted, the importance of the distribution of wealth as a structuring element of society and of the political regimes that govern it.

Regarding political regimes, after enumerating the different social functions endowed with power (magistracies), which must be performed in a society, Aristotle (1998) states:

> And if these functions are to exist in cities, and to exist with efficiency and justice, it will be necessary that those who perform them be men endowed with virtue in political matters. As for the other capacities, in the opinion of many, they can concur in the same persons, that is to say

> that the same can be warriors, farmers and artisans, and also members of the deliberative and judicial bodies; and it is true that all men claim to have virtue and believe themselves capable of carrying out the majority of the magistracies. But what is impossible is that the same should be both poor and rich, and, for this reason, these seem to be par excellence the parts of the city, that is, the rich and the poor. And by the fact, moreover, that the former is ordinarily few and the latter many; these parts are presented as antagonistic classes within the city, so that one and the other establish political regimes with a view to their respective supremacy, and for this reason, finally, it is believed that there are only two forms of government, which are democracy and oligarchy (p. 110).

Now, from the point of view of the concept of justice, the economic theories of the value-power founded on the concept of social system, want to delve into the background of the greater or lesser distributive justice that arises from the structure of society. Therefore, the conditions that determine the degrees of justice prevailing in the structure of society are those that determine the structure of relative prices. In other words, there can be neither fair markets nor fair prices in the framework of unfair societies.

Chapter XVI

Integral democracy and republicanism[50]

Integral Democracy

The notions of democracy and the process of democratization proposed here, which we will call "integral or multidimensional", seek to universalize the notion of democracy not only for the sphere of political regimes, but also by extending it to the other dimensions of human societies.

What characterizes republicanism, as represented in the Judeo-Greco- Latin tradition, is the ethical content conferred on the forms of government, which must be founded on the concept of virtue. It is not always clear what is meant by this term, but it undoubtedly introduces the sphere of morality and ethics into the political forms of power. So, oriented to these roots of the republican notion, the notion of virtue refers us to the idea of justice, loaded with ethical and moral foundations.

The most typical republican features recognized today in this vision of integral democracy are essentially three: a) a strict correspondence or correlation between the validity of human rights and freedoms, on the one hand, and the validity of human duties and responsibilities (associated with the notion of civic virtue), on the other; b) a notion of freedom as non-domination; c) a substantive (as opposed to procedural) conception of democracy associated with the notion of justice (Salvat 2002, Ovejero 2004).

---

[50] Chapter 4 of Poder, "Capitalismo y democracia", Editorial RIL 2013.

Correlation (on a social and not an individual scale) between rights and duties

The right to elect and to be elected to public positions by the citizens of a democratic regime gives a central role to human beings, since the citizen condition is predicated only with respect to human beings. Although not every human being has been invested, in history, with the Citizen condition, it is clear that every citizen must necessarily be a human being. This emphasis on the human condition of any citizen might seem an obvious truism, were it not that in the present day of capitalist mega-corporations the misleading expression "corporate citizenship" or "Corporate citizen" has been coined, confusing the basic meaning of central notions of political science established since Aristotle's time.

Universal suffrage is one of many ways of establishing the centrality of the citizen who, through this mechanism, expresses his sovereign will and constitutes the foundations of the power of the State. If the right to elect and be elected is extended to all human beings, it means that the centrality of the citizen becomes the centrality of the human being as the source of legitimacy and power of political regimes.

The other way of establishing this centrality of human beings in the democratic process is associated with the notion, of liberal origin, of human rights. However, for the republican vision in its modality of integral democracy, this notion lacks effective validity and effective empowerment if it does not correspond to a correlative specification of the duties, obligations, commitments and responsibilities of those in charge of enforcing those rights.

If this central place for the notion of the human being is accepted, then integral democracy must be an expression on a social scale of the defense of those traits that define a human being. Following Aristotle, human beings possess four quite defining traits that are objective and universal: (a) animality with its underlying biological-environmental conditions, (b) moral rationality or the capacity and willingness to propose ends and values that can be judged in the light of ethical principles, (c) instrumental rationality or the capacity to produce instruments designed to satisfy the ends of social life, and (d) "sociality," understood as an objective condition inherent in human nature, as opposed to "sociability," which is a more equivocal term and refers rather to a personal and voluntary disposition to be more or less sociable. Human beings are social animals, but human "sociality" is more complex and developed than the "sociality" of other animal species, and this complexity is expressed in Aristotle's dictum that human beings are "political animals".

Of course, the notion of political animal includes that of social animal, but the reverse is not necessarily true. Therefore, only humans on this planet are political animals. The condition of a political animal is objective and independent of the conscience of those who are it, just as the condition of biped is inherent to the forms of human animality, and not because someone insists on walking like a quadruped, will modify an element that is already inherent to the human condition.

To each of these four features of the human condition (animality, moral rationality, instrumental rationality and "sociality") correspond four social subsystems (biological-environmental, cultural, economic and political). This correspondence is of course presented here in a still blurred way, and expresses no more than a sketch that should be deepened. But it serves to point out the link between the four defining dimensions of human beings and the four constituent subsystems of any human society.

In sum, an integral democracy is one that is understood multidimensionally as democracy postulated and practiced not only in the political sphere, but also in the biological-environmental, economic, and cultural dimensions. Consequently, such a democracy, if it assumes a republican character, should include lists of rights and obligations not only political but also economic, biological-environmental and cultural. Citizen rights must be empowered through the commitment and obligations assumed by those endowed with power. To this end, it is necessary to establish who, when and how assumes the responsibilities required to give effect to these citizens' rights.

The notion of power, understood as an institutionalized social position occupied by a person, is matched at the other pole by the notion of social powerlessness or poverty.

The notion of poverty can be characterized as a lack of power in some sphere of social life. The poor are human beings who have rights (sufficient merits to justify claims) to receive certain goods from society, but they are not empowered by society to make those rights effective.

Poverty is thus a deprivation of something that should necessarily be possessed. The poor, like the rich, have the potential to overcome their cultural poverty (for example, by becoming literate), to overcome their economic poverty (by accessing the resources offered in the markets), to overcome their biological-environmental poverty (by breathing clean air and drinking clean water), and to overcome their political poverty (by accessing basic civil and citizenship rights).

The multidimensional or integral version of republican democracy aims precisely to actualize the potentialities of the poor, incorporating them fully into participation in all dimensions of social life. To this end, they must be empowered, i.e., their biological-environmental, economic, social and political rights must be effectively enforced.

The political role of the State is to set the rules of the game of human societies in all their dimensions. Therefore, the object of action of any State that holds political power (monopoly of coercion) includes the dictation of formal, legal and mandatory rules that determine the dynamics of the four subsystems mentioned above. From this point of view, we can understand Aristotle's reflections that attributed the preeminence of politics above any other practical science.

Politics is indeed a practice and an "enveloping" discipline, so to speak, which sets the basic rules of the game that determine the functioning of all social subsystems and the way in which correspondence between them can be established.

Note, however, that the contents of culture set the values and ends of human action, so that culture also alludes to an enveloping practice and discipline, internalized in everyday human behavior.

Understood in this way, "multidimensional republican democracy" places human beings integrally considered at the center of the ultimate ends that guide the social process.

If this integral humanization of democracy is accepted, then the general objective of the democratic process is associated with the notion of human development predicated for each and every human being that makes up social life.

The notion of human development has a debatable conceptual content and has different meanings, but in any case, it places human beings at the center of the debate. It is not the economic, political or cultural subsystems per se, but human beings themselves, that are predicated on development. Consequently, notions such as economic development, political development or cultural development are purely instrumental and unintelligible if their connection with some socially accepted notion of human development is not specified.

The notion of freedom as non-domination

This book has attempted to unravel the concepts of power and domination. It has done so in relation to the global era of the third millennium and the role played by transnational megacorporation in the current modalities of capitalism. The counterpart of the notion of freedom is the notion of power. The notion of power precedes, in the social sphere, the notion of freedom. And megacorporation expresses the maximum positions of power occupied by an economic agent in the sphere of markets.

In capitalism, the notion of property referring to individuals has been extended by the notion of property referring to organizations. In the early liberal versions, for example, in Locke or Rousseau, the ownership of resources was predicated and legitimized with respect to natural persons, and not to legal persons as is the case with transnational corporations. In Locke, private property was legitimized through the addition of labor to goods or resources that were previously in a "state of nature". This idea also associated the right to the ownership of resources with the individual initiative of those who, through their labor, added value to those resources.

For Rousseau, too, property was predicated of citizens, that is, of persons vested with rights and obligations. But in Rousseau the original predominant notion was the popular will of the citizen, which by means of the social contract created the State. In Rousseau (2010) the notion of liberty is not coupled with the notion of property, and the notion of equality is much stronger than in Locke, for example, when he states: "And let no citizen be opulent enough to buy from another, nor any so poor as to be compelled to sell himself; which supposes, on the part of the great, moderation of goods and credit, and, on the part of the small, moderation of avarice and covetousness". Implicit in these lines is an appeal to the social function of property and to the notion of basic equality among human beings that is not present in Locke.

In Locke's justification of private property there is an appeal to positive liberty, understood as freedom to undertake economic actions that, through personal labor, add value to the natural patrimony. In Rousseau's limitations on the ownership of wealth there is an appeal to negative liberty, understood as a rejection of domination. Thus, Rousseau is closer to what we are calling integral democracy and Locke closer to what today we call liberal democracy.

But it is necessary to emphasize something essential: the actors in the contemporary economic process are no longer natural persons, human beings, but juridical persons, organizations. These organizations have reached such a scale that their existence and performance in the markets cannot be justified, as Locke did, in the defense of people's freedom to undertake, because this freedom to undertake has been institutionalized in rules and limitations to creative work, imposed by the priority of profit over creativity, and secondly, because market power, as it accumulates, creates monopolistic or oligopolistic situations that affect the great mass of micro, small and medium-sized enterprises, mostly made up of people directly responsible for their management, and prevent them from developing their personal creativity.

On these two authors that we have chosen for our reflective counterpoint, both of them are so important in the formulation of the foundations of political liberalism on which contemporary democracies were founded, the notions of freedom are predicated in relation to human beings and not in relation to organizations.

First of all, it is worthwhile to take a historical look at the general relationship of social causality between the notions of power and positive freedom, and the notions of domination and negative freedom. Positive freedom is "freedom to undertake" and is associated with the objectives of expansion of the industrial bourgeoisie, as opposed to the notion of negative freedom, which is liberation on the part of the dominated, with respect to positions or situations of domination. This notion of liberation, at the beginning of the Industrial Revolution, posed the struggle of the nascent industrial bourgeoisie against the oppression or domination of the absolutist regimes of the monarchies supported by the mercantilist economic order. It was the struggle between people-citizens rising up against absolutist states. It was freedom understood as negative freedom, that is, as liberation from pre-existing structures of domination.

It is this language of power and domination that is examined in more detail in this book and linked to the institutions, practices, values and principles of capitalism and democracy.

One can take as a starting point an established situation of domination, where it is reasonably possible to determine who is the dominator and who is the dominated. The rupture of this relation of domination would be a liberation or negative freedom, with respect to the previous dominator. Once this break has been established, a new social positioning emerges that enables the "formerly dominated" (grants him "freedom to"): to autonomously set his ends in the social subsystem where this relation of domination previously took place.

Let us suppose that the dominator in the previous situation is an oligopolistic transnational corporation that limits the radius of action and initiative of small and medium-sized companies operating in the same market, or that affects the power of choice or acquisition of its clients. In short, the dominant corporation commits certain types of abuses (violations of distributive justice) in its relationship with competitors and with suppliers and customers in its own market.

If the legal system establishes legislation to defend consumers and the principles of fair competition, creating new duties, obligations and responsibilities for the dominant company, this process will generate an area of freedom in a double sense.

First, a "negative freedom" as liberation from a previously established situation of domination, and second, a "positive freedom", by making possible the undertaking of new options for small companies and consumers previously dominated in the previous situation. This transition of power positions can be reasonably measured in the prices and quantities traded in the markets and in the distribution of the overall mass of profits or gains achieved by all entrepreneurs.

Similarly, this pre-eminence of transnational corporations in the sphere of ownership of productive resources applied to profit and accumulation affects the freedom of individuals and families by controlling the terms of the private contract. In the case of the granting of consumer credit, the most recent financial procedures have given rise to countless abuses arising from the different positions of power of the contracting parties. Those who grant the credit are huge private corporations, while those who take on the debt are generally middle- or low-income individuals.

But the notions of power and domination are not only explanatory with respect to economic subsystems, but can also be used to understand the injustices that take place in other social subsystems. The above example, referring to the economic sphere, is particularly relevant in a social order where market power is imposed on other social forms of power; however, it can be generalized to all subsystems of social life. Thus, the exercise of choice in the market is preceded by the possession of general purchasing power, required to trade in all kinds of goods; the exercise of freedom in the sphere of culture is preceded by the power to access and use the means of information, communication and knowledge; the exercise of civil and political rights is preceded by the power emanating from the rules of the game, effectively in force, of the State.

The exercise of power is always a relational category, whether it is projected onto things (in which case we speak of possession, production, consumption, etc.), or whether it is projected onto people, in which case we speak of domination.

Never before in human history have the economic forms of power and domination had such an impact on social order. It is not only economic goods, such as the means of life and production, that are increasingly traded in the respective markets.

Cultural goods are distributed through the mechanisms of information, communication and knowledge, and access to these mechanisms is increasingly mediated by markets in areas such as education, art, science and the mass media.

Biological-environmental goods also indirectly acquire a market price. For example, access to clean air, clean water, aesthetic landscapes, squares and gardens, and other similar public goods is increasingly mediated by markets that ration these options.

Finally, certain goods of a political nature, such as public safety or the administration of justice, also tend to pass through the sieve of markets. For example, the hiring of mercenaries for war is a way of commodifying processes that are intrinsically political in nature. Consequently, the forms of domination in this global era pass especially through the sphere of markets and manifest themselves in ways that are different from 19th century theories of exploitation. The most obvious examples of the new conditions of unjust domination (or exploitation) have to do with the mechanism of indebtedness in the sphere of consumption, and, more specifically, with regard to durable goods for individual and family use or consumption.

Consumers have access to an enormous variety of goods, both durable and perishable. The purchase of the first type of goods is based on the use of installment credit which, in general, pledges wages to be received in future months or years. This mechanism of indebtedness traps and subordinate's debtors to new mechanisms of domination and exploitation. This type of situation is related to the crisis of the so-called "toxic mortgages" in the United States (2008) or to the proliferation of credit cards, issued not only by banks but also by retail mega corporations.

The transnational mega corporations of the present global era, when acting in the banking-financial sphere, possess a special form of power conferred by their control of the money market. As Schumpeter (1967) said, "the money market is always the highest state of the capitalist system" (p. 133). However, it was Keynes, in his “Treatise on Money”, who clarified the links between political power and economic power in the monetary sphere.

Although the leading role of the mega-corporations acting in the monetary-financial sphere in the sphere of global capitalist markets is an essential fact for the understanding of the processes of social domination in the third millennium, we remain here in the field of particular processes. In the last part of this book, an attempt will be made to theorize more generally about the notions of social responsibility on the part of those who, in the capitalism of the 21st century, effectively hold and exercise power and domination.

The notion of justice and republican democracy

It is useful to establish a broader generalization between the notions of power and domination, on the one hand, and the notions of justice and democracy, on the other. To this end, we refer again to the Aristotelian notions of legal (or commutative) justice and distributive justice. The central idea that we intend to develop here, already suggested in previous sections, is that the notions of legal or commutative justice refer us to the logic of capitalism, while the notions of distributive justice refer us to the logic of democracy.

Liberal democracy was revolutionary at the end of the eighteenth century precisely because its notion of negative freedom was associated with the breakdown of the domination of the old absolutist regime that sustained pre-capitalist (mercantilist) economic forms, and because its notion of positive freedom was expressed in individual initiative, given through markets, whose "invisible hand" transmuted private interest into public prosperity and development. It was also revolutionary because it attacked the slavish and servile forms of domination in the sphere of labor regimes. In this sense, it practiced negative freedom as a break with a system of domination.

But for the bourgeois capitalists of the 19th century, the notion of positive freedom was linked to the ownership of the means of production and the mechanisms of the market. It was a freedom for the owners. Their motto was not ultimately that of "liberty, equality and fraternity", but that of "private property as the foundation of bourgeois liberty". Later, with the consolidation of capitalism, that ownership of wealth was transmuted into ownership of capital, to accumulate, profit and grow. Finally, in the present era of globalized oligopolistic capitalism, this "freedom- ownership" duo is not predicated with respect to natural persons who can also be citizens, but with respect to those juridical persons (mega- corporations) which are the new organizational forms of transnational capital.

Consequently, today there is an increasingly predominant form of democracy (plutocratic and polyarchy) based on the "freedom-property" duo, which in the field of political philosophy is known as libertarianism, apparently predicated for owners who are natural persons, but practiced as a support for the legitimization of transnational oligopolistic corporations that even claim an "honorary" title of business or corporate citizenship.

The other form of freedom is based on the notion of human being, the only entity on planet Earth that can be a citizen because it is a political animal. The citizen is necessarily a person and not an organizational mechanism subject to the fiction of juridical personhood.

In the republicanism of Greco-Latin roots, the notion of citizen (and not that of owner) is the starting point of all political philosophy. For Aristotle, a condition for being a citizen was to be free from subjections or forms of domination that are preventing the full exercise of citizenship. Aristotle understood this and therefore, from his position as a privileged aristocrat, denied that slaves, servants, artisans and even small merchants could be full citizens.

For the Greek philosopher, justice is the practice of virtue towards the other with whom one lives. Therefore, in order to propose the notion of justice, he takes the notion of virtue as a starting point. In modern terminology this means that he projects an institutional vision on the subject of justice. Indeed, virtue, according to Aristotle, is a habit, it has a recurrent, repetitive character. Likewise, the practice of justice (the exercise of virtue towards others) means that magistrates (those endowed with power such as legislators, judges or supreme rulers) can only practice justice if they are virtuous and, therefore, can project their virtue towards others.

More broadly, in an ideal democracy of citizens, where everyone can actively participate in the government of the polis, a just society would be one composed of virtuous citizens who would also be just by projecting their virtue to others.

If we accept that institutions are social rules in force (i.e., effectively practiced) and, therefore, recurrent, the habitual practice of justice is the habitual practice of virtue projected into the social sphere. There is thus an important link between the notion of virtue, the notion of justice and the republican notion of democracy.

It is for this reason that Aristotle, beyond the type of political regime that is installed (monarchy, aristocracy, democracy) observes that "good" regimes require that the rulers do not act for their own benefit but in the interest of the whole polis. That is, it demands that they be virtuous and that they practice their virtue in front of others. Having thus established the notion of justice and its links with the notion of virtue, he focuses on the two main forms of justice which are, as we have repeatedly pointed out, legal or commutative justice and distributive justice.

The only justice that capitalism recognizes is that which applies to contracts. In opposition, distributive justice is that which is proper to the validity of democracy. The two forms of justice are not mutually exclusive, but in republicanism as a form of government, distributive justice, which is practiced with respect to individuals, must predominate over commutative justice, which is applied to property owners.

Chapter XVII

Corporate Social Responsibility[51]

Reference framework

The issue of corporate social responsibility (CSR) will be approached in this chapter from the following perspectives:

a) A historically and structurally situated perspective, and, moreover, framed within the economic, political and cultural systems that predominate in the global societies of the 21st century with particular reference to the notion of development.

b) An evaluation of the issue of CSR, not from the point of view of the deliberate commitments or strategies of companies to exceed the ethical standards of their management and administration, ***but from the point of view of the objective impact, deliberate or otherwise, that their behavior has on the societies in which they operate. A guiding thread of the discourse will be aimed at revealing the causal correlation between the economic power of companies, the impact of their behavior and the consequent CSR that may derive from it.***

c) A consideration of CSR in the context of the social responsibility of all actors endowed with power in the economic, political, cultural and environmental spheres, as well as in the economic sphere.

---

[51] The content of this chapter, drafted in 2011, received technical and financial support from the Spain-UNDP Trust Fund within the framework of the project "Towards Integrated and Inclusive Development in Latin America and the Caribbean". Its guiding frameworks were the Spanish Cooperation Master Plan and the United Nations Development Programme (UNDP) Regional Programme of the Bureau for Latin America and the Caribbean. Its original title was "Fundamentals of a Latin American approach to teaching corporate social responsibility".

d) A concern for the role that universities can play in the study of these objective impacts and how to channel them favorably to strengthen the principles of democracy and human development.
e) The general intention of this approach is not to exclude or replace the central themes of CSR as it has been approached in the major studies coming from the developed world. However, it is necessary to broaden the field of vision from various points of view, adding a macroeconomic perspective in the field of economic science, and a multidimensional systemic perspective in the field of social sciences. In addition, the aim is to situate these studies in the identity traits of Latin American societies, attending to historical-structural aspects that are specific to us. Contributions in the field of teaching, research and extension should, I propose, bear this Latin American "stamp" those questions and challenges us. It is based on this perspective that we propose this complementary approach to the subject of CSR.

Capitalism and democracy

The issue of companies and their social responsibility can be contextualized in terms of much broader categories, of a transhistorical nature, which are closely linked to the development of Western societies: I am referring to capitalism and democracy. I suggest that an adequate understanding of CSR requires framing reflections in these broad conceptual contexts.

Contemporary human societies can be "read" or conceived of as complex systems composed of economic, political and cultural subsystems, and today, in the face of the crisis of the biosphere, we can also speak of biological-environmental subsystems (Bunge 1997, 1999).

Each subsystem is characterized by the actors that compose it, the structures that frame them, the mechanisms or processes conducted by the actors within the framework of the structures, and the ends or values that guide the actors in their behaviors. The notion of power can be included in this picture, understood as the positions of the actors in the structures, and the strategies and tactics through which they try to impose their wills (their values and their ends) on the dynamics of the systems in which they act (Di Filippo 2009).

In economic and political reflections on power, especially in the Anglo-Saxon literature, the more pedagogical language of games is often used, which corresponds closely to the language of systems. Thus, in this "translation" the system is a game, the actors are players, the structures are the technical and social rules of the game, and the processes and mechanisms that move the system are the moves.

Ultimately the actors are always natural or human persons, but they play analytically different roles depending on the subsystems in which they act. In each of these subsystems there are actors (players) who occupy dominant positions of power, which can be partially or totally counterbalanced by other positions of power corresponding to other actors (players) in the structures of the same or other subsystems.

Capitalism and democracy in the global era

Global capitalism is an economic subsystem in which transnational corporations (TC) occupy dominant positions of power, within the framework of productive and property structures that consolidate their positions. TCs activate mechanisms and processes of great global impact, which are oriented to profit, capitalize and expand their position in the markets.

On the other side, the predominant political subsystems in the West today are based on liberal democracies, understood as regimes or structures in which the citizens of national societies are defined as having rights and assuming obligations that acquire legal form through the regulations of the States, endowed with sovereignty granted by the will of the people.

In a broader sense, the notion of democracy can also be understood as the value substratum of a cultural subsystem, whose actors are natural or legal persons, whose substantive structures are moral and ethical norms that legitimize the rights and duties of actors in society, and whose operational mechanisms (also structured) are information, communication and knowledge.

In the State-citizen relationship, liberal democracy has established a dictum with ethical roots originating in the French Revolution: liberty, equality, fraternity. Today's balance sheet suggests that the three precepts of the dictum of the French Revolution should be considered jointly and interdependently. Liberty without equality and solidarity led to the enormous social injustices that characterized the dawn of capitalism. Equality without liberty and solidarity led to authoritarian collectivist experiences during the first half of the twentieth century. And "selective and authoritarian" fraternity, without freedom or equality, resulted in closed corporate regimes, based on exclusive loyalties and brotherhoods such as those associated with the Nazi-fascist regimes that led to the most devastating world war ever experienced by the human species.

The institutions and organizations of democracy now interact with the institutions and organizations of global capitalism in a way that is defining for understanding the future course of human societies. Current social deprivation, especially in developing regions, is associated with forms of exclusion and inequality, again accompanied by notions of freedom without equality and solidarity. The key to overcoming these new social injustices must be found in democracy understood not only as a political regime for the administration of power but also as a culture that claims transhistorical ethical values founded on justice (Rawls 1979, Sen 2010, Sen and Klicksberg 2010)

The conflictive historical interaction between capitalism and democracy

In the sphere of contemporary capitalist societies, TCs are holders of economic power on such a scale that the only actors capable of counterbalancing these powers (and only to a certain extent) are the national or supranational states where the political power of human societies is rooted.

It is within the framework of these basic positions and relations of power that the meaning of CSR in the global societies of the 21st century can be more clearly understood. A brief historical background to this subject is in order.

One of the great contributions of Keynesian economics was to make it clear that the microeconomic rationality of companies, guided by market signals, is not sufficient for an efficient and fair allocation of resources. The presence of the State as the maker of the rules of the game that regulate markets, for example through laws regulating competition, or those that defend the interests of consumers, becomes necessary.

After Keynes, the Keynesian school, which also dealt with long-term macroeconomic trends, demonstrated that the market lacks self-regulating mechanisms based on a microeconomic logic that can guarantee efficient growth based on the full use of human and material resources. Much less can the market alone guarantee a certain justice in the allocation of resources. Therefore, the State must exercise a regulatory function, as when it enacts laws to defend competition against the abuse of market power, or to defend the interests of consumers, or to protect their health by controlling the quality of the food and beverages that are sold, etc. In addition, the State performs market stabilization functions through its monetary policies, and income redistribution through its fiscal policies.

Before the depression of the 1930s, companies associated state intervention in the economy with the communism prevailing in the Soviet Union, i.e., with an executioner of the market and of capitalist enterprise. At the same time, neoclassical economic theory rationalized and legitimized the magic of the invisible hand of the market.

The aftermath of the crisis of the 1930s was prolonged unemployment, political turbulence, and a slide towards extremist and aggressive ideologies. The balance of state-market equilibrium then shifted in the opposite direction. The installation of statist economies took place in Western Europe, warmongering regimes emerged and led to the Second World War.

Thus, there was a transition from faith in the orthodoxy of the markets, which culminated in the great crisis, to an abuse of state power that culminated in the Second World War.

During the first half of the 20th century, while all this was going on, companies grew in scale, taking advantage of the machining and big industry techniques of the Second Industrial Revolution (electronics, internal combustion engines, development of household appliances, etc.). The markets of the mechanical and electromechanical industries, thanks to increasing returns to scale, quickly reached oligopolistic structures.

After the great catastrophe of the Second World War, the so- called welfare states developed along with the consolidation of democracies. In Western Europe, a virtuous circle of integration and democratization was set in motion that has continued to this day, giving rise to the European Union. It seemed that this time the State- market equation had been balanced, giving rise to a golden period (1945-1975) of capitalist development, in which high economic growth was accompanied by a strengthening of the middle classes and a firm and sustained defense of human rights promoted by the process of decolonization and the brand-new founding of the United Nations.

The moral derived from these findings was that the microeconomic rationality of profit and accumulation, supported by the self-regulation of markets, is not enough to keep the capitalist machine running, and requires the presence of another agent endowed with political power to project a macroeconomic and systemic reading of the same process: the democratic state.

Through the formidable impetus of the UN, ethics began to infiltrate the characterization of development. First came the issue of equity or distributive justice, both nationally and internationally. ECLAC highlighted the impact on the peripheries of the concentration of technical progress and its fruits, making it clear that growth is a necessary but not sufficient condition for overcoming the poverty of nations and people (ECLAC 1949, Prebisch 1949, 1951, 1981).

Following the Second Vatican Council, and several subsequent encyclicals published in the 1960s, Catholic Social Teaching also emphasized the importance of development, making explicit its own ethical foundations to support the notion of democracy.

In particular, it counterposed the notions of human duties and responsibilities as a necessary counterpart to the notions of human rights and freedoms that the UN had re-emphasized. The old ethical notion of virtue was rescued and, in this new perspective, made it possible to contrast the visions of liberal democracy with those of republicanism rooted in the Greco-Latin heritage (Gargarella 2004).

In the UN sphere, the UNDP, starting in the 1990s, focused decisively on the issue of human development. The foundational contributions of Mahbub Ul Haq, after his premature death, were continued by Amartya Sen (Sen 2000). Development was then focused on human beings, instead of being predicated on systems or social structures.

In a broad sense, not only political but also cultural, the notion of democracy became the encompassing category within the framework of which this new vision of development could be put forward.

On the other hand, the reconstitution of post-war capitalism was associated with the founding of other intergovernmental organizations such as the IMF, the GATT (today the WTO), and for economic reconstruction and the promotion of economic growth in the poorest regions, the IBRD, later known as the World Bank, was founded. These organizations channeled the international capitalist order during the so-called "golden period" (1945-1970). The market-State equation was translated into a systemic perspective in the form, more concretely, of the capitalism- democracy equation which, at the level of national States and in the light of Keynesian teachings, allowed the power of large corporations to be subjected to the power of the democratic State.

Transnational corporations (TC)and globalized capitalism

The framing of capitalism within the framework of the so-called welfare states functioned in a relatively sustained manner in the developed world, both in national and international terms, until the onset of the information, communication and knowledge technology (ICT) revolution.

These new technologies favored the globalization of markets and the spread of TC organization and management criteria. In this way, the moderating, regulatory and redistributive power exercised by democratically rooted welfare states over the trends of global capitalism was weakened.

The "genie" (of the market) had escaped from the "lamp" and, freed from the political constraints of democratic national states, the "animal spirits" (Keynes 1943) of deregulated capitalism were expanding on a planetary scale hand in hand with the TCs. Today, this cycle that began in the 1980s has culminated in a great recession that has not yet been overcome and is aggravated by the long-term environmental crisis.

It is not possible to delve here into the new rules of the game of market orthodoxy associated with the so-called Conservative Revolution and the Washington Consensus. We will only say that the balancing equation between capitalism and democracy that seemed to prevail during the so-called thirty "glorious years" (1945-1975) has been broken, and the general orientations of capitalism on a global scale have come to depend once again on the microeconomic rationality of the mega-corporations, now transformed into transnational corporations. The issue of corporate social responsibility acquires topicality and substance if it is linked to these transnational corporations, and, this is the option taken up in this chapter.

Corporate social responsibility: What are we talking about?

What do we mean by "responsibility"?

First of all, the notion of responsibility as it has been used by CSR theorists, especially in developed countries, obeys the intention of creating a corporate or organizational commitment that is incorporated into the company's mission or objectives through each of its different behaviors and actions, and which is of an ethical or moral nature. The real or rhetorical intention of this commitment is to go "beyond" legal responsibilities and the usual levels of management and administration.

A second interpretation, privileged in the present essay, which is generally accepted in other non-business fields, understands responsibility as a moral or legal obligation to answer for certain impacts objectively determinable (actions or omissions, and not for a declaration of intentions) whose breach (of such obligation) gives rise to different types of legal (by the State) or moral (by the public opinion of civil society) sanctions.

It should be stressed that the first notion generally adopted in CSR studies implies the point of view of the company with respect to its explicit commitments on the subject, while the second notion of responsibility implies the point of view of the rest of society.

What do we mean by "social"?

Originally, in the legal terminology of business, the expression referred to the corporate form assumed by the company (limited liability company, joint stock company, joint stock company, etc.).

However, in CSR studies, the term "social" was used to refer to the environment of people or organizations with a direct interest in the behavior of the company (workers, clients, suppliers, unions, shareholders and other people directly affected, usually referred to as stakeholders).

Always from the point of view of the company's intentions to achieve ethically superior performance, the characterization of social issues became increasingly broader and more multilateral. Likewise, the notion of responsibility was applied with the intention of reciprocity, in the sense that ethically compatible behavior was also expected from stakeholders. In any case, the reasoning abstracted from the historical-structural frameworks in which the companies operated, with vague or no reference to the magnitude of economic power they represented.

The notion of the social, in the present work, has been sufficiently developed in the two sections dedicated to the evolution of capitalism and democracy. Based on them, we postulate here that the social scope of corporate responsibility is directly related to the power held by those who contro it. The first to formulate these ideas in the field of CSR studies was K. Davis (1960 and 1975). Later, at a deeper ethical and philosophical level, the German philosopher Hans Jonas also proposed the same relationship between responsibility and power.

On the other side, the social issue as it has been examined in the literature on development and underdevelopment, referring to the poor and peripheral nations of the world, includes a macroeconomic perspective associated with distributive justice, and the strong concentration in the distribution of wealth and income in peripheral countries such as those of Latin America. This other conception of social issues affects the characterization we can make of companies.

What do we mean by "companies"?

Thirdly, the notion of corporate social responsibility obviously refers to companies. But to which companies does it refer? A quick glance at the literature on the subject, especially that originating in the developed English-speaking countries, which is abundant and almost immeasurable shows that it refers to the large corporate firm, and, more specifically, to the Transnational Corporation (TC). The most defining feature of these corporations is that they concentrate the technological and economic power of national societies.

There are legal responsibilities in the sphere of markets on the part of TCs, such as, for example, those derived from antitrust or consumer protection laws, in order to avoid situations of abuse of power, collusion, etc. *However, the impacts of the behavior of these companies are much broader than those derived from dominant positions in the market, especially in relatively less developed regions, such as Latin America.*

It is therefore advisable to start with a reference framework for classifying companies in order to distinguish the institutionalized positions of power of different business strata and to associate these positions with the potential socio-environmental impacts that may arise in each case.

In the thinking of the United Nations Economic Commission for Latin America and the Caribbean (ECLAC), the notion of structural heterogeneity, used since the 1960s and updated to the conditions of the 21st century, refers precisely to this issue. This notion emerges as a structural background, both technological and institutional in nature, of inequality and exclusion at the level of firms, which affects other social forms of poverty and exclusion (Pinto 1965, Pinto and Di Filippo 1974 and 1979, Di Filippo 1981, ECLAC 2010).

The notion of structural heterogeneity makes it possible to distinguish at least three very different strata of firms in terms of their importance in the national economy. The top stratum in terms of economic power and technical productivity corresponds to large TCs, both those from developed countries and those from emerging countries or from other Latin American countries (the latter are often referred to by ECLAC as "trans-Latin"). The intermediate stratum corresponds to small and medium-sized enterprises, and the lower stratum to microenterprises.

The two lower strata (microenterprises and small and medium-sized enterprises, which we could include in the expression MSMEs) are generally in passive and subordinate market positions, both in the real and monetary- financial spheres. Their average productivities and the wage levels that these companies can finance are usually below the national average, and always are in the case of microenterprises. However, their role in job creation is decisive, accounting for between 70% and 80% of total employment in Latin American nations.

The relative economic gravitation of transnational or global companies in peripheral nations is immense given their leading role in exports, macroeconomic profits, investments and technology transfer.

The environmental impact that the behavior of these companies can generate on a national scale in a peripheral country deserves a separate paragraph.

What do we mean by corporate citizenship?

The notion of moral responsibility acquires full meaning when it is linked to natural or human persons (as opposed to legal persons). It is natural persons who can be holders of political and human rights. This topic is directly linked to another term that has proliferated, even in some books on CSR: "corporate citizenship". The term "corporate citizenship", in its different meanings and nuances, has been linked to that of "corporate responsibility", giving the latter the same meaning already criticized in previous paragraphs (Capriotti 2006).

But it turns out that "citizenship" has a specific meaning that has been extensively analyzed in political science since the time of Aristotle, who was the first to carry out a complete and profound study of the notion of citizen. Since then, the entire history of political thought, and also of studies on democracy as a specific system of government, have made use of very precise and profound characterizations of the notion of citizen. The dictionary of the Spanish Academy of Language expresses the most common meanings of "inhabitant or neighbor of a city" or "belonging to the city or to the citizens". But then it includes the precise technical meaning that political science assigns to the term: "The inhabitant of ancient cities or of modern States as a subject of political rights and who intervenes, exercising them, in the Government of the country". Of course, the notion of "citizenship" is defined by the dictionary as "quality and right of citizenship".

However, a TC is not a citizen. In the technical sense of this expression as taught in the schools of political science at universities and academies, a citizen is first and foremost a natural or physical person, or more simply: a human being. Citizen rights and obligations are unequivocally predicated of human beings. However, practically all the literature on CSR refers to legal persons who by definition are not and could never be citizens.

Note that, by contrast, many small and micro-businesses are personal or family organizations in which ownership and management correspond to the same person, who is obviously a citizen. In these companies the legal person of the company identifies itself with the natural person of its owner and manager. But, by definition, the TCs that bear the brunt of CSR are in all cases legal persons, increasingly independent of the natural persons who occupy top management positions or the shareholders of the day.

Therefore, when the expression "corporate citizenship" is used, it is at best a euphemism for a powerful organization that can be a potential benefactor of the community (city, commune, etc.) in which it operates. However, this type of euphemism is not useful for an academic treatment of the subject, especially from the point of view of the multidisciplinary role that the university can play in its relationship with society, in order to explain CSR. In short, the notion of business (or corporate) citizenship, presents serious difficulties, to say the least..

Corporate social responsibility: power and social impacts

The notion of CSR, not from the point of view of business but from that of society as a whole, can be understood as a legal and moral obligation to respond to the societal impact of certain actions or omissions.

The point of view of CSR studies is essentially microeconomic or at most meso-economic (to use a term that came into vogue in the 1990s).

In other words, it refers to the modes of corporate organization, management and administration (microeconomic aspect), or to the nature of the links between the company and its stakeholders (possibly meso-economic aspect).

When the issue of corporate social responsibility is approached only in "microeconomic" or "meso-economic" terms, it leaves out the macro-systemic gravitation of certain TCs on the aggregate behavior of employment, investment and consumption. When TCs decide where to invest, their decisions can greatly affect thc allocation of resources both in the places where these investments are made and in the distribution of these investments on a global scale. When they decide where to invest, their decisions can significantly influence the sectoral structure of production also on a global scale. In both cases, such decisions significantly affect the fiscal and monetary position of the countries involved.

The effective impact of a single transnational corporation in developing countries, for a given sector (energy supply, mining, exports, etc.) is usually more important than all the MSMEs in the same sector, taken together..

Instrumental rationality and moral rationality in TCs

The issue can be approached on the basis of two notions of rationality that inform human behavior in society. On the one hand, the instrumental rationality that predominates in the economic and political spheres of the exercise of power, and on the other hand, the moral rationality that alludes to the fundamental values and ultimate goals that inform and guide human actions.

The instrumental rationality of TC is fundamentally technical and microeconomic. It introduces technology to achieve productivity gains, with the aim of achieving greater competitiveness and better positioning in national and global markets.

To the extent that the mission and objectives of TC´s are limited to increasing profits and expanding their competitive presence, both the integrity of the biosphere and human rights may be affected. This is not a hypothesis but an alarming finding that is calling into question both the legitimacy of TC´s and the survival of human societies.

CSR, seen in the light of TCs themselves, aims to introduce increasing degrees of efficiency and moral integrity in the human beings who run and manage businesses. This task, as evidenced by recent experiences mentioned several times in this paper, is not enough to adequately prevent, much less to prevent, various types of environmental, financial and social disasters. Without prejudice then to recognize the sincerity of many of these efforts (not all) to achieve this goal. The TCs with all their power are but components of a larger systemic framework, and if we look at them from this intrinsic limitation, even if their managers have the best intentions, they cannot replace the breadth of the macro-systemic view of the States, nor the depth of the scientific view of the universities, when they examine the techno-economic and social fields involved in those actions. It is their responsibility to look after the social issues that affect unemployment, underemployment, poverty and social exclusion.

TCs: commitment, responsibility, power and impact

Whether on a national/subnational or international/global scale, from the point of view of the human societies involved, the responsibility of TCs is directly related to two main types of impacts, the first operating on the increasingly artificialized natural order of the biosphere, and the second on economic and social orders.

Although at first sight the environmental issue is more clearly associated with considerations of a techno-economic nature, it is also a profoundly social issue with a direct impact on intergenerational distributive justice. At the rate of environmental deterioration observed with current technologies and microeconomic rationalities, future generations are unfairly deprived and excluded from a natural capital that should be shared. The last periodic meeting of the Global Compact initiative (2010), sponsored by the UN, focused precisely on the theme of long-term sustainable development (UN, Global Compact 2006).

The environmental impacts of the action of TCs are multiple: pollution caused by thermoelectric or nuclear power plants, deterioration of the ozone layer due to the use of chlorine and bromine in industry, greenhouse effects produced by the proliferation of carbon dioxide in the atmosphere, use of transgenic and/or cloned species that replace natural species, loss of biodiversity as a consequence of the combined action of these and other factors, etc. These impacts, therefore, refer fundamentally to the capacity to significantly and irreversibly modify the planet's biosphere.

These and other forms of destructive power of applied technology can only be definitively overcome through deep and structural technological change itself, towards non-aggressive forms that are temporarily and indefinitely sustainable.

The power of TCs in the promotion of new technologies that are less aggressive with the biosphere is obviously enormous, but also ambivalent depending on their specific interests. Large private or state-owned oil TCs, or those that manage nuclear power plants, could, in the short term, be affected in their interests by the proliferation of less polluting and more easily accessible energy sources such as solar, wind, geothermal or tidal energy. On the other hand, other TCs, such as automakers, are more willing to introduce alternative sources, for example for the manufacture of hybrid or electric cars.

If this interplay of interests is left exclusively to oligopolistic market forces, it is unlikely that in the short term political and social concerns for environmental integrity will prevail over the cost-benefit calculations of the TCs. These mega-corporations tend to prefer technological alternatives, which are more polluting but more profitable, given the scale of their operations, and delay the development of smaller-scale alternatives, accessible to some MSMEs that could become profitable as the scale of demand reduces their costs. These calculations are of course affected by the amount of fixed investment in facilities whose amortization is slow over time.

One of the reasons for the proliferation of free trade zones is the reduction of environmental costs. The permissiveness of environmental regulations in the host countries allows these companies to generate profits without assuming the environmental costs incurred by the areas where they are located.

From another angle, there are investment decisions made by TNCs that, in addition to environmental issues, affect the economic and social environments of both the countries where their headquarters are located and the countries where the investment is destined.

Another mechanism associated with the “maquila”, which is detrimental to workers in developed countries, consists of taking advantage of the cheaper labor force in developing countries. Thus, there are industrial districts in the United States in the automotive and textile sectors that languish under conditions of high unemployment as a result of the massive relocation of industrial plants to these free trade zones.

Other strategic decisions, creating objective responsibilities that are directly linked to "our" notion of CSR, can be exemplified by the behavior of banks in recent times, especially with the extension of consumer credit in the form of "plastic money" (debit and credit cards). This modality is associated with short-term financial rationales of high risk for the economic stability of developed economies and for the living conditions of debtors. They have proliferated extremely rapidly in developing economies in general and in Latin America in particular.

This type of credit promotes a consumerist culture where the short-term liquidity transferred to consumers is often far in excess of their long-term solvency. By committing unearned wages to future payments on debts already acquired, less solvent debtors are the first victims of catastrophic speculative "bubbles" such as those produced with subprime mortgages, related to the collapse of U.S. investment banking in 2008.

The social impact of this preponderance of market orthodoxy, which has been manifesting itself since the 1980s, is not only evident in developing regions or in Latin America in particular, but also in the developed economies themselves. The proliferation of situations of poverty and the concentration of income distribution are occurring in developed countries. This trend has been most evident for the last two or three decades in the case of the United States, but it is also currently being observed in Europe, where welfare states are being dismantled to a significant degree.

The above crisis, which is still ongoing on a global scale, highlights the systemic nature of risk with respect to companies that are "too big to fail". It also calls into question the responsibility of their CEOs involved in short-sighted speculative maneuvers, which ended up affecting the economic, social and cultural rights of debtors of lower economic and cultural level.

In this way, the issue of "power in itself" is combined with the issue of "power for itself". For "power in itself" refers to the overall impact on the global economy and society, regardless of the character, conscious or not, deliberate or not, of the generation of this impact by corporate leaders (remember the British Petroleum episode in the Gulf of Mexico, or Tepco in the Fukushima nuclear power plant). The "power to itself" inherent in the intrinsic rationality of these companies refers to business tactics that are at best morally reprehensible and at worst directly criminal recall the behavior of investment banks in the subprime mortgage episode, or "subprime" originated in the Wall Street "environment", which led to the current global financial and economic crisis (2011).

The distinction between the legal responsibilities of companies and the human responsibilities of their leaders requires consideration of the division of powers between the owners of share capital, who may be very numerous and dispersed, and the members of senior management who are in charge of the actual management of the companies.

Shareholders often put pressure on the top management of mega-corporations to generate dividends in the short term to improve their share price. This short-term mentality often leads to speculative management practices that lead to financial collapses such as the one referred to above.

The top management of corporations, i.e., the so-called CEOs (chief executive officers) exercise, through management, enormous personal power in crucial decisions that affect not only the distribution of profits in the form of dividends, or the issuance of shares or bonds, but also the setting of their own remuneration. Their legal constraints and moral values are not always commensurate with the enormous socio-environmental impact of their actions, even when their legal responsibilities are safeguarded by efficient legal teams.

These mechanisms of strategic management by top management are behind the growing concentration in the distribution of wealth and income in developed economies.

MSMEs, commitment, responsibility, power and impact

CSR in the case of MSMEs gives rise to very different issues. On the one hand, the first meaning that we have attributed to the term (the unilateral commitment of the firm to improving the probity and efficiency of its management) is embodied in more easily identifiable human beings, especially in the case of micro-enterprises. The improvement of CSR in this first sense by MSMEs can accumulate merit to gain access to technical or financial support from development agencies and to obtain greater loyalty from their clientele. In this first sense of the expression, responsible business behavior is a condition for survival under reasonable conditions.

The second meaning that we have attributed to CSR (focused from the point of view of the rest of society and measured by the objective impact of its behavior), given the scale of these units, only acquires some meaning when examined in large aggregates, be they sectoral or regional.

In physical-biological-environmental matters, not all the responsibility falls on TCs, since micro-units operating at the subsistence level, especially in rural areas, contribute, for example, to the felling of forests with the consequent desertification, or to the indiscriminate hunting of endangered animal species, etc. However, in the first case (TC), the environmental impact is the result of technological choices of global scope, while in the second case (MSMEs), it is fundamentally a matter of local impacts derived from the need for survival of poor communities. Pollution derived from the use of inadequate, obsolete or poorly maintained production equipment is also an important issue affecting MSMEs in general, but the significance of these effects, from the point of view of their scientific study and of university-society relations, is totally different from that of the impact produced by TCs.

In general, MSMEs in developing regions, and particularly those in Latin America, operate at the subnational and local levels, their productivity, especially in the area of goods production, is much lower than that of TCs in the same branches of activity, and they lack, by definition, the minimum scales required to make a significant impact on the markets in which they operate.

Significant impacts originating in MSMEs can only come from associative mechanisms. Only in this way can they reach the minimum scales that will allow them to export or gravitate in national markets. Consumer or production cooperatives can be mechanisms to increase their market power. In other words, since they lack economic and technological power, they can only make up for it to some degree by generating union or trade union power, understood in a broad sense.

Taken as a whole, the main social impact of MSMEs is of a macroeconomic nature and is related to the high percentage of total employment generated by these units. However, at the individual level of each MSME, the capacity to generate employment or new investment is obviously very limited. Similarly, the CSR of MSMEs in the sense of a unilateral voluntary commitment to generate employment is obviously negligible, given their low investment potential.

Social distribution of responsibilities

If a systemic, multidimensional and historically dynamic perspective is adopted to examine the present historical juncture, it is worth highlighting the interdependence of the economic, political, cultural and biological-environmental subsystems, within which it is necessary to examine the notion of CSR.

The most significant and explanatory issue is that of the responsibility of all social actors endowed with power, and not only of the TCs or their managers. In this regard, see the recently agreed and approved ISO 26000 Standards. In this case, these are voluntary standards with no binding ties or legal sanctions.

TCs and shared social responsibility

The national States and their governments of the day require a macro-systemic "reading" of the same processes that TCs "read" from a microeconomic perspective. This macro-systemic reading, referring to the behavior of the large socioeconomic aggregates, is required to prevent and regulate the cycles that are inherent to the development of capitalism, such as the great crisis of the 1930s or the current crisis of global capitalism that began in 2008.

The concern of democratic governments for the socioeconomic impact of oligopolistic markets generates public policies that, in the short term, tend to have countercyclical objectives and, in the long term, extend towards the promotion of equitable, sustainable and nationally autonomous development.

These public policies have a direct impact on the overall democratic political process and, therefore, on the very stability of the political movements and parties that sustain governments. In a longer- term sense, they also affect the very structure of the political subsystems of democratic states.

A current and relevant example is the way in which European welfare states are currently (2011) being affected by the financial debt crisis that unbalances the fiscal budgets of several peripheral nations of the European Union and threatens the integrity of the euro as a community currency.

The microeconomic behavior of TCs, on global oligopolistic markets, affects the macroeconomy of the nation states where they operate. These impacts of a macro-social nature are verified in short terms (e.g., one calendar year) but also in medium terms (e.g., the recessionary period of the global crisis that began in 2008).

The economic, financial, environmental and socio-political crises currently being experienced on a global scale suggest that the microeconomic (and micro-social) rationality of TCs, based on short- and medium-term visions, and limited to their respective competitive market positions, does not seem to be compatible with the reproduction and sustainable development of the socioeconomic, political and environmental subsystems of human societies in this globalized era

This leads us to approach the issue of CSR by avoiding two extreme positions, both of which are very dangerous. The first is to blame exclusively the TNCs, their shareholders, and their top executives for the enormous crises that global society is facing on a global scale. This would be a biased vision that leads to unfeasible recommendations based on an incomplete analysis of social reality.

The second extreme position would be to promote the most unrestricted entrepreneurial freedom, to deepen the dogma of market self-regulation, and to believe that, through the microeconomic dynamics of these companies, long-term sustainable development can be achieved. This would be an equally biased vision that ignores the enormous social inequalities that are expressed, not only in the sphere of markets, but also in other dimensions such as the political, biological-environmental and cultural.

"It takes two to tango," just as it takes two to play tennis or ping-pong. In more complex social games, competition, cooperation, and also democratic debate by many players may be needed. It is therefore not possible to attribute all the social responsibility to some of them, however dominant their position may be or however selfish we may consider the way they play their game.

This intermediate position means considering TCs as co- responsible in the first place, but not exclusively guilty of the current crises. It means recognizing the shared and non-exclusive nature of this responsibility with other political, social and cultural actors in the global subsystem. Indeed, in a certain sense, both markets and TCs are mechanisms that operate in accordance with the legal and cultural norms that frame them, and in accordance with the cultural values of their direct operators.

It is true that the immoderate craving for profit and market power leads to unsustainable processes that result in increasingly dangerous economic crises. But the idea of "guilty parties" refers to an "ad hominem" consideration, as the ancients used to say. In other words, it is very easy to imprison the culprits of "Ponzi" bubbles or to repudiate the very high remunerations of some CEOs operating in the banking and automotive industries, or energy, among others. In short, the fundamental issue is not that of establishing personal responsibility or specific culpability. It is not a question of judging Shakespeare's Shylock or Dickens' Scrooge, which have always existed and will continue to exist

The structural overcoming of these risks must go far beyond the imputation of certain "scapegoats". In addition to applying legal sanctions, in accordance with the law, to those who abused their positions of economic power, it is necessary to try to modify, through democratic methods, the nature of the rationality of behavior. In short, it is not just a problem of good or bad people, but of the general values that govern the system, and of the main norms that guide people's behavior.

Thus conceived, the issue of CSR involves other structures such as the political structure, the cultural structure and the environmental structure, and the values that guide the actors operating in these subsystems and structures.

However, the idea is not to dilute CSR among a growing number of institutions and organizations, but quite the opposite. The idea is to specify and identify the responsibilities of all powerful social actors, in the field of the rules and values that guide their behavior, which will have a major negative impact on socio-economic structures.

The financial meltdown that triggered the current global crisis in 2008 is a good example of this assertion. In this case, the companies most representative of a "microeconomic" management that implies an enormous social responsibility have been, in the first instance, the giants of the US investment banking industry. More broadly, other public organizations and a large part of the large private banks of the nations involved in the process were involved, especially due to the "domino effects" of the crisis under analysis.

The expression "microeconomic" is in quotation marks because the sheer scale of these companies makes them too large for society to allow them to go bankrupt. They are microeconomic in their basic rationale (to compete in markets, to profit, to accumulate, and to expand their economic power), but they are not microeconomic from the point of view of the global impact of their behavior. A significant indication that the enormous power of these companies is associated with their scale is that they are microeconomic in nature. can be found in the aftermath of the bankruptcy of Lehmann Brothers at the beginning of the 2008 financial collapse.

According to the aforementioned financial debacle, here too, the term "microeconomic" is in quotation marks, because of the strong and direct interdependence between the behavior of these companies and that of other public or semi-public companies such as state-controlled insurers (the case of the Federal National Mortgage Association, commonly known as Fannie Mae, and the Federal Home Loan Mortgage Corporation known as Freddie Mac), or because of the role played by the allegedly independent risk assessment agencies (Moody's, Standard and Poor's, etc.) that did not warn at all of the real estate crisis that had erupted and, consequently, of the financial risk of the large US investment banks.

At best, we could speak of a strategic mismanagement of the companies' operations by their top management, and at worst, of an unscrupulous exploitation of complacent regulations that were not capable of uncovering frauds such as the one, already mentioned, perpetrated by Bernard Madoff, for around fifty billion dollars. In both cases the moral and legal dimensions of corporate social responsibility are at work. Moral because of the recalcitrant individualism of the people who made the decisions, and legal because of the leniency of the rules and controls that governed their actions.

The central point of this section is that, if we are talking about the social responsibility of TCs, then this responsibility is shared with governmental or non-governmental public entities or others of dubious legal and moral status, such as "independent" risk rating agencies

MSMEs and shared social responsibility

This notion of "ex post" objective responsibility that we are applying here, as opposed to the notion more commonly accepted by CSR theorists of "ex ante" subjective responsibilities (commitments, intentions, purposes), also applies to MSMEs. And here too, these companies are not exclusively responsible but, even more so than in the case of TCs, there are other institutions that share this responsibility with them.

MSMEs are responsible for generating around 70% or 80% of employment in Latin America. They are responsible in the sense that it is the actions or omissions of these enterprises that directly determine the employment opportunities of the vast majority of the region's poorest working population. However, given the scarce individual market power that each one of them shows separately, there is an enormous indirect co-responsibility on the part of the public authorities that, through their general macroeconomic policies on the one hand and their specific actions in the MSME field on the other, contribute to generate jobs in these productive strata.

This shared responsibility of MSMEs and government authorities has a greater direct social impact, both qualitatively and quantitatively, than the social impact generated by TCs. Qualitatively because a good part of the employees of MSMEs live at subsistence level and correspond to the poor strata of the region, and quantitatively because they make up the largest fraction of Latin American workers.

Consequently, in the University-Society link, the issue of CSR of MSMEs requires specific consideration in aspects such as access to credit, professional training, training in the exercise of the rights granted to them by law, simplification of the commitments and requirements to be fulfilled for the performance of their activities, and promotion of forms of associativity and cooperativism that enhance their opportunities in national and international markets. These issues have received special attention in EU regulations.

University, civil society and democracy

To situate this complex issue, we can start from an ideal or utopian vision, geometrically represented by three concentric circles. The widest outer circle expresses a civil society endowed with a solid democratic culture, operating within the framework of an equally democratic political system.

A second circle, inscribed within the first, expresses the existence of independent universities that operate above the immediate microeconomic interests of capitalist companies and are institutionally protected against political pressures from the governments of the day.

A third circle, inscribed within the second, expresses the research, evaluations and scientifically based recommendations produced by these public universities, which can be used in the determination of social responsibilities in general (and business in particular), at the service of that civil society.

In this "ideal image", reflections on business management, both public and private, subordinate the instrumental rationality of the market to the moral rationality of democratic culture (Bunge 1997). But obviously the historical reality is much more complex. Therefore, the reflections that follow are no more than very tentative suggestions from someone who is far from being an expert in educational sciences or, in knowledge, of the complex problems facing higher education in Latin America.

We have pointed out two meanings of the notion of CSR, the first commonly accepted in the literature on the subject, is that of a voluntary and unilateral commitment assumed by companies in general and TCs in particular, to go beyond (in the day-to-day management of their businesses) what is legally required of them, in the honesty of their procedures, in the protection of the biosphere and human rights, etc. This is the contribution that companies are currently being asked to make through initiatives such as the United Nations Global Compact.

The second meaning of CSR that we have favored in this paper is based on the effective impact of the actions of TNCs both on the biosphere and on the institutions and living conditions of human societies. This latter notion has recently gained strength and abstracts from the intentions previously expressed by the TCs themselves. It is a concept that has been taken up in the new characterization of the notion of CSR proposed by the European Commission[52].

This is an objective impact that is partly independent of the conscience of the top executives who run the company, and its determination requires a thorough and systematic research that in its general principles can only be developed by universities. Such is the case, for example, with the study of the effects of nuclear energy, biotechnology, molecular biology or genetic engineering on the integrity

---

[52] "The Commission presents a new definition of CSR, namely the responsibility of enterprises for their impact on society". European Commission, Renewed EU Strategy for 2011-2014 on Corporate Social Responsibility, Brussels, 25.10.2011, COM (211) 681 final. Communication from the commission to the European parliament, the council, the European economic and social committee and the committee of the regions, p. 7.

of plant and animal species, or the effects of polluting energy sources and their replacement by cleaner and more sustainable ones. The most complete knowledge possible of these effects is the first condition to be fulfilled by TC if they genuinely and sincerely want to assume their environmental and social responsibilities. To this end, they require the support of independent university research.

A social function of universities (especially the large public universities) in Latin America is to advise companies (especially MSMEs), governments and civil society in general, on the unknown or insufficiently known impacts on the biosphere derived from the technological processes used by these companies (especially TC). All the "hard" sciences (experimental, scientific, quantifiable, objective), such as physics, chemistry, mechanics and biological sciences, can contribute to further clarifying the direct and indirect effects of these insufficiently known forces and processes, within the scope of TC action.

Another function of universities is to inform companies, governments and civil society in general about the unknown or insufficiently known impacts on the social order derived from the microeconomic behavior of companies. All the "soft" sciences, both the social sciences (e.g., sociology and economics, where the application of empirical methods and scientific verifications is more extensive) and the human sciences (associated with politics, ethics and the exercise of human freedoms, rights and duties) are involved in this second type of impact.

Universities that study this kind of impacts through all technical and scientific disciplines must represent the point of view of civil society, beyond the current interests of the political power concentrated in the States, or of the economic power concentrated in the TCs. To this end, they should be as far removed as possible from such interests (limited in time and space to specific positions of power) and try to maintain the scientific independence of their research and teaching bodies.

It is necessary to persuade States and companies, especially those most endowed with power, that, in the long term, the exercise of rigorous and scientific research in all the aforementioned fields generates the best contributions to sustainable and humane development. All social actors benefit from this contribution.

What is the most appropriate approach for the university to be able to effectively assume the long-term interests of civil society in sustainable and human development? This is explored in the next section.

Transnational corporations and civil society

To recapitulate what has been said, two different points of view can be discerned on the subject of CSR. The first is the point of view of the TNCs themselves, which, by assuming voluntary commitments, try to go beyond what the law imposes on them in terms of responsibilities. The second is the point of view of civil society, which experiences the environmental and social impacts of the behavior of TCs.

In the cultural sphere, this point of view is strongly influenced by the organizations that control the means of information, communication and knowledge.

It should be noted that CSR, in the sense accepted by the relevant literature, is above all an ethical and moral issue, and therefore falls within the scope of the cultural subsystem. However, the means of information, communication and knowledge through which the mechanisms of the cultural subsystem operate are also to an increasing degree TC, or non-profit organizations that are frequently financed by TC foundations. Therefore, neither the mass media, shapers of public opinion, nor all universities, especially those financed or supported by private sources, are producing moral evaluations adequate to the enormous impact derived from some actions carried out by TCs. Sometimes the powerful advertising voice of TCs or of governmental agencies linked to certain short-term interests resonates much more loudly and frequently than the voice of independent civil society, which, with the assistance of universities, could evaluate such moral responsibility.

In a broader sense, this issue is inscribed both in the private control exercised by large corporations and in the authoritarian control that, in certain cases, governments may try to exercise over the media, communication and knowledge. The independence and social responsibility of the journalistic profession is vital in this regard.

Precisely what is new in the present global era is the revolution of information, communication and knowledge technologies. The presence of Internet users operating through the different social networks is a new, extremely powerful force that can change the correlations of power in the political and cultural sphere, strengthening the role of the citizen in political democracies and of natural persons (human beings) in democratic cultures. Some examples are at hand: that of the recent mobilizations of societies under former dictatorships in the Middle East, or that of emerging social movements in the battered social democracies of Western Europe. Thus, the "ordinary" citizens of civil society are finding a new and powerful "vehicle" through the control of ICTs.

However, the emergence of new instruments and mechanisms capable of assessing and sanctioning the degrees of responsibility for the behavior of powerful actors is one thing, and the actual cultural content transmitted by the information, communication and knowledge media is another.

A power struggle is developing here to conquer the minds of the youngest people, who are torn between frivolities and games on the one hand and genuine cultural, political and environmental concerns on the other.

It is a permanent and inalienable mission of the University to be at the service of the interests of civil society, in other words, society composed of human beings and citizens. And as we will see in the last point of this work, these interests are determined vis a vis the more circumscribed interests of the companies in the economic sphere and of the governments in power in the political sphere..

CSR and universities: "closed" or "open" issue?

We have characterized two different ways of understanding the notion of CSR. The first is the first meaning of the term. We have defined CSR as a purpose or commitment of an ethical nature unilaterally formulated within companies themselves, or their corporate trade organizations, with the aim of incorporating it into all aspects of their mission, their plans and strategies, and their usual modes of management and administration. In this first meaning, CSR refers to this explicit commitment, and to the effective degrees of its fulfillment. This first meaning refers to CSR from the point of view of companies.

The study of this notion, especially by some private universities, is a subject exclusive to the areas of research in leadership, management and business administration in general. In the field of training, it refers to education for managers. This type of approach to CSR is already highly structured both nationally and internationally. Business schools operating in the developed world, and also in Latin America, are part of this approach. The mission of these programs is to train business executives and, in a broader sense, to train leaders for all types of organizations. The notion of CSR plays here as a dimension of probity, efficiency and initiative required by these future entrepreneurs. This type of business school is strongly linked to, and financed by, foundations and philanthropic funds, closely associated with TC on a global scale. There are international accreditation systems that "certify the quality" of these studies, and among the most important ones are AMBA (International Association of Masters in Business Administration, based in London, Great Britain), EQUIS (European Quality Improvement System with based in Brussels, Belgium), or the AACSB (International Association to Advance Collegiate Schools of Business, based in Tampa, United States). Latin American business schools pride themselves on being able to obtain good accreditation and recognition from these and other agencies. Students who attend these educational centers climb the first steps of a private career that can lead them to the top management of Latin American or global companies.

On the other side, we have understood CSR as a set of moral and legal obligations arising from corporate behavior, in proportion to the socio-environmental impact that objectively results from that behavior. The term "objectively" here means irrespective of the intentions or purposes of those corporate behaviors, and even irrespective of the knowledge of the companies and their representatives of those impacts. From a legal perspective this includes civil and criminal liabilities, and, from an ethical perspective, it also includes moral liabilities.

The systematic study of such impacts by universities does not attempt to establish particular responsibilities, much less specific culpability.

From this second notion of CSR, neither is it a question of organizing complacent apologies nor of awarding prizes for good business performance. It is the task of the judiciary and truly independent public opinion to determine responsibilities and culpability. Recognition and awards for business excellence are the task of organizations dedicated to the evaluation of the quality of performance, or of the corporate trade organizations that bring together private and transnational business interests.

The task of universities committed to society in democratic regimes is to apply scientific knowledge, both in "hard" and "soft" sciences, to a better understanding of the socio-environmental impacts generated by the behavior of TCs from the point of view of the interests, rights and obligations of civil society.

It is also the University's task to promote ethical debates of a cross-cutting nature that bring together the views of businessmen, managers, and other stakeholders, private and public, of professionals, of artists, of intellectuals, etc. In order to seek broad social cohesion, capable of consulting social needs that are not necessarily supported by sufficient acquisitive power.

This means that the real task of universities, which independently represent the interests of civil society, is to study social responsibility in general, not only of businessmen, but of all leaders of organizations, whether private or public, governmental or non-governmental, with special reference to those who are endowed with greater power. As we have tried to express in previous sections, the "logic" of this university mission is to establish a causal link between socio-environmental impacts, positions of power of those "causing" such impacts, and social responsibilities.

More specifically concerning to CSR, both the public management of those working in public-state organizations and the private management of those working in large companies (especially in TNCs) imply positions of power whose impacts must be evaluated in terms of their socio-environmental consequences by public universities operating in democratic societies.

Bibliography

ALADI (agosto de 1980). Tratado de Montevideo. Montevideo.

ALALC (18 de febrero de 1960). Tratado de Montevideo.

Albert, M (1991). Capitalismo contra capitalismo. Barcelona: Paidós.

ALCA (18 de febrero de 2004). Propuesta del Gobierno de Venezuela al Grupo Consultivo Sobre Economías Más pequeñas. FTAA.sme/w/81/Rev.1.

Alonso, J. A., & Garcimartín, C (2005). Comercio y desigualdad internacional. Madrid: Los Libros de la Catarata.

Angulo, N (2005). El derecho humano al desarrollo frente a la mundialización del mercado. Madrid: IEPALA Editorial.

Ara, I (1994). Las transformaciones de los derechos humanos. Madrid: Tecnos.

Aragón, J., & Rocha, F (2004). La responsabilidad social empresarial en España: una aproximación desde la perspectiva laboral. Madrid: Ministerio de Trabajo y Asuntos Sociales.

Aristóteles (1941). The Basic Works of Aristotle. Chapel Hill: Random House, Inc.

Aristóteles (1947). Obras Completas (Tomos I-IV). Buenos Aires: Anaconda.

Aristóteles (1985). Metafísica. Madrid: Editorial Sarpe.

Aristóteles (1995). Física. Madrid: Gredos.

Aristóteles (1997). Moral a Nicómaco. Madrid: Espasa Calpe.

Aristóteles (1998). La política. Bogotá: Editorial Panamericana.

Aristóteles (1999). Metafísica. Madrid: Austral.

Aristóteles (2001). History of Animals. Libro VIII. The Basic Works of

Aristotle (R. Mc Keon, Ed.) New York: Modern Library.

Aristóeles (2003). De Ánima. Buenos Aires: Editorial Leviatán. Aristóteles (2005). Política. Buenos Aires: Losada.

Arnau, A (1998). Entre modernité et mondialisation. droit et societé, LGDJ.

Arnsperger, C., & Van Parijs, P (2000). Éthique économique et sociale. Paris: La Découverte.

Arrighi, G., & Silver, J (2001). Caos y orden en el sistema-mundo moderno. Madrid: Akal.

Arrow, K (1962). The Economic Implications of Learning Doing. The Review of Economic Studies, 29, 155–173.
Arrow, K (1973). Social Responsibility and Economic Efficiency. Public Policy, 21, 303–317.
Ássael, H (abril de 2004). Asimetrías, comercio y financiamiento en el Área de Libre Comercio de las Américas (ALCA), y en América Latina y el Caribe. Serie Financiamiento y Desarrollo. Santiago: Cepal.
Bagú, S (1993). Economía de la Sociedad Colonial. Ciudad de México: Grijalbo.
Balanyá, B (2002). Europa, S. A.: la influencia de las multinacionales en la construcción de la U.E. Barcelona: Icaria.
Balboa, M (1961). Cuentas nacionales. Santiago : Instituto Latinoamericano y del Caribe de Planificación Económica y Social.
Barro, R (1986). Macroeconomía. New York: McGraw-Hill, Versión española, Editorial Interamericana (1986), México.
Bates, C. A (2003). Aristotle's "Best Regime". Baton Rouge: Louisiana State University Press.
Baumol, W (1982). Contestable Markets: An Uprising in the Theory of Industry Structure. American Economic Review, 72(1), 1-15.
Becker, G (1964). Human Capital. New York: Columbia University Press.
Bekerman, M (28 de noviembre de 2004). La economía y las prioridades sociales. Página 12.
Bello, D., & Di Filippo, A (2009). El retorno a la política. Polis, Revista Latinoamericana, 25, 1-15.
Bentham, J (1985). Fragmento sobre el Gobierno. Madrid: Sarpe.
Bentham, J (1991). Introducción a los Principios de la Moral y la Legislación. En J. Colomer, Textos Cardinales. Barcelona: Ediciones Península.
Berlin, I (1967). Dos conceptos de la libertad. En A. Quinton, Filosofía Política (E. Suárez, Trad.). México: Fondo de Cultura Económica.
BID, Cepal, OIM, CELADE, & FNUAP (diciembre de 2001). La migración internacional y el desarrollo en las Américas. Serie Seminarios y Conferencias. Santiago: Cepal.
Bielschowsky, R (1998). Cincuenta años del pensamiento de la Cepal: una reseña. En Cepal, Cincuenta años del pensamiento en la Cepal: textos seleccionados (Vol. 1 y 2, págs. 9-61). Santiago: Fondo de Cultura Económica; Cepal.
Bielschowsky, R (2009). Sesenta años de la Cepal: estructuralismo y neoestructuralismo. Revista Cepal, 97, 173 - 194.
Boatright, J (1993). Ethics and the Conduct of Business. Prentice Hall.
Bobbio, N (1986). El futuro de la democracia. México: Fondo de Cultura Económica.

Bobbio, N (2008). La teoría de las formas de Gobierno en la historia del pensamiento político (J. Fernández, Trad.) México: Fondo de Cultura Económica.

Bourdieu, P (1990). Sociología y cultura. México: Grijalbo.

Bourdieu, P (2000). Poder, derecho y clases sociales. Bilbao: Desclée.

Bouzas, R (22 de marzo de 2003). Mecanismos para compensar los efectos de las asimetrías de la integración regional y la globalización: Lecciones para América Latina y el Caribe. El caso del Mercosur. Milán: BID.

Bowen, H (1953). Social Responsibilities of the Businessman. New York: Harper & Row.

Bunge, M (1961). Causalidad: el principio de causalidad en la ciencia moderna. Buenos Aires: Eudeba.

Bunge, M (1985). Economía y filosofía. Madrid: Tecnos.

Bunge, M (1996). Buscar la filosofía en las ciencias sociales. Buenos Aires: Siglo XXI.

Bunge, M (1996). Ética, ciencia y técnica. Buenos Aires: Editorial Sudamericana.

Bunge, M (1997). Ciencia, técnica y desarrollo. Buenos Aires: Editorial Sudamericana.

Bunge, M (1999). Las ciencias sociales en discusión. Buenos Aires: Editorial Sudamericana.

Bunge, M (1999). Sistemas Sociales y Filosofía. Buenos Aires: Editorial Sudamericana.

Bunge, M (2000). Epistemología. México: Siglo XXI.

Bunge, M (2000). La relación entre la sociología y la filosofía. Madrid: Editorial edaf.

Bunge, M (2001). La ciencia, su método y su filosofía. Buenos Aires: Editorial Sudamericana.

Bunge, M (2002). Crisis y reconstrucción de la filosofía. Barcelona: Gedisa. Bunge, M (2002). Ser, Saber, Hacer. México: Paidós; UNAM.

Bustillo, I., & Ocampo, J. A (mayo de 2003). Asimetrías y Cooperación en el Área de Libre Comercio de las Américas. Serie Informes y Estudios Especia- les. Santiago: Cepal.

CAN (4 de mayo de 2004). El trato preferencial en la Comunidad Andina: un enfoque regional. Documento borrador para discusión interna. SG/di 621. Obtenido de http: //www.comunidadandina.org/DocOficialesFiles/DIn-formativos/SGdi621.pdf.

CAN (1969.). Acuerdo de Cartagena.

Cardoso, H., & Faletto, E (1969). Dependencia y desarrollo en América Latina. Ciudad de México: Siglo XXI.

Caricom (4 de julio de 1973). Tratado de Chaguaramas.

Catro, A., & Lessa, C (1973). Introducción a la economía. Buenos Aires: Siglo XXI.

Cepal (1951). Estudio Económico de América Latina 1949. New York: Naciones Unidas; Departamento de Asuntos Económicos.

Cepal (1959). El Mercado Común Latinoamericano. Santiago: Cepal.

Cepal (1963). El Desarrollo Social de América Latina en la Posguerra. Buenos Aires: Cepal.

Cepal (1990). Transformación productiva con equidad: la tarea prioritaria del desarrollo de América Latina y el Caribe en los años noventa. Santiago: Cepal.

Cepal (1992). Educación y conocimiento: eje de la transformación productiva con equidad. Santiago: Cepal.

Cepal (1998). Cincuenta años de pensamiento de la Cepal. Santiago: Cepal.

Cepal (agosto de 1999). Migración y desarrollo en América del Norte y Centroamérica: una visión sintética. Serie Población y Desarrollo. Santiago: Celade.

Cepal (2000). Equidad, desarrollo y ciudadanía. Santiago: Cepal. Cepal (2002). Globalización y desarrollo. Santiago: Cepal.

Cepal (2005). Balance Preliminar de las Economías de América Latina y el Caribe 2005. Santiago: Cepal.

Cepal (2005). Panorama de la Inserción Internacional de América Latina y el Caribe 2004: tendencias 2005. Santiago : Cepal.

Cepal (2006). Panorama de la Inserción Internacional de América Latina y el Caribe 2005-2006. Santiago: Cepal.

Cepal (2010). La Hora de la Igualdad. Santiago : Documento de Conferencia; Cepal, Naciones Unidas.

Cepal; BID (2005). Heterogeneidad estructural, asimetrías tecnológicas y crecimiento en América Latina (M. Cimoli, Ed.) Santiago: Cepal.

Cepal; IIDH (2004). La igualdad de los modernos: reflexiones acerca de la realización de los derechos económicos, sociales y culturales en América Latina. Revista IIDH(40).

Chavagreaux, C (2007). Los paraísos fiscales. Mataró: El Viejo Topo.

Chenery, H., & Clark, P (1959). Economía Interindustrial. México: Fondo de Cultura Económica.

Cicero (1998). The Republic and The Laws (N. Rudd, Trad.) New York: Oxford University Press.

Cicerón (1997). Sobre los Deberes. Barcelona: Ediciones Altaya.

Comisión Europea (2000). Carta europea de la pequeña empresa. Lisboa: Unión Europea.

Commons, J (1931). Economía Institucional. American Economic Review, 21, 648-657.

Commons, J (1990). Institutional Economics (Vols. 1-2). New Jersey: Transaction Publishers.

Commons, J (1995). Legal Foundations of Capitalism. New Jersey: Transaction Publishers.

Commons, J (2003). Institutional Economics (Vol. 1 y 2). Transaction Publishers.

Cortina, A (2007). Ética sin moral. Madrid: Tecnos.

Crespo Hernandéz, A (2000). El acuerdo multilateral de inversiones: ¿crisis de un modelo de globalización? Madrid: Eurolex.

Dahl, R (1992). La democracia y sus críticos. Barcelona: Paidós.

Davis, K (1960). Can Business Afford to Ignore Social Responsibilities? California Management Review (2), 70-76.

Davis, K (1975). Five Propositions for Social Responsibility. Business Horizons, 18(3), 19-24.

De George, R (1999). Business Ethics. Upper Saddle River: Prentice Hall.

Di Filippo, A., & Ahumada, J (2013). Economía política global I. En D. Bello, Manual de Relaciones Internacionales (págs. 209-254). Santiago: RIL editores.

Di Filippo, A (1980). El desarrollo económico y las teorías del valor. Revista de la Cepal (11), 81-119.

Di Filippo, A (1981). Desarrollo y desigualdad social en la América Latina. Ciudad de México: Fondo de Cultura Económica; El Trimestre Económico.

Di Filippo, A (1981). La tesis del excedente y la realización de la plusvalía en Marx. En R. Prebisch, Capitalismo periférico: crisis y transformación. México, D.F.: Fondo de Cultura Económica.

Di Filippo, A (1993, mayo). "Revolución Informática, Desarrollo Económico y Competitividad". Ponencia preparada para la Reunión Regional sobre Gestión de Información, organizada por Clades y Cepal, Santiago de Chile.

Di Filippo, A (1994). Regionalismo abierto e inversión extranjera en América Latina. Documento de Trabajo N°34. Santiago: Cepal.

Di Filippo, A (1997). Multilateralismo y regionalismo en la integración de América Latina. Cepal.

Di Filippo, A (1998). La visión centro-periferia hoy. Revista de la Cepal, 175-186.

Di Filippo, A (septiembre de 2000). Globalización, integración regional y migraciones. En La Migración Internacional y el Desarrollo en las Américas, Simposio en Costa Rica. Cepal; BID; OIM; FNUAP.

Di Filippo, A (2000). Integración regional, desarrollo y equidad. México D.F.: Siglo XXI; Cepal.
Di Filippo, A (2004). Two Types of Regional Integration Processes, Stanford University, Latin American Studies Center, Lunch Lecture at Bolivar Hou- se. Working Papers of Stanford Center for International Development. California: Department of Economics Landau Building.
Di Filippo, A (2006). La Comunidad Sudamericana de Naciones como Proyecto de Largo Plazo. En A. Fairlie (Ed.), Países andinos frente al TLC y la comunidad sudamericana de naciones (págs. 141-172). Lima: Red Latinoamericana de Política Comercial (LATN); Friedrich Ebert Stiftung.
Di Filippo, A (2006). Las Asimetrías en los acuerdos de integración de América Latina y el Caribe. Caracas: Sistema Económico Latinoamericano.
Di Filippo, A (2007). América Latina: integración regional en la era global. Si Somos Americanos. Revista de Estudios Transfronterizos, 9(1), 143-170.
Di Filippo, A (2007). La escuela latinoamericana del desarrollo: tensiones epistemológicas de un movimiento fundacional. Cinta Moebio, 124-154. Obtenido de www.moebio.uchile.cl/29/difilippo.html
Di Filippo, A (2008). Área de Libre Comercio de las Américas: origen, desarrollo y propuestas de futuro. En J. Vidal-Beneyto, & C. Díaz, América Latina, hacia su unidad. Modelos de integración y procesos integradores. Valencia: Fundación Amela.
Di Filippo, A (2008). La Economía Política Estructuralista Latinoamericana. Encrucijada Americana, 92-103.
Di Filippo, A (2009). Estructuralismo latinoamericano y teoría económica. Revista Cepal (98), 181-203.
Di Filippo, A (2011). "La responsabilidad social empresarial como instrumento de vinculación universidad-sociedad", Conferencia dictada en I Seminario Iberoamericano sobre modelos de docencia e investigación en Responsabilidad social empresarial, Bs. As, junio 2011.
Di Filippo, A (2012). "Fundamentos de un Enfoque Iberoamericano en enseñanza de la Responsabilidad social empresarial", en Licha Isabel, (compiladora): Enfoque y herramientas de responsabilidad social empresarial en Iberoamérica pnud-Santander-aecid. http://www.calidadtenerife.org/?q=node/11944.
Di Filippo, A (2013). Poder, capitalismo y democracia. Santiago: RIL Editores.
Di Filippo, A (29 y 30 de noviembre de 2016). Corresponsabilidad social corporativa y crisis de autorregulación. Ponencia presentada al Diálogo de alto nivel sobre arquitectura financiera internacional: ética y economía. Buenos Aires: Cáritas América Latina; Programa Internacional sobre Democracia, Sociedad y Nuevas Economías UBA;

Centro Regional Ecuménico de Asesoría y Servicio; Red Mundial de Ética – Globethics; la Comisión Episcopal de Pastoral Social.

Di Filippo, A (2017). El estructuralismo latinoamericano: validez y vigencia en el siglo XXI. Entrelíneas de la Política Económica, 48, 3-18.

Di Filippo, A., & Franco, R (1997). Aspectos sociales de la integración regional. En Serie Políticas Sociales. Cepal.

Di Filippo, A., & Franco, R (2000). Integración regional, desarrollo y equidad. México: Siglo XXI; Cepal.

Di Filippo, A., & Jadue, S (1976). La Heterogeneidad Estructural: concepto y dimensiones. Trimestre Económico, 43(169), 167-214.

Donaldson, T (1999). Ethical Issues in Business. Prentice Hall.

Dos Santos, T (1978). El Nuevo Carácter de la Dependencia. En T. Dos Santos, Imperialismo y Dependencia. Ciudad de México: ERA.

Doyal, L., & Gough, I (1994). Teoría de las necesidades humanas. Barcelona: Icaria-Fuhem.

Drucker, P (1984). The New Meaning of Corporate Social Responsibility. California, Management Review, 26(2), 53-63.

Escaith, H (2001). Las economías pequeñas de América Latina y el Caribe. Revista Cepal, 71-85.

Fajnzylber, F (1990). Industrialización en América Latina: de la 'caja negra' al 'casillero vacío'. Santiago: Cuadernos de la Cepal; Naciones Unidas.

Ferrater, M (1999). Diccionario de Filosofía (Tomos I-IV). Barcelona: Ariel.

Ferrer, A (1963). La Economía Argentina. Buenos Aires: Fondo de Cultura Económica.

Ferrer, A (1996). Historia de la Globalización I. México: Fondo de Cultura Económica.

Ferrer, A (1996). Historia de la globalización: orígenes del orden económico mundial. Buenos Aires: Fondo de Cultura Económica.

Ferrer, A (2000). Historia de la Globalización II. México: Fondo de Cultura Económica.

Ferrer, A., & Rougier, M (2012). La Economía Argentina. Buenos Aires: Fondo de Cultura Económica.

Ffrench-Davis, R (2005). Macroeconomía, comercio y finanzas para reformar las reformas en América Latina. Bogotá: Cepal; Mayol Ediciones.

Ffrench-Davis, R., & Di Filippo, A (2003). El Rol de las Instituciones Regionales en la Globalización. Revista de Estudios Internacionales(141), 5-22.

Franco, R (1981). Planificación social en América Latina y el Caribe. Santiago: ILPES; Unicef.

Freeman, R (1984). Strategic Management: A Stakeholder Approach. Boston: Pitman.
Friedman, M (1953). The Methodology of Positive Economics. Estados Unidos: University of Chicago Press.
Friedman, M (1970). The Social Responsability of Business is to Increase its Profits. The New York Times Magazine, 32-33.
Fundación Prohumana (2004). ¿Qué es la Responsabilidad Social Empresarial? Santiago: Fundación Prohumana.
Furtado, C (1959). Formación Económica del Brasil. Fondo de Cultura Económica.
Furtado, C (1964). Desarrollo y subdesarrollo. Buenos Aires: Eudeba.
Furtado, C (1965). Dialéctica del desarrollo. Ciudad de México: Fondo de Cultura Económica.
Furtado, C (1966). Subdesarrollo y estancamiento en América Latina. Buenos Aires: Eudeba.
Furtado, C (1968). Teoría y política del desarrollo económico. Ciudad de México: Siglo XXI.
Furtado, C (1971). Desarrollo y Subdesarrollo. Buenos Aires: Eudeba.
Furtado, C (1976). Prefacio a nova economía política. Rio de Janeiro: Paz e Terra.
Furtado, C (1979). Creatividad y dependencia. México D.F.: Siglo XXI.
Galbraith, J. K (1969). El Nuevo Estado Industrial. Barcelona: Editorial Ariel.
Germani, G (1955). Estructura Social de la Argentina. Buenos Aires: Raigal.
Germani, G (1956). La Sociología Científica. Ciudad de México: UNAM.
Germani, G (1964). La Sociología en América Latina: Problemas y Perspectivas. Buenos Aires: Eudeba.
Germani, G (1964). Política y Sociedad en una Época de Transición. Buenos Aires: Paidós.
Germani, G (1969). Sociología de la Modernización. Buenos Aires: Paidós.
Gilpin, R (1987). The Political Economy of International Relations. New Jersey: Princeton University Press.
Giordano, P., Mesquita, M., & Quevedo, F (2004). El tratamiento de las asimetrías en los acuerdos de integración regional. Buenos Aires: BID-INTAL.
González, P (1965). La democracia en México. Ciudad de México: Fondo de Cultura Económica.
Graciarena, J (1976). Poder y estilos de desarrollo: una perspectiva heterodoxa. Revista de la Cepal, 173-193.
Grossman, G., & Helpman, E (1991). Innovation and Growth in the Global Economy. Cambridge: The MIT Press.

Guerrero Ginel, J (2003). Mecanismos para compensar los efectos de las asimetrías de la integración regional y la globalización: lecciones para América Latina y el Caribe. El caso de Andalucía y la Unión Europea. BID; INTAL.

Gunder Frank, A (1967). Capitalismo y subdesarrollo en América Latina. Ciudad de México: Siglo XXI.

Gurrieri, A (1982). La obra de Prebisch en la Cepal. Ciudad de México: Fondo de Cultura Económica.

Harcourt, G (1975). Teoría del capital. Barcelona: Oikos-Tau.

Hayek, F (1978). Law, Legislation and Liberty. Vol. 2: The Mirage of Social Justice. Chicago: The University of Chicago Press.

Hayek, F (1981). Por qué no soy conservador. En F. Hayek, Camino de Libertad (págs. 121-144). Santiago: Centro de Estudios Públicos.

Hayek, F (1988). The Fatal Conceit. Bartley: Chicago Press.

Hayek, F (1988). The Fatal Conceit: the errors of socialism. The collected works of Freidrich August Hayek, Vol. 1. Londres: Routledge.

Hegel, F (1969). Filosofía del espíritu. Buenos Aires: Editorial Claridad.

Hegel, F (2005). Lecciones sobre la historia de la filosofía II. México : Fondo de Cultura Económica.

Helpman, E (2004). The Mystery of Economic Growth. Cambridge: Harvard University Press.

Hernández Zubizarreta, J (2009). Las empresas transnacionales frente a los Derechos Humanos: historia de una asimetría normativa. Bilbao: Hegoa; OMAL.

Hernández, Y (2005). Un nuevo tratamiento de las asimetrías en la integración sudamericana. Documento de trabajo. La Paz: Secretaría de ALADI.

Hettne, B., & Inotai, A (1994). The New Regionalism. Helsinki: Naciones Unidas; Wider.

Hinkelammert y Jiménez, Economía vida humana y bien común, Reflexiones sobre Economía Crítica. Costa Rica, Enero de 2013.

Hurrel, A., & Woods, N (1999). Inequality, Globalization, and World Politics. New York: Oxford University Press.

Infante, R., & Sunkel, O (2009). Chile hacia un desarrollo inclusivo. Revista Cepal(97), 135-154.

INTAL (2005). Caricom Report N°. 2. Buenos Aires: IDB-INTAL.

ISO (s.f.). Normas ISO 26000 Responsabilidad Social. Obtenido de http: //www.iso.org/iso/social_responsibility.

Jonas, H (1995). El principio de responsabilidad. Barcelona: Herder.

Juan Pablo II (1994). Veritatis Splendor. Santiago de Chile: Ediciones San Pablo.

Kant, I (1998). Fundamentación de la metafísica de las costumbres. Madrid: Espasa.
Katz, J (2000). Reformas estructurales, productividad y conducta tecnológica en América Latina. Santiago : Cepal; Fondo de Cultura Económica.
Keynes, J. M (1943). Teoría general de la ocupación, el interés y el dinero. México D.F. : Fondo de Cultura Económica.
Kicillof, A (2007). Fundamentos de la Teoría General. Buenos Aires: Eudeba.
Kliksberg, B (2002). El capital social. Dimensión olvidada del desarrollo. Venezuela: Universidad Metropolitana.
Kliksberg, B (2002). Hacia una economía con rostro humano. Buenos Aires: Fondo de Cultura Económica.
Kliksberg, B (2005). La agenda ética pendiente de América Latina. Buenos Aires: Fondo de Cultura Económica; BID.
Kliksberg, B., & Tomassini, L (2000). Capital social y cultura: claves estratégicas para el desarrollo. Argentina: Fondo de Cultura Económica.
Kuhn, T (1969). The Structure of Scientific Revolutions. Chicago: University of Chicago Press.
Kymlicka, W (2002). Contemporary Political Philosophy: An Introduction. New York: Oxford University Press.
Leontief, W (1973). Análisis económico Input-Output. Barcelona: Ariel.
Lessa, & Castro (1973). Introducción a la Economía. Buenos Aires: Siglo XXI.
Licha, I (1999). El enfoque de gerencia social. BID; INDES.
Lipietz, A (1991). Audacia: Uma alternativa para o século XXI. Sao Paulo: Novel.
List, F (1856). National system of political economy. Philadelphia: J. B. Lippincott & Company.
Los, B (2001). Crecimiento endógeno y cambio estructural en un modelo dinámico de insumo producto. Momento Económico, 2-28.
Lozano, J (1999). Ética y empresa. Madrid: Trotta.
Lozano, L (1993). La iniciativa para las Américas. El comercio hecho estrategia. Revista Nueva Sociedad(125), 121-134.
Lucas, R (1988). On the Mechanics of Economic Development. Journal of Monetary Economics, 3-42.
MacIntyre, A (1994). Historia de la ética. Barcelona: Paidós.
MacIntyre, A (2001). Tras la virtud. Barcelona: Editorial Crítica.
Mallorquín, C (2006). En Resguardo de lo herético: el estructuralismo latinoamericano y el institucionalismo latinoamericano. En R. Sánchez, & C. Mallorquin, Estructuralismo Latinoamericano e Institucionalismo Norteamericano ¿Discursos compatibles en la teoría social contemporánea?. Puebla: Benemérita Universidad Autónoma de Puebla.

Mankiw, N (2007). Principios de economía. Madrid: Editorial Thomson.

Marini, R., & Dos Santos, T (1999). El Pensamiento Social Latinoamericano en el siglo XX. Caracas: IESALC.

Martin, R., & Sunley, P (1998). Slow convergence? The new endogenous growth theory and regional development. Economic Geography, 201-227.

Marx, C (1946). El capital. Crítica de la Economía Política. Tomo I. México: Fondo de Cultura Económica.

Marx, C (1969). El capital. Tomo II (W. Roces, Trad.) México: Fondo de Cultura Económica.

Marx, C (1971). Elementos fundamentales para la crítica de la economía política. Siglo XXI.

Medina Echavarría, J (1963). Consideraciones sociológicas sobre el desarrollo económico de América Latina. Santiago: Cepal.

Medina Echavarría, J (1973). Aspectos Sociales del Desarrollo Económico. Santiago: Cepal.

Medina Echavarría, J (1980). La sociología como ciencia social concreta. Madrid: Cultura Hispánica.

Mercosur (1991). Tratado de Asunción para la Constitución de un Mercado Común. Asunción.

Mill, J (1997). El Utilitarismo. Madrid: Alianza Editorial.

Minsky, H (1992). The financial instability hypothesis. Jerome Levy Economics Institute Working Paper (74).

Monza, A (1971). La validez teórica de la idea de función de producción agregada. Económica, 17(3), 315-328.

Myrdal, G (1961). El Estado del futuro. México: Fondo de Cultura Económica.

Myrdal, G (1968). Teoría económica y regiones subdesarrolladas. México D.F.: Fondo de Cultura Económica.

Neffa, J (2000). ¿Qué hacer para mejorar la competitividad de las Pyme argentinas? Buenos Aires: Asociación Trabajo y Sociedad; Programa de Investigaciones Económicas sobre Tecnología, Trabajo y Empleo (CEIL-PIETTE CONICET).

Nixson, F (2006). Rethinking the political economy of development: back to basics and beyond. Journal of International Development, 18(7), 967-981.

North, D (1981). Structure and Change in Economic History. New York and London: Norton & Company.

North, D (1990). Institutions, Institutional Change and Economic Performance (Political Economy of Institutions and Decisions). Cambridge: Cambridge University Press.

North, D (1993). Instituciones, cambio institucional y desempeño económico.México: Fondo de Cultura Económica.

Noyola, J (1957). Inflación y desarrollo económico en México y Chile. Panorama económico (170).

Nun, J (1969). Superpoblación relativa, ejército industrial de reserva y masa marginal. Revista Latinoamericana de Sociología, 180-235.

Ocampo, J (1998). Cincuenta años de la Cepal. Revista Cepal, 11-16.

Ocampo, J (1999). La reforma del sistema financiero internacional: un debate en marcha. Santiago: Fondo de Cultura Económica; Cepal.

Ocampo, J. A (2001). Raúl Prebisch y la agenda del desarrollo en los albores del siglo XXI. Revista de la Cepal, 25-40.

OEA (1998). Mecanismos y medidas para facilitar la participación de las economías más pequeñas en el área de libre comercio de las Américas: actualización. OEA; Estudios de la Unidad de Comercio.

OIT (2003). Superar la pobreza mediante el trabajo. Ginebra : Conferencia Internacional del Trabajo, 91ª reunión 2003. OIT.

OIT (2004). Por una globalización justa: crear oportunidades para todos. Suiza: Comisión Mundial sobre la Dimensión Social de la Globalización.

Olson, M (1965). The Logic of Collective Action. Cambridge: Harvard University Press.

ONU (2010). Global Compact. Obtenido de http: //www.unglobalcompact.org/

Ovejero, F., Martí, J. L., & Gargarella, R (2004). Nuevas ideas republicanas: autogobierno y libertad. Barcelona : Paidós.

Paladino, M (2004). La responsabilidad de la empresa en la sociedad. Construyendo la sociedad desde la tarea directiva. Buenos Aires: Ariel Sociedad Económica.

Paladino, M., & Mohan, A (2002). Tendencias de la responsabilidad social empresaria en Argentina. Buenos Aires: Documento de Investigación de IAE; Universidad Austral.

Pasinetti, L (1978). Crecimiento económico y distribución de la renta. Madrid: Alianza Editorial.

Pasinetti, L (1985). Cambio estructural y crecimiento económico. Madrid: Pirámide.

Perroux, F (1981). Poder y economía. Madrid: Ediciones ICE.

Pinto, A (1965). Concentración del progreso técnico y de sus frutos en el desarrollo latinoamericano. El Trimestre Económico, 32(125), 3-69.

Pinto, A (1968). Raíces estructurales de la inflación. Estabilidad monetaria y desarrollo económico. México, D.F.: Arte y Cultura.

Pinto, A (1973). Inflación: raíces estructurales. México, D.F.: Fondo deCultura Económica.

Pinto, A (1991). América Latina: una visión estructuralista. México, D.F.: Facultad de Economía; Universidad Nacional Autónoma de México.

Pinto, A., & Di Filippo, A (1974). Notas sobre la estrategia de la distribución y la redistribución del ingreso en América Latina. El Trimestre Económico (162), 357-375.

Pinto, A., & Di Filippo, A (1979). Desarrollo y pobreza en América Latina, un enfoque histórico-estructural. En A. Pinto, América Latina: Una visión Estructuralista. Ciudad de México: Universidad Nacional Autónoma de México.

Pinto, A., & Di Filippo, A (1979). Desarrollo y pobreza en América Latina: un enfoque histórico. El Trimestre Económico, 46(183), 569-590.

Pinto, A., & Di Filippo, A (1991). Notas sobre la estrategia de la distribución y la redistribución del ingreso en América Latina. En A. Pinto, América Latina: una visión estructuralista (págs. 535-554). Ciudad de México: Universidad Nacional Autónoma de México.

PNUD (2010). Informe Regional sobre Desarrollo Humano para América Latina y el Caribe 2010: Actuar sobre el futuro: romper la transmisión intergeneracional de la desigualdad. San José: PNUD-OEA.

Polanyi, K (2006). La Gran Transformación. México D.F.: Fondo de Cultura Económica.

Porter, M (1991). La ventaja competitiva de las naciones. Buenos Aires : Editorial Vergara.

Posner, M (1961). International Trade and Technical Change. Vol 13(3), 323-341. Oxford Economic Papers.

Prebisch, R (1947). Introducción a Keynes. México D.F.: Fondo de Cultura Económica.

Prebisch, R (1949). Estudio Económico de América Latina. New York: Cepal/ ONU.

Prebisch, R (1951). Problemas teóricos y prácticos del crecimiento económico. México D.F.: Cepal.

Prebisch, R (1962). El desarrollo económico de América Latina y algunos de sus principales problemas. Boletín Económico de América Latina de la Cepal VII, 7(1).

Prebisch, R (1963). Hacia una Dinámica del Desarrollo Latinoamericano. México: Fondo de Cultura Económica.

Prebisch, R (1970). Transformación y desarrollo: la gran tarea de América Latina. Ciudad de México: Banco Interamericano de Desarrollo y Fondo de Cultura Económica.

Prebisch, R (1980). Biosfera y desarrollo. Revista de la Cepal (12), 73-88.

Prebisch, R (1981). Capitalismo periférico: crisis y transformación. México D.F.: Fondo de Cultura Económica.

Puiggrós, R (1986). De la Colonia a la Revolución. Buenos Aires: Sudamericana.
Ramonet, I (2003). Un mundo sin rumbo. Madrid: Debate.

Ramonet, I (2002). Guerras del siglo XXI. Nuevos miedos nuevas amenazas. Barcelona: Mondadori.

Rawls, J (1979). Teoría de la Justicia. México: Fondo de Cultura Económica.

Rawls, J (1993). Political Liberalism. New York: Columbia University Press.

Rawls, J (1996). Liberalismo Político. México: Fondo de Cultura Económica.

Rawls, J (2000). Teoría de la justicia. México: Fondo de Cultura Económica.

Razeto, L. 1 (1984). Economía de solidaridad y mercado democrático. Santiago: Academia de Humanismo Cristiano.

Red Jesuita Internacional para el Desarrollo (2006). Deuda externa y comercio mundial. Bilbao: Ediciones Mensajero.

Reich, R (2007). Supercapitalism: The Transformation of Business, Democracy, and Everyday Life. N New York: Knopf.

Reyno, M (2010). Responsabilidad social empresarial como ventaja competitiva. Universidad de Málaga.

Riaza, A (2001). Las transnacionales españolas en América Latina y el Caribe: Orientaciones para una estrategia de cooperación al desarrollo. Madrid: IS- COD.

Richards, H., & Swanger, J (2006). The Dilemmas of Social Democracies. Londres: Lexington Books.

Rodríguez, O (1993). La teoría del subdesarrollo de la Cepal. México D.F.: Siglo XXI.

Rofman, A (1999). Economías Regionales. Revista Realidad Económica (162).

Rofman, A (2000). Desarrollo regional y exclusión social. Buenos Aires: Amorrortu.

Rojo Duque, L (1966). Lecturas sobre la teoría económica del desarrollo. Madrid: Editorial Gredos.

Romer, P (1986). Increasing Returns and Long-Run Growth. Journal of Political Economy, 94(5), 1002-1037.

Romer, P (1990). Endogenous technological change. Journal of Political Economy, 98(5), 71-102.

Rouquie, A (1989). América Latina: Introducción al Extremo Occidente. México: Siglo XXI.

Salazar-Xirinachs, J (2003). Las asimetrías en los TLCs contemporáneos y el TLC Centroamérica-Estados Unidos (CAFTA). OEA.

Salvat, P (2002). El porvenir de la equidad. Aportaciones para un giro ético en la filosofía política contemporánea. Santiago: Lom Ediciones; Universidad Alberto Hurtado.

Samuelson, P (1951). Economics, An Introductory Analysis. New York: Mc Graw Hill.
Samuelson, P (1971). Fundamentos del Análisis Económico. Buenos Aires: El Ateneo.
Santos, F (1992). El Orden Monetario y Financiero. En J. Guzmán, & A. Rallo, Estructura Económica Mundial (pág. 132). Madrid: Mc. Graw Hill.
Schumpeter, J (1939). Business Cycles. New York; London: McGraw-Hill.
Schumpeter, J (1967). Teoría del desenvolvimiento económico. México: Fondo de Cultura Económica.
Schumpeter, J (1971). Capitalismo, socialismo y democracia. Madrid: Editorial Aguilar.
SELA (2005). Análisis de las Disposiciones de trato especial y diferenciado. Caracas: XXI Reunión Ordinaria del Consejo Latinoamericano.
SELA (2005). Arquitectura institucional de la integración para la articulación y convergencia. Reunión Ordinaria del Consejo Latinoamericano. SELA.
SELA (2005). La institucionalidad de la integración en América Latina y el Caribe: posibilidades de articulación y convergencia. Caracas: SELA.
SELA (2005). La Institucionalidad de la Integración en América Latina y el Caribe: posibilidades de articulación y convergencia. Caracas: Secretaría Permanente del SELA.
SELA (2005). Propuesta para el tratamiento de las asimetrías en la Comunidad Sudamericana de Naciones. Montevideo: Documento preparado para la Re- unión de Seguimiento sobre el Tema de las Asimetrías; Secretaría General de ALADI.
Sen, A (1997). Sobre ética y economía. Madrid: Alianza Universidad.
Sen, A (2000). Desarrollo y libertad. Buenos Aires: Planeta.
Sen, A (2010). La idea de la justicia. Madrid: Taurus.
Sen, A., & Kliksberg, B (2008). Primero la gente. Barcelona: Ediciones Deusto.
Smith, A (1983). La Riqueza de las Naciones. Buenos Aires: Editorial Orbis Hyspamerica.
Smith, A (1994). La Riqueza de las Naciones. Madrid: Alianza Editorial.
Smith, A (1997). La teoría de los sentimientos morales. Madrid: Alianza Editorial.
Smith, A (1999). La riqueza de las naciones. Madrid: Alianza Editorial.
Solari, A., Franco, R., & Jutkowitz, J (1976). Teoría, acción social y desarrollo en América Latina. México D.F.: Siglo XXI.
Solow, R (1988). Growth Theory and After. The American Economic Review, 78(3), 307-317.

Stavenhagen, R (1965). Siete tesis equivocadas sobre América Latina. En R. Stavenhagen, Las clases sociales en las sociedades agrarias. Ciudad de México: Siglo XXI.

Stavenhagen, R (1972). Sociología y subdesarrollo. Ciudad de México: Nuestro Tiempo.

Sunkel, O (1958). La inflación chilena: un enfoque heterodoxo. El trimestre económico, 25(100), 570-599.

Sunkel, O (1958). La inflación chilena: un enfoque heterodoxo. El Trimestre Económico, 25(100), 570 – 599.

Sunkel, O (1970). Desarrollo, subdesarrollo, dependencia, marginación y desigualdades espaciales: hacia un enfoque totalizante. EURE, 1(1), 13-49.

Sunkel, O (1972). Capitalismo transnacional y desintegración nacional en América Latina. Buenos Aires: Ediciones Nuevas Fichas.

Sunkel, O (1978). La dependencia y la heterogeneidad estructural. El Trimestre Económico, 45(177), 3-20.

Sunkel, O (1980). La interacción entre los estilos de desarrollo y el medio ambiente en la América Latina. En O. Sunkel, & N. Gligo, Estilos de desarrollo y medio ambiente en América Latina (págs. 9-67). México, D.F: Fondo de Cultura Económica.

Sunkel, O (1989). Institucionalismo y estructuralismo. Revista de la Cepal(38), 147-156.

Sunkel, O., & Infante, R (2009). Hacia un desarrollo inclusivo: el caso de Chile. Santiago: Cepal; OIT; Fundación Chile 21.

Sunkel, O., & Paz, P (1970). El subdesarrollo latinoamericano y la teoría del desarrollo. México: Siglo XXI.

Tobin, J (1980). Financial structure and monetary rules. Kredit und Kapital, 16(2).

Tobin, J (1984). On the Efficiency of the Financial System. Lloyds Bank Review, 1-15.

Tugores, J (1994). Economía Internacional e Integración Económica. New York: Mc Graw Hill.

Tussie, D (2004). La política comercial en un contexto de federalismo. Integración & comercio (21), 69-84.

UE (2001). Libro Verde: Fomentar un marco europeo para la responsabilidad social de las empresas. Bruselas: Comisión de las Comunidades Europeas.

UNCTAD (1991). World Investment Report 1991. The Triad in foreign direct investment. New York: United Nations.

UNCTAD (1992). World Investment Report 1992. Transnational Corporations as Engines of Growth. New York: United Nations.

UNCTAD (1993). World Investment Report 1993. Transnational Corporations and Integrated International Production. New York: United Nations.

UNCTAD (1994). World Investment Report 1994. Transnational Corporations, Employment and the Workplace. New York: United Nations.

UNCTAD (febrero de 1995). Recent Developments in International Investment and Transnational Corporations. UNCTAD.

UNCTAD (1995). World Investment Report 1995. Transnational Corporations and Competitiveness. New York: United Nations.

UNCTAD (2007). The "New Regionalism" and NorthSouth Trade Agreements. En UNCTAD, Trade and Development Report 2007 (págs. 53-86). New York; Ginebra: Naciones Unidas.

Vaillant, M (2008). How to rescue the trade agreement between the EU and Mercosur. BID.

Veblen, T (1904). The Theory of business Enterprise. New York: Charles Scribner's Sons.

Veblen, T (1963). Teoría de la clase ociosa. México: Fondo de Cultura Económica.

Verger, A (2003). El sutil poder de las transnacionales. Lógica de funcionamiento e impacto de las grandes empresas en un mundo globalizado. Barcelona: Icaria.

Vernon, R (1966). International Investment and International Trade in the Product Cycle. The Quarterly Journal of Economics, 80(2), 190-207.

Viner, J (1950). The Customs Union Issue. New York: Carnegie Endowment for International Peace.

Viner, J (1952). International Trade and Economic Development. Oxford: Free Press.

Vives, A., Corral, A., & Isusi, I (2005). Responsabilidad social de la empresa en las PYMEs de Latinoamérica. Washington D.C.: Ikei.

Weber, M (1964). Historia económica general. México: Fondo de Cultura Económica.

Weber, M (1973). Ensayos sobre metodología sociológica. Buenos Aires: Amorrortu.

Weber, M (1974). Economía y sociedad. México: Fondo de Cultura Económica.

Williamson, O (1989). Las instituciones económicas del capitalismo. México:Fondo de Cultura Económica.

Wolfe, M (1976). El desarrollo esquivo: exploraciones en la política social y la realidad sociopolítica. México D.F.: Fondo de Cultura Económica.

Zaiat, A (2014). Economía a contramano. Buenos Aires: Planeta-Bookest.

Made in United States
Orlando, FL
04 November 2026

90219984R00207